D0897740

The Idea of LYRIC

EIDOS | Studies in Classical Kinds

Thomas G. Rosenmeyer, General Editor

The Idea of
LYRIC

Lyric Modes in Ancient
and Modern Poetry

W. R. Johnson

University of California Press

Berkeley • Los Angeles • London

University of California Press
Berkeley and Los Angeles, California
University of California Press, Ltd.
London, England
© 1982 by
The Regents of the University of California

Library of Congress Cataloging in Publication Data
Johnson, W. R. (Walter Ralph), 1933–
    The idea of lyric.
    Includes bibliographical references and index.
    1. Lyric poetry—History and criticism.
2. Classical poetry—History and criticism.
I. Title.
PN1356.J6   809.1′4   81-3384
ISBN 0-520-04462-2   AACR2

Printed in the United States of America

1 2 3 4 5 6 7 8 9

For Nick Papayanis

Oh, morning, at the brown brink eastward, springs—

Contents

Preface   ix

I.   Swans in Crystal: The Problem of Modern
Lyric and Its Pronouns   1

II.   Praise and Blame: Greek Lyric   24

The Fragments and the Music   24
Archilochus and Pound and *Ethopoeia*   29
The Rhetoric of Sappho   38
The Waning of Song and Its Last Renewal:
    Anacreon, Simonides, and Pindar   49
The Genius of Greek Lyric   71

III.   On the Absence of Ancient Lyric Theory   76

IV.   In the Birdcage of the Muses:
Ancient Literary Lyric   96

Where the Sea Is Remembered:
    Callimachus and Meleager   96
The Sparrow and Nemesis: Catullus   108
In the Deserts of the Heart: Horace   123

V.   The Figure of Ariadne: Some Lyric Mongrels
and Lyric Monologue   146

VI.   The Amplitude of Time: Whitman
and Modern Choral   176

Notes   197

Index   211

Preface

When I was sorting through what my predecessors had to say about lyric, was pondering their definitions of it, I kept wondering, naturally, vaguely, pompously, if I could not somehow correct them, improve on them. Of course, I have not. Essences—which I believe to exist in some fashion—elude us. Our vision is, for the most part, conditioned by the times and the spaces we happen to inhabit; and this means that we see vividly (chronotopically) only a part or parts of the whole, the part or parts that are ours. That and that only— the rest, in varying degrees, we see dimly, see wrongly, or see not at all.

I have tried to *imagine* (Herder's *einfühlen*) what ancient classical lyric was and in its fragments remains by contrasting it with what I and many, perhaps most, of my readers know thoroughly—because we were born into it, breathe it, and live it. Modernism, a fascinating phase of romanticism, may have ended, but romanticism itself— which is not the least of the glories of the human spirit—continues its blossomings. This, then, is a book on lyric, on Western classical lyric, by a later romantic Latinist, offered to his siblings.

To August Frugé and T. G. Rosenmeyer, I give thanks once again for their unending kindness, their wise patience and their sweet determination. I am also very grateful to the following friends for having given me their generous counsel and encouragement: Nell Altizer, Gordon Kirkwood, Françoise Meltzer, William Mullen, James Powell, Pietro Pucci, Sandra Siegel, Martin Stiles, and Sabina Thorne. Finally I thank the editors of *Occident* for permission to reprint my first chapter, which first appeared in that magazine in a somewhat different form.

"Then, Sir, what is poetry?"

"Why, Sir, it is much easier to say what it is not. We all *know* what light is, but it is not very easy to *tell* what it is."

Samuel Johnson, Boswell's *Life*,
April 11, 1776

I

Swans in Crystal:
The Problem of Modern Lyric
and Its Pronouns

In his lecture "The Three Voices of Poetry," while in the process of
fabricating one of the last and the most effective of his smoke-
screens, T. S. Eliot has occasion to examine the *OED*'s definition of
the word *lyric* and decides that the word, and with it the concept of
the lyric genre, will not do, must pack up its bags, and depart forth-
with into outer darkness. In Eliot's view, what finally distinguishes
poems that are neither didactic nor dramatic (his second and third
voices of poetry) from those that belong to the poet of the first voice
is that the first-voice poet is expressing "his own thoughts and sentiments to himself or to no one." This voice, this poetic genre, he
elects to designate as "meditative verse," and it is meditative verse
that for him replaces outmoded lyric, which was perhaps never quite
genuine in any case. For in Eliot's view the older meditative poets,
when they pretended to address their poems, their sentiments, and
their thoughts to another person, were in fact disguising their interior monologues by presenting them as utterances of praise or blame,
as attempts at communication with other beings, as shared speech.
Eliot's abnormal reticence, which is, of course, one of the sources of
his lyric power, contributes in large measure to his redefinition of
lyric, but that reticence does not concern us here.[1] What matters
here is that Eliot's rejection of lyric is representative of a central,

1

perhaps of the central, trend in modern theory and practice of lyric, and Eliot's formulation of his attitude toward old lyric and new meditative verse is, as usual, as perfect as it is deceptive and oblique.

There is no question but that the forms of lyric poetry have met with remarkable changes in modern times. Have these transformations of lyric form advanced to such a point that the substance of lyric itself has been transformed utterly, even annihilated? Or, to put it another way, in Eliot's way, was there ever a lyric genre at all? If there was, what was it? Or, as I prefer to ask, what is it? I regard this genre as immutable and universal. Its accidents may and always do show extraordinary variations as it unfolds in time, but its substance abides. As an emblem of this changing permanence, I take Tertullian's brief meditation on the peacock:

> multicolor et discolor et versicolor, numquam ipsa, semper alia, etsi semper ipsa quando alia, totiens denique mutanda quotiens movenda.[2]

Our ancestors, who imagined that bees were ruled by kings rather than by queens, naturally assumed that the vain peacock must be female, not male. My translation of this passage, in the spirit of the times, reverses these mistaken and sexist genders of the original:

> Multicolored, particolored and versicolored, never utterly himself yet always most himself when in his changing he becomes another: changed, utterly changed (or so it seems) with every step he takes.[3]

When I try to think about the problem of lyric or the problem of genre in general, it is often the image of Tertullian's peacock that comes to me—not as a solution, of course, to the problem, but rather as a reminder of the wonderful impossibility of the problem.

In my search for this invisible ideal, let me begin with the visible, with what can be observed and counted. Let me begin with the obvious. And I look for the obvious in Catullus, not because he is really obvious, but because, as compared with the subtlety and confusing fragmentation of Greek lyric or with the subtlety and intricate presence of Horace, he seems almost obvious. I am looking for pronouns in Catullus, as I shall look for them in other poets who seem to me representative of their age, or of a certain crucial shift in the treatment of lyric. (My statistics are offered less as data than as meta-

phors for the forms of lyric I am looking for; as an earnest of my sincerity here, let me confess that my arithmetic is poor, and that my
categories seem somewhat dubious even to me, and, finally, that I
have sometimes pigeon-holed certain poems in a whimsical, arbi-
trary, even tyrannical way.) My categories for examining lyric pronouns are three: The first is the I-You poem, in which the poet addresses or pretends to address his thoughts and feelings to another
person—in William Wordsworth's phrase to Samuel Taylor Coleridge, "as if to thee alone"; in this category the person addressed
(whether actual or fictional) is a metaphor for readers of the poem
and becomes a symbolic mediator, a conductor between the poet
and each of his readers and listeners. This pronominal patterning
(*ego-tu, ego-vos*) I take to be the classic form for lyric solo, or, as the
Greeks came to call it, monody. But for my immediate purposes I
don't distinguish between I-You poems singular and I-You poems
plural. What concerns me in this category is a speaker, or singer,
talking to, singing to, another person or persons, often, but not always, at a highly dramatic moment in which the essence of their relationship, of their "story," reveals itself in the singer's lyrical discourse, in his praise or blame, in the metaphors he finds to recreate
the emotions he seeks to describe. The second category for examining lyric pronouns is Eliot's meditative poem, in which the poet talks
to himself or to no one in particular or, sometimes, calls on, apostro-
phizes, inanimate or nonhuman entities, abstractions, or the dead.
In this category, the person or thing addressed, when it exists, is
often no more than a focusing device, an object of meditation. Finally, the third and last category is the poem cast as a dialogue, dramatic monologue, or straight narrative, in which the poet disappears entirely and is content to present a voice or voices or a story
without intervening in that presentation directly. Such a poem is
sometimes lyric, sometimes not, depending on what the poet is trying to do.

Back now to Catullus. Of his 112 poems, 70 percent are I-You
poems, 14 percent are meditative poems, and 16 percent are in the
miscellaneous category. Because Catullus is among the most personal, exuberant, and extraverted of poets (unless we choose to emphasize the long poems 63, 64, and 68), in one's memory he is always present before us, talking to us by talking to others, shouting,
giggling, whining, burbling, praising, and blaming—Catullus's pas-

sion for sharing thoughts and feelings is at the core of this extraordinary, strangely limited, yet wonderfully varied personality. But that
memory is, in a way, imprecise. Ten of his meditative poems Catullus addresses to himself, and these soliloquies account for some of his
finest poems (for example, poems 8 and 76); his habit of arguing
with himself is one of his most powerful attractions and, aside from
the great long poems, is what helps give depth to a collection that
might otherwise seem, in a casual reading, rather frivolous, despite
its high spirits and its fireworks.[4]

Horace, on the other hand, talks to himself very rarely (*Odes* 1.35
and 2.5 seem to me the clear occurrences here). Of his poems, 9
percent are meditative as against 87 percent I-You and 4 percent
miscellaneous. Of the I-You poems, eleven are essentially choral
poems, mannered imitations of Pindaric themes and Pindaric manner. (I assume that Horace's decided preference for the I-You poem is
strongly influenced by his Greek models, from Archilochus through
the writers of Hellenistic elegiac epigram, but the pitiful state of the
fragments leaves this question uncertain: Archilochus, Sappho, and
Alcaeus seem to have used the form extensively; Anacreon and Simonides seem not to have done so. But the fragments provide us
with no real evidence one way or the other.) It is true, of course,
that some of Horace's poems addressed to a You seem rather perfunctory as living speech, as if the vocatives and proper names were essentially ornamental or mere devices to generate the poem. Nevertheless, the sheer bulk of his I-You poems provides a constant,
unified impression of living speech, of intimacy, exchange, and
discourse.

The most usual mode in Greek lyric (probably) and in Latin lyric
(certainly) was to address the poem (in Greek, the song) to another
person or to other persons. What this typical lyric form points to is
the conditions and the purposes of song: the presence of the singer
before his audience; his re-creation of universal emotions in a specific context, a compressed, stylized story (I love you, hate you; You,
I, We feel awe in the face of this hero's splendor as we feel awe at the
gods who bestow this splendor); and, finally, the sharing, the interchange of these emotions by singer and audience. The specific context, the fiction of I and You and their situation of discourse, concre-
tizes the universal, makes it perceptible and makes it singable. In
Rainer Maria Rilke's phrase, "feelings are shaped" that were else

shapeless. Where there is, usually, in our hearts and minds, a bound-
less, depthless indistinction of feelings and thoughts, suddenly, in
the lyric story, at its essential, dramatic moment, emotions and
thoughts are organized in lyrical discourse[5] and find in metaphors—
in correlatives that are neither purely objective nor purely subjective—intelligible re-creations, visible patterns for the inner tem-
pests and stillnesses, configurations that are at once ordered and dynamic. Complex thoughts and feelings that have no name find
perceptible re-creations and patterns in the sung story that the
singer and his audience share.

In Rome, even after the singer sang no more, the old audiences
had vanished, and song lived primarily in books and in libraries, this
musical intimacy, this rhetorical, pronominal patterning, this dialectic of I and You, this lyrical discourse, remained the typical form
for a poetry that re-created common yet complex emotions in particular fictions, that made visible the invisible forms and rhythms
of personality, that incarnated and affirmed the misery and beauty
of the individual's existence in a world that delighted and terrified
him, that confessed the greatness of the soul's becoming under the
sign of being—"Infinite passion, and the pain / Of finite hearts that
yearn. . . ."

Thanks in part to Catullus, but mostly thanks to Horace, this typical ancient lyric form is handed down to Western Europe in its literary perfections, even after the ruin of the Greek lyric that inspired it
and that it managed in some sense to re-create and in some sense to
preserve. When Pierre de Ronsard and Ben Jonson began their own
re-creations of lyric, it is to this Latin re-creation that they inevitably turn, just at the moment of that spectacular lyric flowering when
medieval song is wedded to classical literary lyric.

And where did medieval song come from? No one seems to know;
at least the passionate arguments continue, as they doubtless will
continue. If one can hazard a guess—and classicists who cannot
solve their own problems are never shy of solving everyone else's—
medieval song will have begun in the same place that Greek lyric
began, in what Sir Thomas Browne calls "that vulgar and Taverne
Musick, which makes one man merry, another sad"[6] and which reminds him of "the sensible fit of that Harmony, which intellectually
sounds in the eares of God." An ancient tavern in Mesopotamia, in
Arabia, in Provence, in China, or in Browne's own England—or

some low bar anywhere in America where the juke box shrieks, "I need you baby / And if it's quite all right, I want you, baby"—various changes in various places at various times, but the essential form endures.

Or did endure, until Browne's own time, when literary lyric began a slow alteration that continued imperceptibly until Eliot's time, when it reached its perfection and caused Eliot, among many others, to try to find a warrant for it. Initially, John Donne talks to himself occasionally, but he talks more to his women and to his friends; later, he talks mostly to God and to himself. George Herbert talks to himself and to no one in particular often enough (39 percent), but he talks mostly to God (I-You, 54 percent; miscellaneous, 7 percent). With Henry Vaughan we find that the poet talking to himself or to no one is the characteristic lyric mode, a mode that even brief apostrophes at the beginnings and ends of poems (rather like the later romantic apostrophes to absent friends or natural phenomena) do not restore to the older rhetorical, pronomial, social form. The figures for Vaughan are 46 percent I-You, 51 percent meditative, 3 percent miscellaneous, and these figures are slightly deceptive because, as contrasted with Donne or even with Herbert, where one almost always feels an urgency of speech and an intensity of listening even in the meditative poems, many of Vaughan's poems in which God is addressed might easily be shifted from the I-You to the meditative category; in these poems (for example, "Morning Watch" and "The Relapse"), the apostrophes to God seem almost separate from the poem, a result, not an organic part of the meditation proper.

This is a full-fledged meditative verse, both in Eliot's sense and in the sense of the "greater romantic lyric," as M. H. Abrams has defined it.[7] The poet in a landscape chances on something in nature that takes hold of him as he describes it to himself, for himself; from that description comes a vision, his inner state revealed by the outward sign; and from that vision in which the inner and outer blend comes an evaluation of the poet's life, of his renewal, perhaps of his transformation. In short, this poetry is, in a way, mystical. The poet has removed himself (or has been removed) from the world into a private vision of nature in which he sees himself reflected. At best, the audience is extraneous to this poetry; at worst, all sense of the audience has vanished. We can describe this poetry in various ways. We can speak of Puritan sensibility and of the individual and his inner light; we can speak of a fragmentation of society and culture and a consequent alienation of the poet; we can even, glancing at Andrew Marvell, speak of the growth of a secular individualism; and one might even want to speak of the Gutenberg revolution and its effect on the ways lyric poetry began to be experienced in the seventeenth century. I would like to approach this phenomenon in a Marxist way,[8] but amateur historicity and amateur anthropology would only blur these issues further: the "simultaneity of multiple processes" is too powerful here to allow for even unglittering generalities. So, causes I take here for granted, and I concentrate on effects. Despite the rather feeble continuation of the older, classical, universal lyric form, after the near dormancy of lyric in the eighteenth century (notwithstanding the efforts of Robert Burns and William Blake), after Jean-Jacques Rousseau's philosophical warrant to the supremacy of meditative verse, after the brilliant triumphs of Wordsworth and Coleridge, the young Goethe, Alphonse Lamartine, and Giacomo Leopardi, the meditative lyric, the "greater romantic lyric," becomes the dominant form in modern lyric. The poet now talks to himself or to no one about his experience, which may or may not reflect emotion in compressed story—and he finally tends to dispense with both story and emotion, even as he dispenses with the second-person pronouns, singular and plural.

A precise adumbration of this process, an emblem of what this shift from the I-You pronominal form to the meditative form means and does to lyric poetry, is the fate of *The Prelude* as Wordsworth continued to work at it throughout his life. Those of us who grew up with the 1851 edition, and even those of us who had the fortune to move on to the 1805 edition, rejoice in the publication of the one-thousand-line version, the original version, of 1798-1799.[9] This poem seems to me to be very possibly the freshest, the greatest lyric poem in the language. I don't suggest that it is the weakening of the pronominal form in the course of revisions that accounts for what I regard as the final ruin of the poem (until the recent resuscitation); it is not Wordsworth's growing failure to speak his poem to Coleridge that causes the poem to disintegrate—Wordsworth murders his poem with insipid philosophizing and destructive moralism and demented religiosity. But one cannot help but feel that the destruction of the pronominal form (Wordsworth no longer addressing his poem to Coleridge, as if to thee alone) is symptomatic of the larger ruin of this poem's initial transparencies and unique exultations. The later versions of *The Prelude* are meditative poems with a vengeance—and they contain, in microcosm, much of the later lyric catastrophe.

Since its romantic flowering meditative verse has itself changed in various ways, but common to these changes are the isolation, the self-sufficiency, of the lyric I and the virtual disappearance of the lyric You. If Eliot's view is correct, if the lyric You was always mere ornament in lyric poetry, if the self talking to self or to no one was always of the esssence for lyric, no great harm was done when lyric poets increasingly ignored the older rhetorical form of I and You. But the loss of the lyric You had consequences that Eliot and his allies have not reckoned with. When the lyric You vanished from the centrality it had shared with the lyric I, something peculiar began to happen both to the lyric I and to the content of its private meditations. What happens to the lyric I and to the content of its meditations is clearest seen, I think, in the work of Stéphane Mallarmé, and that work, as it happens, has been through most of this century of paramount importance in the life of the lyric. Before glancing at Mallarmé, however, I want to offer a few more percentages: for John Keats, 24 percent I-You, 53 percent meditative, and 23 percent miscellaneous; for Charles Baudelaire, 44 percent I-You, 49 percent meditative, 7 percent miscellaneous; for Mallarmé, 25 percent I-You, 70 percent meditative, 5 percent miscellaneous. We note here the continuing trend away from I-You (though Baudelaire seems to hold the line here) and toward meditation. But these figures are, in fact, rather deceptive. If both Keats and Baudelaire conform to the nineteenth-century trend in formal principles and extend the sway of the meditative poem, it is, nevertheless, true that even when they are talking to marble statues or to nightingales, to the gutters of Paris or to mangy swans, or even when they are talking to themselves or to no one in particular, we sense the old rhetorical urgency; in these two poets the sense of the I is extremely strong, and the sense of the need for discourse is extremely powerful. With Mallarmé, as his famous swan sonnet shows, the case is very different:

> Le vierge, le vivace et le bel aujourd'hui
> Va-t-il nous déchirer avec un coup d'aile ivre
> Ce lac dur oublié que hante sous le givre
> Le transparent glacier des vols qui n'ont pas fui!

Un cygne d'autrefois se souvient que c'est lui
Magnifique mais qui sans espoir se délivre
Pour n'avoir pas chanté la région où vivre
Quand du stérile hiver a resplendi l'ennui.

Tout son col secouera cette blanche agonie
Par l'espace infligé à l'oiseau qui le nie,
Mais non l'horreur du sol où le plumage est pris.

Fantôme qu' à ce lieu son pur éclat assigne,
Il s'immobilise au songe froid de mépris
Que vêt parmi l'exil inutile le Cygne.

The virgin, spirited, beautiful today, will it then tear apart for us with drunk wingbeat this hard forgotten lake which, under frost, the transparent glacier of unknown flights enghosts?

A swan of past times recalls that it is he himself, splendid, yet passive, in despair—for he did not incant the climate of living when impotent winter shone with boredom.

His neck will completely shake away that white pain which space inflicts on a bird who refuses—yes, but it cannot deal in this way with the terror of the ground where its plumage is entrapped.

A phantom who by his own pure gleam has been relegated to this place, he hardens in the cold dream of disdain, in which during his futile exile, the Swan has garbed himself.

This extraordinary poem seems to me the precise emblem of the impersonality that has increasingly become the characteristic mode of modern lyric, a mode that has impressed itself on the poetry of all Western nations, on the poetry of all modern schools of poetry. "Ce lac dur oublié," "vols qui n'ont pas fui," "sans espoir," "l'ennui," "stérile hiver," "blanche agonie," "horreur du sol," "songe froid de mépris," "l'exil inutile." This is a kind of tortured gnosticism, a litany of impotence, futility, isolation, despair. The poet here closes with the uselessness, the unreality, of identity (his own, as man and as poet; everyone's). This is a common enough, recurrent mood for many people; it is, indeed, a necessary, an inevitable part of being alive. But the power, the great tragic power, of this sonnet is rooted in something more than a recurrent but passing mood; it is rooted in a profound and agonizing intuition that this state, this unalterable frozen state of existing (not of living), *is* the human condition. The isolation re-created here with such consummate art is seen as *the* truth about being human. In other poems (for example, "L'azur" and "Brise marine") we find an impulse, thwarted but strong, to flee from the dreadful impossibility of bad selflessness ("Où fuir dans la révolte inutile et perverse?" or "La chair est triste, hélas! et j'ai lu tous les livres. / Fuir! là-bas fuir!"), but there is never any real possibility of escape in these poems from what Baudelaire, in "Le voyage," calls "un oasis d'horreur dans un désert d'ennui." What is the nature of this isolation, this radical inability of the identity, of the person, to break from its terrible confinement and return to the outer world?

There are many ways of reading this dense, violent, multifaceted poem, but I choose to interpret the poem as being essentially about the uselessness, the impossibility, of writing poetry, which, for Mallarmé, would be equivalent to the uselessness of living his life. This is, again, doubtless a common enough experience for poets, at some times in their careers, or when their careers, in effect, have ended. What matters here, however, is the extreme sensitivity, the ruthlessness, with which this grief is faced up to and then re-created. "Language in pieces, culture in pieces," said Roland Barthes. I think that—beyond the merely personal, beyond the unique sensibility and great genius of Mallarmé—it is the fragmentation of language and culture that Mallarmé feels with such extraordinary intensity, that this poem reflects perfectly, that gave Mallarmé his awful and unique vision of himself as being irrelevant as poet, as human being. Not, then, a poem about the human condition (as it has come to seem to some people in this century); rather, a very special nineteenth-century mood, here distilled to its quintessential shade. The myth of the romantic artist as outcast and exile has become, in this poem, reality (of a kind) because Mallarmé has seen with horror that society and culture are themselves disintegrating, becoming unreal along with the artists that they first mocked and then ignored (or so the myth runs).

The Renaissance, it lied; the Enlightenment, it lied: the truth, the only truth, is bad mortality and complete loneliness while we live through the death we call life. These presentiments of cultural ruin, and the radical anxieties and despair they engender, are neither quite accurate nor quite inaccurate. All men are brothers, but, in another way, all men are alone. What is terrifying here is that the dynamism and the dialectic, the rhythms, of identity and of living have ceased utterly to function, and the effort to know one's self and to live one's life, the effort to try for joy and for communion with others, is totally rejected. Not unsimilar intuitions inform the poetry of two other very different, equally great and equally brave and original poets contemporary with Mallarmé, Emily Dickinson and Gerard Manley Hopkins. In their poems, too, the fact of identity becomes problematic, frightening, and there is nothing to connect with, to relate to: no escape. They, too, are, or would like to be, in Nathaniel Hawthorne's phrase, "citizens of Somewhere Else."

The fact of culture in its disintegrations and the self in its fragmentations (or, more precisely, in their dynamic changes) is incontestable in modern times.[10] But Mallarmé's almost univocal response to these difficulties becomes poignant, indeed, tragic, by virtue of its fierce purity. As it happens, the major themes in Mallarmé's sonnet are prefigured in the poetry of Baudelaire, but Baudelaire, though he, too, writes of a tragic swan (as he writes of a sad albatross), is not himself a swan in crystal. He is *un flâneur*, God's spy roaming the streets of the Paris he hates and loves, *looking outward* as well as inward (see, for example, "Les petites vieilles" and "A une passante"), gazing steadily at realities that often frighten and disgust him but which, nonetheless, he cannot help but love, feel compassion for, praise. He may sing of flight and boredom and vicious, destructive anodynes for the pain of existing (*mal*, not *Flowers of Evil* but *Flowers of Pain*), but he never stops embracing present realities and re-creating them into poetry. Nor, as any reader of "Préface" remembers vividly, did he forget his audience—he thumbs his nose at the fragmenting audience, re-creating them also, for good and all.

A very different poet, but also *un flâneur*, reaches a similar solution through quite dissimilar means. Pacing the streets of Alexandria, C. P. Cavafy also looks outward as well as inward (always seeing, looking, gazing), not at the present exactly, but at what remains of the past (ancient and medieval Alexandria, the recent past of the Alexandria of his youth and of his loves, all of Greece that Alexandria summons up for him), and his memory transforms these various pasts into poems and thus into present realities.[11] Both these poets are, then, social beings, that is to say, in the true sense, political animals. Their concern for, their obsession with, their love for, realities outside them, does not prevent them from being lonely, but it does safeguard them against the bad solitude and the anguished yearning for unreal transcendencies, unreal beauties, that Mallarmé fastens on in his swan sonnet and in much of his poetry. Solitary though they are, loners though they are, Baudelaire and Cavafy are "capable of entering into partnerships" (*koinōnein*)[12] with the worlds outside them, and are thus neither beast (*thērion*) nor god (*theos*) but men capable of seeing the world and of discoursing about it, through poetry, with their fellow human beings.

The power of Mallarmé's tragic intuition of aloneness (and of the futility of his art) precluded his attaining the freedom that Baudelaire and Cavafy struggled to achieve. He invented his *grimoires* ("conjurer's books"), he became, not a god, but the hierophant of a new religion, that of pure poetry. But even the famous *mardis* ("Tuesdays"), when he performed his poetic rituals for his converts and disciples, could not bring him to fellowship with the worlds around him, outside him. To blame him for this solution to his dilemma would be not only to judge him arrogantly and falsely but would also be to deny him the depth and the power of his vision in the swan sonnet. He had seen, from a very special angle of vision, things as they are (or, rather, as they began to seem to many intelligent people in late nineteenth-century Europe); and he re-created, magnificently, what he saw and what he felt about what he saw; and were proofs of the authenticity of his vision required, the discipline and dedication of his art and of his entire life would easily supply them.

The trouble came, as it very often does, with his epigones (many, many of them, but I think in particular of the German poet Gottfried Benn and his awful *Verlorenes Ich*—"Lost I"), who attempted to ape, and succeeded only in wallowing in, the despair of the master. In this fraudulent pure poetry (wandering monads muttering to themselves), it is very seldom that we meet with a You of any kind, nor are we likely ever to encounter an authentic I. And that means, almost inevitably, that these epigonic poems are possessed by and feed on an intellectual sentimentality; they are sorry, in a way, for alienation, for being alone. So, they look for genuine emotion, for the content of their discourse, and what they find is their feelings about writing poetry or, rather, about not being able to write poetry. Now, no one is talking to no one about nothing[13].

There are later, frailer descendents of this pure, absolute, un-pronominal poetry—imagism in its minor clones or what Stephen Spender calls "inevitable today," "a deliberately conscious, limited poetry of experience, carefully chosen, rationally explored": our poetry, the cool poetry, the poetry of the snapshot, in which I *is* the camera, and the camera has no emotion, no values, no hopes.[14] The disintegration of pronominal form entails the disintegration of emotional content, for in lyric, too, form and content are interdependent.

It goes without saying that images are of the essence for poetry: from the doctrine of *ut pictura poesis* ("as in painting, so in poetry"), to the modern notion "No idea but in things," and its various cor-relatives—expressive imagism (whatever that may mean), objectivisms, neosurrealism—the image, most particularly in lyric, has en-joyed a secure and necessary centrality, for lyric poetry is about the world as we see it.[15] But it is also about our feelings about, our judg-ments on, the world we see, and about our relationship to that world. And it is surely a misreading of Chinese or even Japanese po-etry to suggest that there the picture is all, that emotions and moral discourse have no place in this poetry, or if they do, exist only to serve and enhance the poem's images. Rather, the picture in lyric exists for the emotions and for the values that the image configures and reveals. Not the least important part of Yvor Winters's critical efforts was his insistence on the function of discourse, of moral ac-tion and moral imagination in lyric poetry (for him this essence of poetry shines brightest in Ben Jonson; but for a Latinist it will be found, of course, in Horace—in those perfectly achieved lyric po-ems where emotions, so far from being excluded, as some have imag-ined, are distilled to their richest purity, where the balance and the tension between picture and reasoned speech find their most dy-namic equilibrium). As a rule, poets do not merely present enchant-ing pictures without commenting on their presentations. Instead, they qualify and test their pictures; they refine and purify the images they offer. They disenchant no less than they enchant. A totally un-rhetorical poetry will be, as we have come to know all too well, a poetry void of passion, void of choosing, void of rational freedom—

it will be, in Paul Valéry's metaphor, the rind of the orange without the pulp and the juice. We want the pictures, yes, but we also want the hates and loves, the blame and the praise, the sense of a living voice, of a mind and heart that are profoundly engaged by a life they live richly, eagerly.

On the face of it, the varieties of imagism might seem a modern reassertion of the classical doctrine of mimesis that the romantic doctrine of artistic autonomy (the artist not re-creating, but creating, reality) had supplanted. But this view of imagism and its objective impersonalities rests on a misunderstanding of what mimesis meant to the Greeks, what it always means in art. Perhaps the people who painted bisons on the walls of their caves were engaged in sympathetic magic; but perhaps they were trying, with great success, not so much to imitate what they saw as to organize their perceptions of what they saw, what they valued in life or rejected. When Myron, the fifth-century Greek sculptor, carved an athlete at the moment of his maximum exertion and tension, yet represented his face, his body, and its struggle with a perfection of grace and repose, he was hardly imitating what he or anyone saw; rather, he was organizing his perceptions of what he thought really was, of what might be; organizing these perceptions for himself and for others, and organizing, too, his feelings about these perceptions, and his thoughts about these feelings. When Paul Cézanne designed that garment tossed randomly on that chair, he was not trying to reproduce, to represent, the naturalistic look of that garment on that chair; rather, he was, like the cave dweller and the Greek sculptor, patterning what he and, potentially, all humans see and feel and think about their lives; he was, in the simplest and profoundest sense of the word, *helping* us to *see* chairs and garments as they are, life as it is, ourselves as we are.

Art, then, any art, is not a reproduction of what is seen: it is a highly complex action (action both by artist and audience) in which what is outer and what is inner—things, perceptions, conceptions, actualities, emotions, and ideas—are gathered into and made manifest by emotive and intelligible forms. The artist cannot be undisciplined in searching for such forms; he can no more be slovenly in his habits of feeling and thinking than he can be slovenly in his habits of looking and listening or of using the implements of his craft; but neither can he be dispassionate, emotionless, unconcerned. The lie in modernist imagism is that no one snaps the picture. But the difference between a bad or mediocre photo and a good or great one is precisely who takes the photo—and the photographer, like any other artist, is defined not merely by his technique or his mastery of his instrument but also by the quality of his feeling, by the precision and vitality of his feelings and thoughts, all of which his composition captures and reveals, even as it captures and reveals certain aspects, certain angles, of the thing that called his mind and heart into action. Even here, one is tempted to say, most especially here, the I is no less indispensable than what it perceives or than the camera that helps to organize what it perceives, conceives, composes. If this sounds like someone trying to reconcile neoclassicism with romanticism, yes, alas, that is what I am trying to do, since neither of these entities is hale without the other. And, as I see it, the chief obstacle to the reconciliation I want is the bad fiction of impersonal art, in which dead emotions and ideas replace live emotions and ideas.

Dwarfed by a gradually infinite universe; dwarfed, too, by a mechanistic science that turned out to be hybristic, in bad repair, and inexpressibly dangerous; overwhelmed by its greedy, disobedient engines and by Gothams that knew and cared nothing for best-laid plans; dissolved by the speculations of, among others, Hegel, Marx, and Darwin, the lyric I grew first ashamed and bewildered, then terrified, by the idea of saying I, forgot how to say You, systematically unlearned emotions and their correlatives and their stories. Translated itself into, annihilated itself for, a technological mode for a technological age. That is decorum, perhaps, but decorum is sometimes indecorous.

Various poets tried, of course, to continue the old pronominal forms of solo lyric.[16] William Butler Yeats, having grown tired of poetry as picture and of impersonal poetry, began to make strenuous efforts to create for himself a vital, commanding, intimate presence as lyric performer. Yeats does not constantly address his hearer (or the hearer's surrogate, the You of the poem) because he does not need to. Once he has invented the singer that he envisioned in his essay on William Morris, once that many-voiced and irresistible fiction has been perfected, our sense of our presence as an audience is so exact and so constant that it need not be frequently dwelt on: the force of the singer's own presence, this perfectly imagined lyric personality, is sufficient to sustain the fiction of the performance.[17] Some of the strategy here, as Richard Ellman has shown, depends on the sudden, dramatic beginnings of the poems and on the frequent use of "now" and of "this" and "that," a technique—but it is more than that—which guarantees a sense of urgency and immediacy and guarantees also the reality, the presence of the singer and of our presence before him.[18]

By the time of Yeats's *Responsibilities* (1914), this fiction of the singer and his audience has been completely realized, and it will never desert him. In a sense this fiction of the live performer had been lurking even in the early lyrics (we catch a glimpse of him, we almost hear him in *The Wind Among the Reeds* and, more frequently, in *The Green Helmet*), but it is not until *Responsibilities* that he stands before us, the many-minded identity forever secure. What this performer does in his prime is to insist, again and again, on the reality of his experience (I see, I name, I bid, I hear, I know, I understand) and to emphasize his energy and his action (I walk, I pace, I climb, I choose, I mock, I turn, I stalk, I seek, I summon, I declare, I proclaim, I find). Yeats uses such verbs more frequently than other modern lyric poets tend to use them because, like his peculiarly effective blend of the diction and syntax of common speech with classical English, they ensure a sense of personal presence and of the immediacy of his performance. Even when Yeats takes up the "greater romantic lyric," his singer transforms it. He is never merely the dreamer in a symbolic landscape—he masters the song, the landscape, and himself, transmuting his experience and ours. It is true that the performance sometimes goes farther than enough, that one sometimes gets the impression that a real rabbit is being yanked from an unreal hat—but even this fraudulence has its charm.

Yet despite its occasional successes in adapting itself to the fragmentation of communities and the habits of reading that are fostered by the printed page and by technological education, the purely literary lyric, even in the hands of Yeats, remains an essentially unsatisfactory genre. The absence of a real audience and the failure of performance engender an anxiety, a kind of bad conscience, a sense of the poet's irrelevance, impotence, and unreality—a frustration of function that the printed page, so far from being able to mitigate, can only intensify. This normal condition of the modern lyric poet, who refuses impersonalism and imagism, this condition which Yeats and a few others escaped only through extraordinary genius and extraordinary effort, was splendidly imagined by Delmore Schwartz, whose sensitivity and honesty both as poet and critic cannot be buried by the unhappiness of his life or the myths that preserve and falsify that unhappiness.

Let us look first at Schwartz's "Tired and Unhappy, You Think of Houses." The poet, in his depression, summons up a scene in a pleasant house on a winter's evening, where a young girl sings "That song of Glück where Orpheus pleads with Death" to an appreciative audience of her elders. This vision dissolves as the figures retire:

It is time to shake yourself! and break this
Banal dream, and turn your head
Where the underground is charged, where the weight
Of the lean buildings is seen,
Where close in the subway rush, anonymous
In the audience, well-dressed or mean,
So many surround you, ringing your fate,
Caught in an anger exact as a machine![19]

The old conditions of lyric performance (note that the singer and her song are quintessential in their pathos), the closed circle, the sympathetic audience "nodding their happiness / To see time fresh again in her self-conscious eyes," the order and comfort of this "ideal" society ("The servants bring coffee, the children retire, / Elder and younger yawn and go to bed"), are poignantly evoked and bitterly spurned. The reality of performance for Schwartz is the silent, unknown, menacing crowd that surrounds him on the subway, all of them packed into, become indistinct from, the loud machine that hurtles them along.

Nor was this, though he distills it here perfectly, an unusual feeling for Schwartz as he contemplated his function as a lyric poet in the modern city. Again and again, the audience is sinister and hostile, and the poet (performer, for Schwartz's images of the poet are often theatrical)[20] is ridiculous and incompetent. This obsession with the gulf that separates poet and audience becomes in a poem

like "Parlez-Vous Français?" paranoid delusion. In this poem, some
men in a fascist state lounge easily in barber chairs as they listen to
Caesar haranguing over a loudspeaker; they are, in a parodic way, an
ideal audience:

> The barber firmly
> Planes the stubble with a steady hand,
> While all in barber chairs reclining
> In wet white faces, fully understand
> Good and evil, who is Gentile, weakness and command.

At this point in the poem a poet enters, tired, unshaven, "shy, pale,
and quite abstracted," almost a cartoon of the popular image of the
romantic poet, and, hearing the dictator, he begins to speak—in
French. His passionate denunciation is, naturally, totally ineffectual:

> He stands there speaking and they laugh to hear
> Rage and excitement from the foreigner.

Schwartz's may seem a very special case, yet it is more than co-
incidental, I think, that he wrote extremely sensitive poems about
both Friedrich Hölderlin and Baudelaire and that the problem of the
lyric poet and his audience (it was not merely anti-Semitism or "personal" problems or normal artistic anxieties that hounded him) remained central to him until the end of his career. In one of his last
and most beautiful poems, "Seurat's Sunday Afternoon Along the
Seine," most of his anger at and much of his fear of the monstrous
audience have disappeared, but its complacency (which he ponders
in Georges Seurat's figures in a landscape, "The Sunday people are
looking at hope itself"), though it can no longer hurt him, still
puzzles him, invokes in him a feeling of resignation that is very close
to despair. Seurat's picture, with its images of ordinary human beings
(and it is such people who view the picture, who are *its* audience) is
filled with "icons of pure consciousness":

> *Ils sont dans le vrai!* They are with the truth, they have found
>   their way.
> The kingdom of heaven on earth on Sunday summer day.
> Is it not clear and clearer? Can we not also hear
> The voice of Kafka, forever saying in despair's sickness trying
>   to say:

"Flaubert was right: *Ils sont dans le vrai!*
Without forbears, without marriage, without heirs,
Yet with a wild longing for forbears, marriage, and heirs:
They all stretch out their hands to me: but they are too far
    away!"

(lines 187–94)

"There is no city!" cries one of the characters in Schwartz's story, "The World Is a Wedding," and a novelist in an early poem, "Far Rockaway," gazing out at the "fun, foam, and freedom" of the summer bathers, asks himself questions he cannot ask the people on the beach below him who, seeming to know what their lives are for, though they are at once the subjects of his stories and the audience for his stories, are irreparably distant from him: he is a disembodied spirit, "that nervous conscience," ineffectual, silent, "a haunting, haunted moon" at sunny midday.

Schwartz's intense, profoundly troubled awareness of his inability to find and comprehend his audience is closely connected with an equally painful intuition of the uncertainty of his own poetic identity. This uncertainty, very clearly, has something to do with Schwartz's doubts about his poetic gifts, about his distrust of poetic politics and the velleities of literary fashion that preciosity and an easy early success did nothing to alleviate. But the anguish of Schwartz is essentially rooted in his grasp of a problem that has always engaged artists and writers, though perhaps seldom so insistently as it has since the Industrial Revolution, and that has especially afflicted lyric poets—what is the role of the artist in society? what is the value (to others and to himself) of what he does? who is he?

Schwartz could not answer these problems that haunted his poetry and life as they haunt all modern lyric. Nor has anyone else solved them. Modern lyric tends to be bereft of its singers and its audiences. But Sylvia Plath closed with these questions with a fatal gallantry. What she sees and organizes is the decomposition of her personality *as a poet*. Where Yeats recovered and systematically enlarged the lyric I by "imagining personality," Sylvia Plath imagines the dissolution of the lyric I by imagining *how* it dissolves and *why* (in few volumes of lyric after Yeats is the lyric I so powerfully presented, in none, so frighteningly realized). Plath does not bother much to talk directly about her art in *Ariel*—she does not have to, because it is ubiquitous in these ferocious poems ("The blood jet is poetry, / There is no stopping it" in "Kindness"). In "Fever 103°," she imagines the final annihilation of the lyric I with an irony that is at once brutal and delicate, mocking and tragic (self-pitying it is not):

> I think I am going up,
> I think I may rise—
> The beads of hot metal fly, and I, love, I
>
> By kisses, by cherubim,
> By whatever these pink things mean.
> Not you, nor him
>
> Not him, nor him
> (My selves dissolving, old whore petticoats)—
> To Paradise.[21]

The lyric pronouns and the lyric form they proffer are negated, are exploded, in this strictly patterned, deranged baroque parody. So, in a poem that dispenses with entertaining ironies ("Ariel"), the lyric I, at the completion of its lonely poetic journey, dissolves again into fire and silence:

> And now I
> Foam to wheat, a glitter of seas.
> The child's cry
>
> Melts in the wall,
> And I
> Am the arrow,
>
> The dew that flies
> Suicidal, at one with the drive
> Into the red
>
> Eye, the cauldron of morning.

The emphatic I's dissolving into the punning "red Eye," the unintelligible absorbed into the unintelligible, the alone with the alone, the ruin of lyric form unsentimentally observed: no one to sing, no one to sing to, nothing to sing.

Nor did she forget to imitate her "audience." She writes of her personal despair (her emotions), of her cruel sense of artistic futility—what kind of audience can want to hear that song? In "Lady Lazarus" the modern lyric audience (beyond even the nightmares of Schwartz) find their ultimate metaphor:

> What a million filaments.
> The peanut-crunching crowd
> Shoves in to see
>
> Them unwrap me hand and foot—
> The big strip tease.
> Gentlemen, ladies,
>
> These are my hands,
> My knees.
> I may be skin and bones,
>
> Nevertheless, I am the same, identical woman.

The poet, this main attraction in the sideshow, is a freak. What then are the audience? No matter, for this poet, like the other lyric I's in these savage expressionistic poems, vanishes into flame and silence:

> Out of the ash
> I rise with my red hair
> And I eat men like air.

Plath, better than any poet, understood the death of lyric. The isolations, the futilities, the suffocations of this closed, meaningless, terrifying world quickly became unsupportable to its most exact and powerful artificer. She was too intelligent and too honest not to see and to acknowledge this hopelessness, and she was, fortunately, so perfectly gifted and disciplined that she was able to represent it flawlessly, unforgettably.

Fortunately, Plath's re-creation of the death of lyric is not the last word on the subject. Although the snapshot lyric of the past forty years or so has been characterized by a gray anonymity that parallels the anonymity of symbolism even while it differs from it in its purposes and modes, there have been, in the same period, small signs of a renascence of lyric identity and its pronouns. Even while Benn, on whom Eliot leaned heavily in his discussion of the three voices, was announcing that the change from pronominal to absolute lyric was permanent and irreversible (the discredited, unreal identity forever forgotten, forever replaced by a world of objects and a disembodied voice to report them), even then, William Carlos Williams, purest of the imagists, was shifting back, in his final volumes, from pictures to pronouns and identity and to their discourses. In a selection of 113 poems, made by Williams himself,[22] only 15 percent are I-You poems as against 81 percent meditative and 4 percent miscellaneous. These statistics are, again, rather deceptive, for in Williams's final poems, most notably in the lovely "Asphodel, That Greeny Flower," the poet is, again and again, an I speaking, singing to a You (yes, singing, even though the triadic foot, an improvement over the earlier monotone, is feeble as far as music goes). In the most vital of his followers, most especially in Allen Ginsberg, this trend continues, and in the work of such diverse poets as Etheridge Knight and Adrienne Rich, attains something of the passion and precision that is normal for classical lyric. (By *classical* here, I mean not only the lyric of Greece and Rome, but of T'ang China, of Persia, of Arabia, of Provence, of Elizabethan England, of Germany and Russia in the early nineteenth century.) This is the rebirth of lyric vitality that Josephine Miles calls for in her auspiciously titled volume, *Poetry and Change*, when she dismisses the poetry of snapshots and demands more poems about more people.[23] Looking over recent poetry in 1974, she said: "There are many I's, some we's, some you's, especially as loved, a few grandfathers and other remembered relatives; but not a great variety of complicated live characters." The perfunctory pronouns do not fool Miles. From these poems, she says, "the sublime is missing, any heartfelt, soulswept elevation of spirit." These words are at once an exorcism and an incantation: they speak of thaw, of melting snowmen and of swans released from their crystal bondage. We feel that thaw, we hear it, in the lyrics of late Williams, Ginsberg, Knight, and Rich.

But it is not, of course, merely the restoration of the pronominal form that effects this liberation of the lyric spirit. Much bad poetry, now and always, has employed the pronominal frame. What there must be in good lyric is "the sublime," a "heartfelt, soulswept elevation" (how wonderful to have the flavor and the power of Longinus restored to us!). Once that sublimity and elevation have been felt, found, recaptured, what is needed to make them visible and audible is something that Ezra Pound called logopoeia and that our ancestors called rhetoric, that is, the vitality of language gathered into and strengthened by the patterned variations of disciplined speech. What is essential, then, to lyric is rhetoric, and essential to this lyrical rhetoric, as we shall see in the next chapter, is the pronominal form and lyric identity, the dynamic configuration of lyrical pronouns that defines and vitalizes the situation of lyrical discourse.

II

Praise and Blame:
Greek Lyric

The Fragments and the Music

There have been many translations in our time from the Greek. I have no Greek and so come to these translations as I come to those from the Japanese or the Nahuatl. But the poems will find few readers as careful, as interested, or as ready to be convinced. Yet the translations from Greek lyric poetry leave me unimpressed.

Having allowed excellence to the translations of Homer and the tragedians by Richmond Lattimore, Francis Fergusson, and Robert Fitzgerald, Yvor Winters goes on to remark that all modern translations of Greek lyric, from H. D. through Dudley Fitts and beyond:

leave me wondering if Greek lyric poetry deserves its reputation. . . . The Ojibways are more impressive. . . . I have never seen a translation of Sappho or Pindar that made either poet appear interesting, although, as a reader of *Arion*, I have, heaven knows, seen many translations of both. I do not know whether this trouble lies in the poems or in the translators, but I strongly suspect the poems. . . . [1]

On the infrequent occasions when Winters descends to this depth of silliness, he is usually proffering a new variety of sour grape or puffing the wares of his versifying friends. Since neither motive seems to account for these views, we must look elsewhere for an explanation. Is it possible that Winters was unaware that, with the single exception of Pindar, he was reading translations of fragments and then comparing these translations with the translations of complete texts of Oriental and Native American originals? This suggestion may, at first glance, seem absurd, but nowhere in his discussion does Winters give any indication that he knows of the wretched condition of Greek lyrical texts, and it therefore seems likely that he has succumbed to an illusion which has haunted literature and literary studies since the Renaissance. We are all in some sense disappointed when we read Greek lyric: not because the poetry is unimpressive—because it is supremely beautiful—but because it exists for us only in shards and tatters. The corpus of Greek lyric, meagerly augmented from time to time by the sands of Egypt, survives in ruins, and when we compare Greek lyric with the other remains of Greek literature and Greek culture, those ruins are heartbreaking. No experience in reading, perhaps, is more depressing and more frustrating than to open a volume of Sappho's fragments and to recognize, yet again—for one always hopes that somehow this time it will be different—that this poetry is all but lost to us.

This is a fact we choose not to face, not head on or constantly, and we therefore devise a fiction, the fiction of which Winters, too, was victim, which we call Greek lyric poetry. Even though we know that Greek lyric is mere fragments, indeed, *because* we know that Greek lyric is mere fragments, we act, speak, and write as if the unthinkable had not happened, as if pious bishops, careless monks, and hungry mice had not consigned Sappho and her lyrical colleagues to irremediable oblivion. C. M. Bowra's *Greek Lyric Poetry*, for instance, consists of some four hundred pages, in which everything that antiquity and modern times knew or suspected or invented about the lyricists and their songs is tirelessly elaborated and patiently embroidered. The book is an act of piety, perhaps, a scholar's veneration of what was, and is no more, and should still be; it is also an engrossing and deceptive work of fiction, grounded in ancient gossip that was both serious and unserious, and in modern conjecture and wishful thinking.

It may be argued that Bowra's book is an extreme case, that his fervor for restoration and his critical biases are no longer fashionable; but his craving for recovery represents a central trend in the criticism of Greek lyric. Both before Bowra and after him there is a strong desire to use the fragments of Greek lyric to design its vanished integrities. We do not want to admit the fact of this loss, so we open the fragments and try to read in Greek, as Winters tried to read in English, poems that are not there. This habit of restoration of a given fragment moves easily after a while into fantasizing the existence of a poet and an *oeuvre*, then into the illusion that the entire ghost, Greek lyric itself, has been totally retrieved. Naturally, any Hellenist you might ask will admit the fact of fragmentation, may even delight in rehearsing the actual state of the texts and the fascinating uncertainty of restorations and conjectures; but if you persist in your scrutiny and talk about the poetry, about the nonexistent poems, as the conversation warms, the skeleton will take on flesh and color, and the ruin will fade. This is not prevarication or trickery, this is human nature: we want those poems, and, in unguarded moments, we imagine them back into existence.

If I warn the reader at such length about what may seem, but is not, obvious, it is because when I begin my discussions of Greek lyric, I will inevitably lapse into the sins I here inveigh against. It is the reader, then, who must remember, when I forget, that Greek lyric, whatever the reader may find about it in these pages, is essentially inaccessible to us.

Another, lesser difficulty that attends our efforts to grasp what remains of Greek lyric is its intimate connection with music and performance. If we have little or no experience of contemporary popular music, whose poetry, though crude, is often genuine; if our sense of poetry is limited to the printed page; even if we have endured poetry readings in which poets read from the printed or typed page —the idea of poetry *and* music, performed before an audience, is strange to us, makes us think vaguely of lutes and viols and countertenors, of long programs of Schubert, and we must rethink what musical poetry might be; we must perform a hard act of historical imagination. But before we attempt that, before we think of Sappho and her audience, Anacreon and his, Pindar and his, a brief consideration of certain technical differences between Greek and modern verse is necessary.

"What music does to words, in any language, is to define the length of each syllable, to impose a precise quantitative scheme."[2]

But in a purely quantitative system of metric, such as existed in Greek, it is the time patterns of long and short syllables that create the rhythms of the verse and impose that rhythm on the music. When Sappho wrote a stanza in the meter that takes her name, the time patterns, the quantities of the syllables, defined a rhythm that music could do little to alter. On the other hand, like any reader who reads it aloud, a composer wishing to set to music a line like

A shadow like an angel with bright hair

has considerable freedom in deciding how he wants to define its essential rhythm. He may decide to treat the line as pure iambics or to diminish its metrical accents from five to as few as three (shádow, ángel, bright hair); he may decided to read the line without any pause, or he may break it in several ways:

A shadow
                    like an angel
                                        with bright hair,

or

A shadow like an angel
                                        with bright hair,

or

A shadow
                    like an angel with bright hair.

Finally, the composer may use several notes for a single syllable, and he may accent or lengthen unaccented or short syllables as he chooses.[3] Working with the accentual-syllabic meter that is the norm in classical English verse, the composer may do with rhythm —as he does with melody—exactly as he pleases. In the songs that we are used to, the words (our "lyrics"), if they are not actually swallowed up by melody and rhythm, serve chiefly to adorn or to illustrate their music. In Greek lyric, however, the music existed for the sake of the words—melody, rhythm, voice, dancing, lyre, and *aulos* ("oboe") all conspired to reinforce and emphasize separate syllables and to augment the clarity of the sung words. What mattered was the performance of the poem, and what mattered in the performance was that the words of the song should be as clearly intelligible as was possible.[4]

The meters of the solo poems[5] were, for the most part, rather simple, and for solo poems the stanza was the norm. In the performance of this poetry the lyre served chiefly to ornament and supplement verbal rhythms that were familiar to the audience or (even when they might not have been familiar) were so uncomplicated that they quickly became intelligible. In choral poetry, however, the verbal rhythms were complicated, and (in theory at least) each new choral poem might have an entirely new metrical pattern.[6] This freedom was required because the poet's rhythms had to accommodate both his words and the movements of his singing dancers. The unusual complexity and the novelty of these rhythms were compensated for by the precision of the movements themselves: the choreography reinforced the singing and the instruments and thus allowed the rhythms of choral lyric to approximate the clarities of those of solo lyric. In choral poems of some length, triadic composition (repetition of strophe, antistrophe, and epode) further facilitated the clarification of unfamiliar metric patterns. To what extent the word managed to hold its own against the dance in performance (it is a question we want always to bear in mind when we read Pindar and Bacchylides) we cannot, of course, be sure; but it is clear enough that, in theory at least, even in this "hybrid" lyric genre that drama arrogated to itself, it was "Song that the Muse made Queen";[7] it was the sung word for which all other parts of the performance existed and which they served.

In trying to grasp the nature of Greek lyric, we have somehow to imagine musical performance without obscuring our imaginations with what we know of contemporary music and its performances. In Greek lyric as it was performed and written to be performed, there were no slurred words, no vocal or instrumental virtuosities;[8] rather, the word, magnified, illumined, and framed by melody, instrument, and, sometimes, by dance. In sum, music intensified the words that the poet and his audience shared; it did not substitute for them or suborn them as decoration. In this sense, what we must bear in mind is that this was not so much a musical poetry (in our sense of the word *musical*) as a performed poetry, a poetry with music.

Once we have grasped, then, the importance of music in Greek lyric, it is essential that we do not exaggerate this importance. First, Greek lyric shares its use of music with many other bodies of high lyric poetry (Hebrew, Chinese, Provençal) even into the Renaissance, and this is therefore not (pace Pound) a truly essential hall-

mark of Greek lyric. Second, the music of Greek poetry is irremedia-
bly lost to us and we cannot, therefore, unless we delude ourselves,
be greatly concerned with it. (And, if we had it, it is doubtful that
we would much want it, except in order to satisfy curiosity: the
chances are that it was almost as monotonous and predictable as is
much of our currently fashionable pseudo-folk music.) What concerns us here is the clarity and immediacy of lyric performance,
which music enhanced. If we can learn to imagine the ways in
which this immediacy of performance influenced Greek lyric form,
we shall perhaps be in a good position to enjoy something of what
remains to us of Greek lyric and to appreciate the achievement of its
poets.

Archilochus and Pound and Ethopoeia

> You can have your bulky brigadier, your mincing staffer,
>   Complete with permanent wave and clean-shaven jowls;
> I want my soldier short, a squat, bow-legged
>   Type, with his feet firm on the ground, a real man.
>   (Fragment 60)[9]

> One of the natives flourished my shield. I lost
>   The glorious baggage in the brush, alas.
> My life—and that's what counts—I saved. They can have the
>   shield!
> There's many a better shield where the old one came from.
>   (Fragment 6)

This voice, these fragments of a shrewd, confident voice, come
down to us from the middle of the seventh century B.C. Archilochus
tells us something about himself, and ancient and modern scholars
tell us considerably more; but our sense of this poet depends not so
much on the facts about his life that he and others offer us, as it does
on the intensity of his various complaints about the world and of his
affirmations of self, on his singular, vital insistence on the clarity of
his perceptions of himself and of the world. What we know about
Archilochus, then, is not really his life, but rather his temperament,
his sensibility, something he created in part from his life, and something that, fixed in language that is usually clear and always vig-

orous, survives the ruin of time and of texts. In this extraordinary phenomenon, the strange permanence of Archilochus in ruin, we confront at once something about the nature of Greek lyric and about the problems of the lyric genre.[10]

This purity, this pure force of sensibility in Archilochus, has little or no connection with the pure lyric spirit that C. D. Lewis posited as being of the essence for lyric poetry. In Lewis's formulation such a spirit will fashion "a poem which expresses a single state of mind, a single mood, or sets two simple moods one against the other"; such poetry is "simple, pure, transparent, impersonal after the best lyric model."[11] What strikes the reader of Greek lyric fragments is that this kind of poetry, the expression or imitation of an anonymous *cri de coeur*, a disembodied extended cry, seems to have had no place in the lyrics of Greece. The voice of the medieval Latin songsters or of "Down by the Salley Gardens" or "Il pleure dans mon coeur" is not heard in the fragments of Greek lyric poetry. Part of the difficulty with Lewis's formulation, at least as far as Greek lyric practice goes, lies in the word "expresses," for Greek lyric is never concerned with expression; it is, true to its rhetorical bent, always concerned with discourse, with describing the reality of the inner passions and with deliberating on their nature and meaning.

In defining the nature of oration, Aristotle remarks: "Every speech is composed of three parts: the speaker (*ek tou legontos*), the subject about which he speaks (*peri hou legei*), and the person to whom he speaks (*pros hon*)—that is, the hearer (*ton akroaten*), to whom the end, the purpose (*to telos*) of the speech refers.[12] Where romantic theory puts the emphasis on the speaker, indeed, tends to eliminate all but the speaker, classical theory carefully divides the emphasis among speaker, discourse, and hearer; if there is a particular emphasis in Aristotle's formulation, it is upon the hearer for whose benefit the discourse exists. Although it may seem perverse to connect Aristotle's concept of oratory with lyric, I think it can be argued that Greek lyric shows a "situation of discourse" (speaker, discourse, hearer) similar to that which obtains in oratory. This similarity is most pronounced in "epideictic" or "display" oratory, in which the speaker, as against the legal or political orator, is not attempting to persuade his hearer to make a judgment on a practical matter (guilt or innocence in the courtroom, war or peace in the assembly) but is praising or blaming some quality or mode in human nature with a view to educating his hearer, to helping him to see what sort of person he can or should become, what sort of person he should not be. In short, the epideictic orator, like the lyric poet, is concerned to offer paradigms of identity, patterns of schooled volition, and he does this by exalting or by censuring certain traits in human character with vivid, dramatic examples of what these traits are like, *may be* like, when we experience them in others or in ourselves. Similarly, in the Greek idea of lyric, then, the business of the lyric poet is to provide a criticism of human passion that will indicate which passions are to be embraced and which are to be shunned: the purpose of this demonstration is the education of the hearer, a process of education that functions not by the poet's stating what must be done or learned but rather by his showing what sorts of behavior, what configurations of identity, are possible or preferable.

In Greek lyric, the more exact and intense the speaker's concentration on his hearer and his discourse, the more completely fixed is his mind on adjusting itself to his purpose in speaking, the more clearly defined and the more powerful the sense of his personality becomes. By focusing on what he has to say, on why he is saying it, and on the person *for* whom—not so much *to* whom—he is saying it, the speaker discovers the exact, the proper, form for his own character as speaker on this particular occasion, in this particular discourse; and, in fact, the purpose of discourse and the presence of the hearer furnish the speaker with enormous power and vitality. In a sense, the act of discourse clarifies the speaker's personality, he learns who and what he is by yielding himself wholly to the act of discourse; in performing his proper funciton properly, by discoursing, describing, deliberating, he becomes himself.

This sketch of lyric as discourse (description and deliberation) rather than as expression offers some correction to romantic notions of lyric poetry as unpremeditated warblings, but it needs to be modified in order to escape the contrary errors of neoclassical theory, in which rhetorical modes are seen as ends rather than as means and in which, moreover, the speaker becomes wholly lost in, wholly indistinguishable from, his discourse and the technical repertoire that structures and ornaments it. Oscar Wilde, that extraordinary fusion of romantic and neoclassical, whose *Intentions* is one of the great English critical works, was superbly trained as a Hellenist and well understood both the spirit and the letter of Greek poetry. Yet his statements on poetry, designed to countervail the excesses of romanticism in its decline, propel the pendulum much too far in the opposite direction: "All bad poetry springs from genuine emotion"; "All fine imaginative work is self-conscious and deliberate. A great poet sings because he chooses to sing." Yes, but—. A great, or good, poet does not create his poems merely out of other literature, out of the "tradition," nor does he create them out of nothing. In the case of Archilochus, it is true that, fresh and vital as his voice sounds to us, very much of his language and many of his themes are borrowed from Homeric epic.[13] But that does not mean that Archilochus never felt any of the emotions that his imagination shapes and to which he adapts his borrowings. We may never know much more than we know now, and it is precious little, about his engagement to Neobule, about the duplicity, if that is what it was, of her father, Lycambes; but we do not need to know anything more, unless "facts" interest us more than poetry does. Whatever happened or did not happen between Archilochus and his fiancée, whatever her father did or did not do, the violence and the outrageous wit of the fragments in question, this perfection of anger, remain—because Archilochus chose to find permanent and powerful shape for something that he had felt and that many humans feel. In this sense, it would not even matter if Neobule and her father were entirely fictitious, though I tend to doubt that they were; what matters only is that this complex cluster of emotions—love, rage, humiliation, loneliness, grief, bewilderment—whatever its origins, whatever its occurrence in place and time, finds answering form when Archilochus ponders it, seeks to make it available for contemplation by others in describing it to them, in imagining it for them in its purest form.

That Archilochus had felt such a configuration of emotions seems to me beyond doubt; he would scarcely have been human had he not. That this particular situation elicited the configuration of emotions is possible, even probable, but hardly certain. The task of the lyric poet is neither to report accurately, in the false sense of mimesis, an actual event and the emotions it gave rise to (which is not really possible, in any case, as anyone who has tried and failed to do this knows); nor is his task to invent emotions that he has never experienced (which is neither really possible nor, so limitless the supply of experience for poet and nonpoet alike, necessary). What distinguishes the lyric poet from people who are not lyric poets is perhaps, in part, his extreme sensitivity to emotions; but more important here is his ability to arrange his perceptions of emotion into clear patterns by means of precise language. In shaping emotions, then, the lyric poet performs two very different, indeed, opposite, functions simultaneously: he particularizes a universal emotion or cluster of emotions, such as all men share—that is to say, he dramatizes the universal, makes it vivid and plausible; and, at the same time, he universalizes an experience that is or was peculiarly his own, thus rendering it clear and intelligible. It is this delicate yet powerful fusion of the individual and the universal that characterizes good lyric poetry.

Eliot, modifying in 1927 the impersonalist theory of his most famous and most influential essay, defines the motive and method of the lyric poet by transforming Shakespeare and Dante into lyric poets rather like himself:

> What every poet starts with is his own emotions. . . . [Shakespeare was] occupied with the struggle—which alone constitutes life for a poet—to transmute his personal and private agonies into something rich and strange, something universal and impersonal. Dante's rage and Shakespeare's general cynicism and disillusionment are merely gigantic attempts to metamorphose private failures and disappointments.[14]

This is a shade too sour perhaps, but we can use it to reform Wilde's dictum in this fashion: all good lyric poetry springs, but seldom if ever directly, from personal feeling. What counts is the transformation of the personal into the impersonal or, better, the tempering of the personal with the universal, a union in which what is temporal and what is timeless strengthen one another, in whose coinherence the individual, the merely personal, and the universal find new meanings. It is the rhetorical situation and the rhetorical purpose of lyric that allow, that require, this marriage, and it is when the poet chooses to submit his private feelings, or his memory of them, to the needs of discourse that he discovers the necessary indirection that gives order and solace to personal uncertainties or personal dismay, and, at the same time, gives life and brilliance to what were otherwise an abstraction.[15]

Since modern theories, both neoclassical and romantic, obscure what the ancient Greek poet thought about the origins and the processes of his lyric creation, so they obscure the elements of the lyric creation itself. Where neoclassical theory will insist too heavily on rhetorical patterning and traditional themes and structures, romantic theory will overemphasize aspects of sound or aspections of imagery (as well as direct expression of "genuine" emotion). Here again, the rhetorical, lyrical triangle of speaker, discourse, and hearer is the essential feature of Greek lyric, of the Latin lyric that continued and refined the Greek tradition, and of the medieval and early modern European lyric that inherited and further refined the Graeco-Roman lyric tradition. In his struggle to reestablish, to make new, the lyrical tradition that he found moribund, Pound came gradually to lose interest in the lyrical identity and its discourse and to concentrate more and more on the *means* of lyrical discourse. Perhaps with an eye to Coleridge's poetries of the word, the eye and the ear, Pound became preoccupied with formulating his famous triad of "kinds of poetry": *phanopoeia* ("image making"), *melopoiia* ("music making"), *logopoeia* ("word making"; "style making").[16] What is missing from Pound's theory of poetry is the character (ethos) of the speaker: the words and sounds and pictures of a lyric poem are spoken to someone about something by someone, and that someone who speaks is, or should be, an integral part of what he speaks.

When Archilochus says:

> . . . tossed by waves,
> And then, I hope, in Salmydessos
> The Hairy Thracians
> Will play the perfect host to his
> Nakedness.
> He'll taste much trouble, and feed on
> A slave's ration.
> But first he'll freeze, there on the beach,
> Lying face down,
> Like a dog, his teeth a-rattle, seaweed
> Glued to his slack
> Flesh. That's what I want to see, because
>
> He did me wrong,
> My one time friend; he ground his heel
> In our love—
>> (Fragment 79a)

the sounds, the verbal patternings (that is, the rhetorical syntax), and, finally, the pictures are agents of the speaker's bitter volition, of his outraged identity, and of the emotions, mixed, torn, violent, that shake it.[17] Behind every lyric, sometimes vaguely sketched, sometimes clearly defined, is a story that explains the present moment of discourse and accounts for the singer's present moods and for his need or choice to sing. But in lyric poems, as against, say, ballads,[18] the story exists for the song, not the song for the story, and what gives the poem its form, its resonance, and its texture is the sensibility of the singer; what reveals and illumines that sensibility is its selection of language, sound, and image, which in turn reveal and illumine the passions that the singer imagines and orders. What the shape of this particular poem was we cannot, of course, even begin to guess at. But the controlled fury of the language and the speaker's clarity of vision and of volition survive this fragmentation. *That's what I want to see, because*: I want to see it happen in time and space; if I should fail of that, I want to see it now, here, in this moment of my discourse; I want somehow to eternize it, his suffering, my suffering, the power and the precision of my feelings and of my perceptions of my feelings and my selfhood. "All this I swallow, it tastes good, I like it well, it becomes mine; I am the man, I suffer'd, I was there."[19] I was there, I am here, to sing it, to fix it forever in language, to form it as surely in your mind as in mine: that is what Greek lyric insists on, the integrity, the heartwholeness, the purity of will, of the singer. Greek lyric is not mere *Gefühlpoesie* ("poetry of feeling") or *Erlebnislyrik* ("poetry of experience") because it insists on universalities and on universalizing rhetoric, on the triangle of discourse and on exact refinements of speech.[20] On the other hand, Greek poetry is not absolute poetry of the kind I have discussed in the previous chapter: *because* it is supremely rhetorical it will not, cannot, do without the lyrical I or without the passions that the lyric I shares with, communicates to, the lyrical You. This Greek idea of lyric unifies what is divided in the modern lyric consciousness; it connects ("Only connect") *Erlebnis* at its most intense with art at its most pure.

The secret of this connection was one that eluded Pound for most of his career; and this failure to reconcile opposites accounts for the deficiency in his poetic theory and also for the gallant yet finally imperfect struggles of his poetic practice.

In "the search for oneself," in the "search for sincere self-expression," one gropes, one finds, some seeming verity. One says, "I am" this, that, or the other thing, and with the words scarcely uttered, one ceases to be that thing.

I began this search for the real in a book called *Personae*, casting off, as it were, complete masks of the self in each poem. I continued in long series of translations, which were but more elaborate masks.[21]

This description of what he did in poetry (until *The Pisan Cantos*) is as accurate and honest as it is sad. *Personae* is, to my mind, one of the great books of monody since Baudelaire, and the translations, in particular that of the Roman poet Propertius, have done more for the lyric tradition than we can now accurately assess. But despite these triumphs Pound was not satisfied, wanted still the wholeness of an Archilochus, of a Catullus or a François Villon, or even of a Heinrich Heine. And could not have it because, like most moderns, he suffered from the "peeling-onionskins" theory of personality, in which the real me lies smothered, frustrated, impotent, under the dreadful layers of time and other unintelligible phenomena. This hopeless search for the real, for oneself and for the sincere, leads finally to a total separation of life from art, or poet from poem, and of both from their audience. This is not something that bothered Archilochus since he understood that identity was compounded of, among other things, accident and diversity, of the *polytropon*, the "many-mindedness" that Odysseus so admirably incarnates.

Our uniqueness, like our freedom, is genuine, but it is not a static entity, or is not merely a static entity; it is also, it is more nearly, a dynamism, a peculiar series of actions and of conflicting wills, of aggressions and submissions, of expansions and contractions—this balanced tumult or tumultuous balance we call, quite rightly, ourselves and our lives ("I like it well, it becomes mine"). This dialectical tension between what we think we are and what we in fact want and do, this fertile stress caused by the mysterious countervailing of our constancy by our changes, exhilarated Archilochus. Pound, like most of us, it bewildered, as a reading of *Mauberley* will perhaps show. Who is the speaker of the first set of twelve poems: Mauberley or Pound and his fictive creature named Mauberley? H. N. Schneidau, not unreasonably, insists that the poems "are all spoken by Pound, who holds up various masks which are not so much identities as accents or tones of voice."[22] Precisely: but this frantic puttering with masks was not a solution to the problem that Pound had defined for himself and us in the passage just quoted. "The search for the real" is, as Archilochus or Dolly Parton or Jimmy Buffet could tell Pound and us, is, in effect, a wild goose chase. The real—all that most of us can have of it, all that anyone but the saints can have of it—is here and now (*hic et nunc*); it is what you and I see about ourselves and about the world we inhabit. The greatness of *Personae* is rooted in Pound's grand determination to find, and near success in finding, this lyrical immanence and the *ethopoeia* ("making of character, of personality") it requires; when Pound began "imitating" Catullus, he almost found his own ethos, as he would almost find it again when he recovered Propertius for us by reinventing him. *Mauberley* is a very great poem, but it is not a sustained, organic unity; it is a violently mannerist poem about not being able to find masks and voices that are sufficient to the lyrical task; it is about the search for the impossible real seen as folly and failure and hence discontinued. The really real would be found, because it could no longer be fled, in the cage at Pisa—but that is another story.

To imagine personality—not, again, to express it—in order to be able to imagine human emotions, our emotions, as they are and may be, really and ideally, is the task of lyric poetry. "To imagine," here, does not mean "to invent" or "to fabricate" or "to photograph" or "to represent"; it means, as Cézanne tells and shows us, to order perceptions in a satisfying, that is to say, pleasing and disturbing way— for we need to be irritated into thinking and feeling no less than we need to be solaced or entertained or comfortably instructed. At the heart of Greek lyric, and of its beginnings with Archilochus, is the imagination of personality:

> My heart, heart, fouled by trouble, do not give in!
> Arise! Beat off the enemy! Eyes straight ahead,
> Make contact, block their pressure, take on the foe's attack
> And hold!
>   And when you win, don't gloat for all to see;
> Nor, when you lose, lock yourself in to cry your heart out!
> Keep a sane check on what you feel, in luck but also in
>   failure,
> And learn to know the seesaw structure of man's life.
>   (Fragment 67a)

Perfect control here, as he rides the vortex. The *rhysmos* ("rhythm") of things, the zigzaggedness of reality, is threatening, exciting, and infinitely mysterious. We cannot know reality as it is, for it is queerer, as John Haldane said of the universe, than we imagine, and queerer than we *can* imagine; but we can know that it is and we can even know something of our relationship to it and thereby know something of ourselves: by living the *rhysmos* from moment to moment, by moving with it and against it. *Gignoske*: "learn to know"! Here, where the poet addresses himself with the imperative, by the ruthless grace of the command, the poet and his hearer are made one, soul speaks to soul (*thume! thume!*). This is the core of Greek lyric, and it defines precisely the meaning of *ethopoeia* and confirms the centrality of rhetoric for lyric.

The Rhetoric of Sappho

In turning to the fragments of Sappho, we encounter an emphasis on and mastery of *ethopoeia* that are similar to those of Archilochus, but Sappho's modes of constructing and arranging poetic personality differ strikingly, so far as we can tell, from his. It is a pity to descend to sexism in discussing her, for she was not easily mistaken for a "poetess" even in times when the vile word seemed to have meaning; but she brought to poetry a subtlety of observation, without the loss of any of lyric's proper powers, that other Greek lyricists seem not to have had in anything like equal measure or that would be found again in European lyric only rarely; and in trying to glimpse the springs of this subtlety, it is difficult not to invoke the idea of the feminine. In any case, this delicacy of contemplation, allied with musical form and with the natural self-assertion of Greek lyric, spells lyric perfection.

We look first at her most famous fragment, in which her special qualities seem distilled:

> I think that man is like a god
> Who faces you, and sits by you,
> And listens to your gentle words,
>
> And to your silver laughter. But I—
> My heart explodes within my breast;
> One timid glance, and all my voice is gone,

My tongue breaks, and a subtle flame
Races below my flesh, my eyes
Refuse their sight, my hearing is a gong,

Cold sweat clings to me, and I shake
From head to toe, my skin the color
Of grass: I am about to die, I think. . . .
        (Fragment 31)[23]

Although it seems likely that we have the beginning of this poem, we cannot be sure of the story, real or fictive, behind it, and therefore we cannot establish, beyond doubt, the exact situation of discourse. Is the speaker jealous of the man who sits beside the girl whom the poet addresses, or is he merely a part of a moment, another moment that illumines and foils the beauty and value of the girl whom the poet has seen before a hundred times, loves and admires? Jealousy seems, at first, only a peripheral matter since the poet immediately loses interest in the man and concentrates her entire attention upon her own response to this moment. But then, does she not also lose interest in the girl herself? The event, briefly yet powerfully sketched, becomes internalized: the moment of intimacy between the girl and the man, together with the girl's quiet speech and delicate laughter, dissolve, or rather, they "explode," into a chaos of violent physical sensation that tell the poet (and us) what is happening in her mind, what is happening *to* her mind. What has, finally, created this explosion of body and mind is the moment and its beauty and anguish—the poet has allowed herself the briefest glance at the girl she admires, has caught, tried not to catch, in the corner of her eye, the image of the lucky, the divine, rival—then, the explosion and the pieces of sensation of thought in their dissolution. From the outer perception, the poet turns inward to her own reaction, finds ruin, and tries, vainly, it seems, to order it. She cannot, she finds, speak or see or hear, fever and chills fasten on her body, her blood rushes from her head, she is near fainting, she is near death. The details of her suffering are swiftly, breathlessly announced, and the experience of complex admiration, anxiety, lust, and jealousy is thereby accurately portrayed: consciousness plunges into darkness in a confused configuration of sensation.[24]

Confused, but not confusing either to her or to us. The welter of discordant feelings is mastered by her swift perception of them and by her uncanny ability to reflect on these disordered experiences without robbing them of their intensity or their rich tangle. This is not "emotion recollected in tranquillity," for the disorder and the erotic anguish are presented in their full immediacy; it is this moment, here and now, that she imagines for her hearers, causes them to see and to feel with her; and she accomplishes this, not as Longinus and some other critics have suggested, by distancing herself from what she imagines (and perhaps re-creates) but rather by mastering the cluster of emotions from inside them; that is, the shock of recognition is imagined as being all but inseparable from the terrible glance, even as the moment of mastery is all but simultaneous with the moment of complete helplessness. She is utterly a victim, but she refuses to see herself as a victim. At its core, the personality remains unshaken. Part of this indomitable selfhood is grounded, as Archilochus tells us it must be, in a sense of *rhysmos* ("rhythm"); we surmise that this is probably a recurrent experience, this man or other men have sat by the girl before, Sappho has dared a glance at them, and she has suffered like this before, has lived this moment before and lived through it. But in its essential strategy the poem dramatizes a particular moment with its particular passions and sudden clarity of knowledge and volition.

The last line of the fragment reads, *alla pan tolmaton, epei—kai peneta*: "But all this must be endured, since. . . ." [25] Where the poem went after this we cannot tell, but what we sense is that the terrible moment has been survived, by the force of will and intelligence that would not yield to what had first seemed inevitable defeat. A moment of supreme erotic frustration, imagined in all its bitterness— what does that moment mean? It means several things: it means, because this *is* a love poem, a poem of high praise, that the nameless girl is infinitely lovable, and it means also that the poet, both in her violent response to the girl and in her command of her own complex, dangerous emotions, is worthy to offer such love to such a girl. The truth of what the poet values has been confirmed by the truth and the power of her response; the measure of that truth and value —the girl's being, what Sappho admires and wishes to possess—is discovered both in the pain this love inflicts and in the courage and honesty that close with this pain. One is almost tempted to say that what is unique in Sappho's poem is its bravery and its gentle authority. Her singer—partly herself perhaps, the woman Sappho; partly an ideal, universal fiction: their fusion in imagination—refuses to lie to herself about her emotions and also refuses to be destroyed by them. To find anything remotely resembling this combination of profundity of feeling and unpersuadable intelligence, we must go to the sonnets of Shakespeare where passion, compassion, and intellectual power find a similar interdependence.

That, as I see it, is what she does in this poem, this fragment; that is how her handling of *ethopoeia* manifests itself. But how, on the level of style and structure, does she achieve this miracle of complexity and seeming ease? The answer to that question is probably beyond us, for poetry of this level of perfection does not fully yield itself to stylistic or structural analysis. But one may venture a few suggestions. Though we do not really know what Greek sounded like, the apparent ease of patterning that caused Dionysius of Halicarnassus to marvel at it,[26] some shadow of this grace, paradoxically at once austere and rich, can be heard even now. This grace was not achieved by Sappho's having imitated a living voice; it is rather a question of Sappho's having imagined an ideal living voice: this facility and precision of euphony and pause, of balance and momentum, of restrained sonority are what we would like to be capable of and never are. The secret of her diction is entirely mysterious. D. L. Page defines its central characteristics well when he speaks of her style in this fragment as being "realistic, severely plain and candid," but when he further remarks that it is "unadorned by literary artifice," that it is the product of "nature, not of artifice,"[27] we cannot agree, for here he describes the effect, not the cause. The language is, indeed, "independent of literary tradition," so far as we can tell, and "apparently . . . close to the speech of everyday," but, once again, this is an ideal simplicity that Sappho has invented. Here, the audacity is breathtaking. These words and phrases ought to seem flat or ordinary or banal, but in fact that language is as unfadingly fresh as it is rigorously selected and meticulously arranged.

Her audacity succeeds in hiding her high artifice of style only because Sappho is in complete control of what one is forced to call something like structure but which were better called dynamic form, which is one aspect of her rhetoric. This fragment is possessed of an extraordinary violence which breaks upon us unexpectedly. Yet the violence is prepared for, as it is tightly contained, by the gentle understatement, the severe simplicity of the first five verses. To put it another way, her major stylistic strategy is to stick to the essentials, to choose her emphasis and her angle and unfolding of visions with supreme care, and then to let the bare, simple words absorb their shining and their resonance from the singer's clear conviction and lucid articulation of detail. Poets who have attempted something of this kind in English, though they may achieve an admirable dryness, a lean, satisfying clarity, can seldom lay claim to anything like this strange union of severity and luxuriance. In this sense, style and form are exactly matched to content. Both in her manner and her matter, Sappho reconciles opposites: her gentleness, grace, and tact take on intensity from her violence, and her violence, though it endures no weakening, is wholly contained by her delicacy: impeccable decorum and ferocious truth.

> Some like the horse, others the infantry;
> And some say ships are the finest things in the world;
> But I say: best is what you love.
>
> And it's quite easy to make this clear to people.
> The famous Helen, paragon of beauty, left
> Her excellent husband, and took ship
>
> For Troy, and never once did she remember
> Her little child, or even her parents, but
> She strayed into forgetfulness.
>
> One lover's glance, and hearts rise up like birds
> With Aphrodite's help. So now I dream
> Of absent Anactoria.
>
> How much do I prefer to see her charms,
> Her dainty step, her radiant face, than all
> The Persian panoply of War!
>   (Fragment 16)

Though it is not certain, this poem, saved for us on papyrus, is probably complete, except for its ruined fifth stanza. One reason for believing in the poem's essential integrity, beyond wishful thinking, is that the poem, or the fragment, shows a favorite structural device of archaic and classical Greek lyric, namely, that of ring composition: the poem begins and ends with the same imagery, that of the splendor of military forces. Furthermore, we find here the no less popular structural device of the preamble or priamel, in which what is not to be elaborated on—here, cavalry, infantry, ships—is used to introduce and then to foil the actual subject of discourse—here, the singer's feeling for Anactoria. Emphatic in the preamble is the first-person singular pronoun which, also part of the ring composition, returns in the final stanza to help round off the poem.

But the first person in this poem, in contrast with that of the previous poem, lacks, or at first seems to lack, vividness and definition. Part of this difficulty may lie in the ruin of stanza five, but it seems doubtful that even if we had this stanza complete we would have a full sense of the occasion of discourse, the origin of this lyric moment. The singer addresses not Anactoria but herself, and the poem seems formally, in Eliot's sense of the phrase, to be meditative; viewed in this way, the singer seems impersonal, hidden in what she sings. Yet for all its apparent obliquity, the poem has its own intensity and its own strong *ethopoeia*. Crucial here is the exemplum, Helen, who abandoned her husband, children, parents, and city to go off to Troy with Paris, who, so far as we can tell, was not even mentioned in the poem. Helen forgot what, in the world's eyes, she should never have forgotten; and the singer, recalling this famous, this notorious, forgetfulness, suddenly remembers her own love, and in so remembering, feels again both the glory of that love and her anguish in being separated from it.

But this separation, though it has prominence by virtue of its place in the penultimate stanza and therefore in the poem, is less important than the feeling of composed exultation that suffuses the poem. The singer begins by rejecting the values of other people—of most men certainly, and perhaps of many women as well—although she claims at the beginning to be tolerant of other, conventional values. Yet this apparent relativism vanishes as she adduces the clear, unarguable proof of her own system of values. Helen had looked at Paris or Paris had looked at Helen or the gaze was mutual: and from this fatal glance came the flight from Sparta, the sailing for Troy, the destruction of the city, together with the countless deaths of both Trojans and Greeks. The terrible price that Helen, or rather Helen's victims, paid for her yielding to love is not of the slightest interest to the singer. The common, ordinary person, who has perhaps not experienced this extraordinary, this divine, moment of erotic vision—seeing the beloved, seeing the beloved return this gaze—feels excitement and admiration only when he looks on the pageantry of war, the massing of brute power, and thereby feels, perhaps, the normal patriotic emotions—his city's force and wealth, the value of his citizenship, the safety of his family. This is love, perhaps, sings Sappho: *ego de ken' otto tis eratai*—"But I say: best is what you love." Yet having said this and having undertaken to prove it, she transvalues all values, ruthlessly, joyously, by choosing the most controversial and most radical example of one who loves and for whom the world is well lost for love, and by ignoring, as utterly irrelevant, what everyone knows: that Helen's love is destructive love at its most destructive. The singer does not care about such destruction: she, like Helen, has experienced the moment of revelation, the moment of glory, which nothing, not separation, not destruction, can take from her. She has, unfailingly, in her mind's eye, the complete presence of what she loves and desires, for the sake of which she, like Helen, would instantly abandon kin and country: she possesses, in its fullness, the beautiful way Anactoria walks, the radiance of her face.

Once again, the subject of discourse and, in a peculiarly oblique way, the emotion that engenders it are violent—a total rejection of the way most people live, the way most people think, a total affirmation of private passion that is of no value to the outer world. And once again, this violence is presented with a perfection of calm and of understatement. As before, the language is simple, is given the appearance of natural speech, but in this poem a powerful force of feeling, the intuition of a unique destiny, radiates from the quiet surface of the language. The singer has no need to raise her voice even as she feels no need to defend her outrageous exemplum; the witty choice of her exemplum is, in fact, the measure of her conviction, of her self-possession and her faith in this love, and of her own worth because of this love. This public poem, which will be sung for an audience and is therefore addressed, in part, to them, is clearly, on one level, an attempt to persuade, to change, and to mold opinion ("And it's quite easy to make this clear to people"); but the poem is also, on another level, a love poem addressed to Anactoria alone. Here the private transvaluation and the triumphant free emotions that achieve that transvaluation can be publicly announced even while the singer also sings to Anactoria the song that she has inspired and that she alone will fully comprehend. In this sense, this is a poem within a poem, a private love song cast as a piece of public argumentation. That wit is part of Sappho's strategy of indirection and of understatement, a way of assuring that the passion will be shaped, will not burst its proper limits and then dwindle to unintelligibility and into crude shapelessness. This wild love and this radical individualism are fully controlled by an intelligence whose grasp of lyrical compression and rhetorical precision is incomparable. If we want to know what lyrical rhetoric is, how *logos* ("speech") is shaped for lyric imagining of emotion, how choices of angles of vision and of modulation and emphasis contribute to that shaping, this poem can tell us. And here *ethopoeia* and lyrical rhetoric find a fixed and splendid harmony.[28]

> Immortal Aphrodite, elegant daughter
> Of Zeus, goddess of guile, I pray to you:
> Do not, my lady, break my heart with sufferings,
>
> But come to me, if once before you heard
> My voice from afar, and listened to my speech,
> And left your father's house and yoked your car
>
> And came. Beautiful, lightning-swift they were,
> The sparrows that drew you over the black earth,
> With wheeling wings, from heaven through the fiery air.
>
> Suddenly they were here. But you, my lady,
> Turned on me your immortal face and smiled,
> And asked, why was I calling you again, and what
>
> Was my complaint, and what did I have in mind
> For my grand passion? "Who is it now that I
> Must lure into your arms? Who is the culprit, Sappho?
>
> If she's avoiding you, she'll seek you out;
> If she disdains your gifts, she'll be the giver;
> If she won't kiss, she'll kiss you yet despite herself."
>
> Come now again, my lady, and set me free
> From anxious troubles, and help me to achieve
> The longings of my heart: Be my ally, in person!
>
> (Fragment 1)

This poem, for it is almost certainly complete, is neither an example of a cult hymn to Aphrodite nor an expression of Sappho's desperation as she finds herself "at the height of her suffering."[29] Instead, the process of indirection that we saw in the previous poem is here carried to its exquisite limits. The moment of discourse and the lyrical situation are not difficult to determine: once again Sappho, or her singer, finds herself utterly, and interestingly, thwarted in her pursuit of the loved one, and here again, as often in the past, she seeks to undo her frustration with a prayer to the only being who can help her, Aphrodite, goddess of love, of erotic encounters. But the statements about suffering are carefully distributed throughout the poem and so endure considerable dimunition of their force, while Sappho carefully positions herself, her singer, and us at special angles of vision from which amorous suffering may be pondered, qualified, and wittily reformulated. When the poem is ended, erotic suffering, like the purity of erotic volition that nourishes such suffering, is seen to be, in many cases and at most levels of its operation, illusion. Yet this process of disillusionment is neither mocking nor cruel, for Sappho designs a humorous and tolerant fiction by means of which this lover, and so, any lover, can move from illusion without losing proper self-esteem.

Central to this fiction is Sappho's prayer to Aphrodite, which is conventional in its structure: invocation, with mention of the deity's special attributes (here, *doloploke*, "weaver of wiles," is crucial); reminders of the deity's previous assistance; then a request for similar assistance in the present crisis. What has nothing to do with convention is the turn the prayer takes at the end of the second stanza. In recalling to Aphrodite her past succor, Sappho imagines what appears to be a series of past epiphanies in which the goddess descends from Mount Olympus in her sparrow-drawn chariot and meets her devotee face to face. The memory of these past epiphanies is distilled into a single epiphany in the present moment and the present prayer; it is as if the goddess has come again in answer to this prayer, whirling down into the poem to overwhelm it with her radiant presence and her amused wisdom. The goddess smiles, as she always smiles when answering this cry *de profundis*. Why shouldn't she smile her rich, deathless smile at this desperate, silly woman? What worshipper is more attentive than Sappho, more pious in her devotion to the goddess's name and nature, more, in her whims and passions, like herself? And who should understand Sappho better than the goddess whose special poet she is? Hence the smile, which is mocking, affectionate, admiring.

Suddenly, in the midst of the prayer, in a burst of radiant movement, we see the goddess of love through Sappho's eyes; then, when the goddess begins speaking to her, we see Sappho through the eyes of Aphrodite. She is extraordinarily passionate, this woman whom love grieves, beyond measure, beyond hope: a fitting celebrant, then, of the power and the truth of erotic passion. But isn't she also—and this is part of passion's truth—governed by caprice? "Yes, once again you've found your own true love. Miss Right has come along—again. What do you want me to do this time, as if I didn't know?" The truth of passion and its violence are here carefully balanced against caprice and its cunning, and only a poet who was herself *doloplokos* ("goddess of guile"; "weaver of wiles") could possibly achieve such precision of balancing. This poem is a poem within a poem within a poem. The song about Sappho's passion (and caprice) is sung before an audience; it is reflected in and reflects a fictional epiphany of Aphrodite, which suddenly, without quite denying passion, sets passion in a new, equivocal light; and this fiction, in turn, is reflected in and reflects a more private poem, written for and sung to the person who (actually or fictively) has inspired the passion and its poem. For the prayer to Aphrodite turns out, on close inspection, to be, among other things, an elegant seduction poem. If Aphrodite has often (always?) helped Sappho in the past, it is reasonable to assume that she will honor this present supplication as well (*su d'auta / summachos esso*—"be my ally, my companion-in-arms, my fellow warrior"). Through Sappho's lips we hear what Aphrodite has said to her before, that the beloved will yield, and will more than yield, against her will. Through Sappho's lips, here and now, in this public song, the goddess speaks the same speech— in the girl's hearing, as she sits with the amused audience; whether or not this is an actual girl or a conflation of girls or an ideal, fictive girl, makes no difference at all to the success of the poem; for the poem, whatever its actual inspiration, is a paradigm of the spectrum of passion, an imagination of what is universal in the human heart: *hoia an genoito* ("what might be").[30]

The poem, then, is crystalline, not merely in the precision of its forms and in the clarity of its surfaces but also in its various angles and its shifting integrities. The strategy of *ethopoeia* achieves here a peculiar complexity. We, the audience, first see Sappho as a conventional lyric singer, beset by love's anguish, praying for deliverance; we see her next through Aphrodite's eyes, a foolish woman, tormented by whims she encourages but cannot master; and we see her finally through the eyes of her beloved, as she sits listening in the audience—in this final vision the singer is a woman both passionate and cunning, both serious and capricious, who invents this complex *don du poème* ("gift of a poem") and who will not take no for an answer. Whether there was a girl to reject or accept the gift is beside the point. What the poem shows, among other things, is that this gift is precious and that the giver is possessed of a clear understanding of a complex mystery. No one of these pictures of Sappho explains who Sappho is and what she knows; but the three pictures, merging in their endless mutual reflections, fuse through rhetorical sophistication in an accurate picture of an intricate clustering of human feeling and human intellection. Are we foolish when we love? Yes and no, maybe and maybe not. We look into this mirror not to see what we look like and what we are but to see, more clearly than we ever can, from moment to moment, in our lives, the possible shapes of what we feel and think, of what we blame and praise, of what we wish to be and wish not to be. We can do this because Sappho has caught this eternal moment in the mirror of imagination, has precisely focused, as naïve mimesis never could, every shade of this intricate inwardness: the bewildering varieties of love and selfhood clarified, compressed into twenty-eight verses.

One complaint lodged against Sappho—it is lodged against Emily Dickinson too, and that tells us something about the complaint—is that her range is narrow. Even if the charge could be proved correct, and it cannot, we would want to remember that lyric poetry cares very little for breadth and width, everything for depth and height. Whatever the mysterious criteria for great European lyric may be, compression, intensity of feeling, and complexity and subtlety of reflection are surely high among them. But I want to emphasize complexity and subtlety of reflection. In Greek lyric and in the later lyric that flows from it, sound and picture and various kinds of rhetorical ingenuity, all informed by a strong sense of the person of the speaker, together with a strong sense of the occasion, situation, and purpose of the discourse, are inseparable. Their fusion and the strength that grows from that fusion are grounded in a rhetorical sophistication, which, though it hardly precludes sincerity, shows

Lewis's notion of pure lyric to be inadequate even as it shows Pound's
divisions of poetry and his glorification of image to be yet another
kind of harmful simplification. The term "rhetorical sophistication"
may sound both hurtful to romantic and postromantic ears and re-
ductionist in its own way, but I am not engaged here in constructing
Latinist wargames. What I am calling rhetorical sophistication is as
evident in Chinese and Arabic lyric as it is in the classical lyric tradition of Europe. Nor, in making these claims for rhetorical sophistication, am I attempting to deny greatness to lyric that might be
described as, depending on one's view, naïve or pure, or, in the best
and highest sense, primitive. The lyrics that Ruth Finnegan has collected in her anthology *Oral Poetry*,[31] and folk lyric anywhere, any-
time, have no apologies to make to anyone. The problem is that
simplicity cannot, usually, handle complexity of reflection whereas
complexity of reflection, which is naturally allied with rhetorical sophistication, can handle, can attain to, certain kinds of simplicity.
Because Sappho and the voices from whom she is, for all intents and
purposes, indistinguishable are best defined by their elegance, conscious artistry, and rhetorical sophistication does not mean that they
fail of genuine feeling or heart-wholeness. It means, on the contrary,
that their freshness and purity of experience are, *because* of the elaborations they accept, precisely formed in ways that naïve lyric and its
naïve rhetoric can seldom if ever approach.

The pattern for and the standard of monody was, so far as the fragments of Greek lyric will permit us to judge, set by Sappho. That
standard has often been met by later lyric poets and has occasionally
been surpassed. But it is she, as antiquity well knew, who set the
standard. In her poetry, complexity and simplicity mingle; she knew
how to imagine and to order emotion because she knew how to
imagine and to order lyrical *logos* ("speech"; "pattern"). When that
knowledge has been grasped, adapted, refined, and passed on, European lyric has thrived; when that knowledge has been lost or has
faltered, the power of European lyric has suffered diminution.

*The Waning of Song and Its Last Renewal: Anacreon, Simonides, and
Pindar*

Since our effort here is to search for the outline of the poetics of
Greek lyric, we avoid, as best we can, the history of Greek lyric and
so ignore not only the elegists and the iambic poets, who are often

taken as part of that history, but also most of the lyricists themselves.
Anacreon we will not omit, for he is both the last of the great monodists and, so far as we can tell, the inventor of a major lyric mode
that was to have a long and fertile life in European lyric. The reasons
for the decline in monody, and, more slowly, the decline of choral as
well, I will presently sketch when discussing Simonides. There I will
be forced to entertain certain sociological and political possibilities,
but, for the case of Anacreon, it is perhaps sufficient to recall that
the time of vital lyrical flowering in a given literature as in the life of
a given lyric poet is usually fairly brief. Indeed, most genres flourish
superbly only for short periods; but lyric, not surprisingly, given the
requirements of intensity and compression, tends to have an unusually short fruition. What may sound, then, like hostile criticism
of Anacreon is not really that; for, coming at the end of the tradition
of monody, when its themes and modes and perhaps even its welcome were wearing thin, when newer, rival genres were discovering their essential forms and gathering their audiences, Anacreon
turned his disadvantages of time and place—he was, essentially, an
entertainer at the courts of tyrants—into brilliant assets. At a moment when, so far as we can tell, lyric inspiration was all but exhausted and aesthetic and intellectual fashions were moving away
from what lyric needs for its life and from what it has to offer, Anacreon faced his predicament squarely and created, from this complex
impoverishment, the ideal mask of hedonism.

Here is a poem by Anacreon that recalls something of Sappho's
prayer to Aphrodite and may even depend on it for some of its
inspiration:

> My Lord, you whom Eros the Tamer
> And the Nymphs with indigo eyes
> And bright Aphrodite
> Join with in your games,
> You haunter of mountains' lofty heights,
> I pray you, come kindly to me,
> Come hear my prayer:
> Be to Kleomboulos a timely mentor—
> O Dionysus,
> Counsel him honor my passion.
>> (Fragment 301)

Though this is most likely a poem, not a fragment, for the conventional structure of the prayer-poem seems complete, except for mention of past services rendered, a comparison with Sappho may seem unfair since the two poets clearly have very different aims. Yet it is aims and means, not talents, that I am focusing on. Where Sappho presents us with a rich complexity of views and emotions, Anacreon distills tradition and emotion to a single view, which crystallizes in an elegant joke: the seduction prayer is addressed to the wine god, who is asked to assure that the beloved's inebriation at the next symposium will be adequate to the purposes of seduction. This joke, this poem, with its deft handling of religious decorum and literary reminiscence, is charming in its gentle wit and in its assured compressions. The small irony, lust faintly masked in piety to the god and concern for the boy's welfare, is caught up in language of incomparable delicacy, and the refinements of sound and syntax recall the mastery of Sappho and challenge it. But the joke remains, for all this artistry, no more than a joke. If the essential strategy here is the same as Sappho's—for Kleomboulos is to be thought of as sitting in the audience to whom the song is sung—the poem neither attempts the levels that Sappho's poem achieves, nor is it possessed of the singer's dramatic presence, as *this* speaker, *this* singer. Instead, the voice from the mask recalls Lewis's pure anonymous singer in a paradoxical manner—paradoxical because while Sappho's consummate illusion of a natural voice is ironically rehearsed, where her artifice was all but imperceptible, Anacreon renders his ornaments conspicuous, boldly, zestfully. For Anacreon, *ethopoeia* has become irrelevant, if not impossible: what he can do and do well, what he delights in, is, to misuse an ancient term, *prosopopoeia*, "the making of a mask."[32] Where Archilochus and Sappho, in their different ways, are concerned to find the proper form for emotions, to order and clarify emotions by ideal dramatizations of their manifestations and their dynamics, by giving them bodies and voices *hic et nunc* ("here and now"), Anacreon finds that his lyric task is to invent varied forms, not for emotions, but for an attitude or a configuration of attitudes.

It is idle to say of Anacreon that his range is small; even if, as the fragments indicate, he limited himself chiefly to wine, girls and boys, death, old age, and song, we must admit that this spectrum is wide enough, that the range of Li Po or Robert Herrick or the Archpoet or Robert Burns is scarcely wider. But it is not merely his themes that are constant; it is also his tone, a fact which his inge-nuity tends to hide and was doubtless carefully trained to hide. What is the tone, behind this mask? It is a kind of genial despair—since there is nothing really to despair of, nothing really to win or to lose; a kind of frivolous stoicism, of intelligent stoicism. What the mask hides—or rather, what it reveals, for, like Wilde, Anacreon knew that masks, unless they are worn by bandits, exist to reveal what were else incapable of revelation—what the mask reveals is weari-ness, indifference, and a lethargy that is, aesthetically, energetic. *L'art pour l'art.*

> Blond Love has aimed and hit me squarely
> With his little crimson ball—
> He summons me to share his games
> With that girl in the fancy sandals.
> But she—for she was born in splendid Lesbos—
> Has scorned me for my ivory hair,
> And hankers after one of her own kind.
> (Fragment 302)

Passion? Anacreon is fond of *paizein*: "to play," fun and games. Eros plays with the singer, and the singer, in turn, plays with the charm-ing girl, whose slippers confer on her a small but adequate immor-tality. It is not his age that she holds against him; he loses the game because of her notorious preferences. It is a sly, wry malice that anni-hilates her refusal, together with his own emotions and love poetry itself. What is, or was, passion if not this: the games people play out of boredom, out of having nothing to do, games for which there are no prizes and no winners? But if no winners, then no losers either. Tolerant, good-natured, he shrugs and walks away—from perfection of utterance.

Aside from its own artistic creed, this art seems to have nothing to work with, or better, nothing to work against: the ingenuities en-counter no useful resistance. That should, in my view at least, spell sterility of some sort, but this poetry, as I mentioned earlier, was not barren. If it had done nothing more than to provide Horace with one of his favorite instruments, that would have been enough and more than enough. But, in fact, Anacreon's shaping of an attitude accomplished much more than that; it gave European lyric one form of the genuine and abiding gaiety that is one of its chief glories. Anacreon is not, then, merely a dirty old artiste camping it up for the idle rich, a clockwork bird in a gilded cage. The sense of life as a pastime without meaning or purpose is very strong, but no less strong, and flawlessly achieved, is an almost unfailing cheerfulness, something that partakes of courtesy and self-discipline and even, in a way, of courage. Anacreon, even he, is a moralist of sorts. A moralist without a whip or megaphone. We need him, and it is lucky we have even a little of him.

The mask of hedonism is not the only ironic lyric form that evolves in the last quarter of the sixth century B.C. In turning to choral poetry and to Simonides, we encounter another, ironic lyric mode. But before we focus on Simonides, we must first glance at the nature and development of choral poetry from its beginnings, or what we know of them, until the time when Pindar bestowed on choral poetry its great, permanent form.

The prime function of Greek choral poetry was religious and ceremonial, and its essence was legends of gods and heroes. When the Greeks worshipped the gods at their festivals or honored men at special moments in their lives, it was natural that the story of why the worshippers and celebrants came to be gathered on a particular occasion should become the nucleus of the musical, danced poetry that defined that worship and celebration. In distinguishing lyric from drama and epic, Plato will, naturally center on this narrative lyric poetry (see Chapter 3 below), but, so far as we know, it was only in Stesichorus, and, possibly, in Ibycus, that all, or almost all, of the entire choral poem was given up to divine and heroic legend. Even in Bacchylides, who is extremely fond of narrative and extremely good at it, the story is broken up, varied, foiled by prayers, maxims, statements about the poet's craft and the power of art, remarks on members of the choir; and when the poem celebrates a human being rather than gods, on the person being celebrated, or his family and his city. It is this form of choral lyric, in which the narrative yields more and more to its adornments and modulations, that gradually supplanted purely narrative choral poetry and that Pindar would make supreme among all lyric forms.

But in the chorals of Alcman, the first great representative of the form whose work survives (again in fragments), we are still very far from the splendor of Pindar. In the charming "Partheneion," from which the legend has been lost, the religious and social occasion, the act of devotion and the festal mood that enforms this devotion, are mirrored in a poem that is "at once the object and the medium of presentation."[33] In what remains to us of this poem, it is the performers themselves, their self-confidence in their beauty and in their vocal and dancing skill, their gaiety, and their eagerness to triumph in the choral contest—it is this moment in time, when the performers and audience gather both in solemnity and in a spirit of fun to celebrate the glorious dead, that is being imitated even as it is being performed, experienced, lived. In a way that may seem strange to us, the present moment is eternalized and ennobled, all its ephemeral charm and mortal existence gathered into the immortal legend it recalls and affirms; and the rhythms, the melody, the legend, the prayers, the dancers, and the dance have become, for all the discrepancies that obtain among them, for all their discord, a concordant, rhythmical metaphor for a particular feeling—the celebration of gods and humans, of their kinship with the cosmos. In the brilliance of the occasion and the poem that immortalizes that occasion—not because the poem will be written down, or later performed, or remembered in any way—the energy and beauty of the singing, dancing girls, their delight in life and their reverence for divine and heroic being, are transformed into a *rhysmos* ("rhythm") that is at once dynamic and at rest. The legends of *illud tempus* ("that time") evoke a heightened sense of *hoc tempus* ("this time"); these two mirrors, past and the present, reflect one another, and in that reflection is discovered the perennial rhythm where gods and humans, past and present, are united in the unchanging now.

The societies for which Alcman, Stesichorus, Ibycus, Simonides, Bacchylides, and Pindar composed their choral poems were based upon a profound belief in human greatness, upon shared, enduring metaphors for the fellowship of gods and men, for the beauty of the cosmos, and, most particularly, for the worth and the grandeur of the lucky individuals whom the *Iliad* and the *Odyssey* had endowed with powerful and significant form. In the great ages of colonization, of the great nobles and the great tyrants, these ideas and metaphors had been modified, revised, and adapted to changed conditions by lyric poets and by early "philosophers" in various ways, at various times; but the substance of these metaphors, which Nietzsche be-

yond all others, has so eccentrically and so skillfully described, remained essentially intact throughout all their crises and alterations.
But from about the middle of the sixth century B.C. until the Persian
Wars, early in the fifth century B.C., we can dimly see the power of
these shared metaphors begin to weaken and disappear. The gradual
emergence of rationalism, combined with a complex network of political and economic crises, creates an intellectual and social atmosphere in which the old legends of the divine and the heroic no
longer furnish adequate nourishment for the survival of the shared
metaphors and the communities that they had made possible. This is
the beginning of what will be in the middle of the fifth century, particularly in Athens, the Greek enlightenment, a period, an intellectual and emotional movement, in which Homer and his world are
first questioned, then criticized, then supplanted by science, by
logic, by rationalistic metaphysics, and by prose. It is during this re-
hearsal for the age of reason that Xenophanes closes with the problem of the "immorality" of Homer's gods and the "arrogance" of his
anthropomorphism, thereby undermining the validity of the legends
on which both Greek society and choral poetry were founded. But
Xenophanes was not alone in performing such scrutiny (he is as
much a part of the spirit of his age as he is an adumbration of the
later enlightenment in full flower), and Hermann Fränkel is clearly
correct in seeing Simonides as Xenophanes's collaborator in disman-
tling the old, ruining structures of thought and feeling and in dig-
ging the foundations for the new structures that will replace them.[34]
In the splendors and miseries of the Homeric world and of the archaic world that inherited, changed, and preserved that world, man
is at once ineffably wretched and ineffably grand. One of the major
tasks of the enlightenment and the preenlightenment was to refor-
mulate the questions about man's nature and condition, about the
metaphors that supported Greek society, and to devise answers to
the new questions about the peculiar interdependence of human
splendor and human misery.

Nothing in Greek lyric is more paradoxical or more fascinating
than the situation of Simonides. Here was a choral poet, part artist,
part priest, part sophisticated shaman, forced to analyze the legends
that his predecessors had praised and sung, forced to redefine his
own function as a singer of legends, as a worker of the miracle of
incantation. In answering the questions: Are men and gods of one

race? Is a poetry a means, a magical means, of bringing individuals and communities in touch with their own rhythms, of transporting them, out of past and present, into the eternal now? Is poetry, both as memory and prayer, a method of becoming beautiful and good and of knowing the truth?—in trying to answer these questions, Simonides might very well have availed himself of the complicated and lovely ironies that enabled Anacreon not to answer such questions but to avoid them. But he did something harder: he said neither yes nor no to such questions; he used a dialectical rhythm, a dialectical voice, to force us to ask and to answer these questions for ourselves. This mode of poetry, which is as rigorous as it is charitable and which, as Fränkel, again, suggests, Horace was to take for his favorite mode,[35] is essentially Socratic, that is to say, the humanistic poetic mode par excellence.

Seen in this light, it is not surprising that although Simonides showed wide mastery in various lyric forms, though he was, apparently, excellent in traditional choral poetry and in the triumph songs (*epinikia*) that he invented or at least elaborated, his special interest lay in dirges (*threnoi*) and in epigrams for the dead, forms where, because advice, reflection, solace and exhortation to perserverance and common sense are of the essence,[36] the dialectical mode has special prominence and special importance. The magnificence of man?

> For even those ancient creatures, half divine,
> The sons of the high gods who govern all,
> Not even they could reach their final years
> Exempt from envy, hazard and harsh toil.
> (Fragment 357)

The old magnificence is not sneered at; rather it is placed in a new focus, and the limitations of human life are redefined, the old exultations and the old lamentations are subjected to new ponderings, new balancings:

> A fable tells us Virtue lives
> high amid pathless rocks, protected by
> a blessed band of Nymphs—
> she is not manifest to mortal vision,
> except to him who strives from his heart's core,
> who has dared climb the furthest crag of courage.
> (Fragment 386)

The ancient *arete* ("virtue"; "bravery"; a natural yet spectacular ability to fulfill one's special function, to exercise one's gifts and thereby become and be oneself) is here an ideal to be striven after, not an inheritance to be taken easily and thereafter enjoyed. And the old luck, the old destiny?

> Since you are human, never try to tell
> what tomorrow may proffer—
> nor if you see a fellow creature's luck,
> pretend to say how long that luck will last,
> for luck is swifter in its changes than
> the wink of the wings of a fly.
>
> (Fragment 355)

The old vision of helplessness is reaffirmed, but *sub specie rationis* ("under the sign of reason"), some helplessness, much helplessness, belongs to that area of men's lives that is out of their control and therefore not worthy of consideration, much less of bitterness. If our brains, energy, strength, and will are to be used rightly, they must be used decorously: the grand Homeric extravagances, both of joy and suffering, are no longer, whether fortunately or unfortunately, available. Neither angels nor beasts, we have only this ordinary human life, in all its bafflements, confusion, weaknesses; and it is enough. This life, too, no less than the brighter (and darker) life of the past, is part of the cosmos, part of the eternal now. But to find the present, to master this future and revere this past, we must labor, with all our intelligence and all our emotions, to become what we are. To be truly human, we must work to become human. To live our lives, we must take care neither to squander our lives in the stupid hope of snatching hold of some superlife nor to die each day by fearing to live. It is a message of guarded hope, it is an active, critical—as against a passive, acquiescent—appreciation of ourselves and our lives. Schooled in this poetry, we are prepared, or can prepare ourselves, to listen to and be questioned by a Socrates or a Christ. Without losing their gods or their pleasure in and reverence for being, men are now ready to take on, again, in new ways, the responsibilities and the dignities of human beings.[37]

Are the old legends, then, and the poetry that illumined them, obsolete? No, even without the aid of allegory, the legends and the poems aid us to discover our lives, to order ourselves and change our lives.[38] The legends contain, and will always contain, the ancient wisdom and the history of its subsequent growth and flowerings, the traditions of human experience. But this wisdom cannot be directly handed on, cannot be swallowed, digested, possessed. For poetry—or at least this poetry—is not moralistic, or is not, in the usual sense, didactic. It is, rather, dialectical and maieutic: *verba admonent tantum ut quaeramus res, non exhibent ut norimus*[39] ("For words only urge us on to look for realities; they do not explain realities so that we comprehend them"). The legends and the poets' meditations on the legends can persuade us to ponder the realities outside us and inside us that the makers of legends imagine in their proper forms and that the poets re-create, but these are the limits of poetry; for poetry, like men and their lives, has strict limitations that must be carefully observed. Did the old poetry seem to promise immortality? If it truly promised that, it was wrong and we were foolish to believe it.

> What sensible man would commend
> that simile of Kleoboulos, citizen of Lindos?
> This man compared
> strong rivers in their flood and flowers in springtime,
> sunshaft and moonlight and the spindrift sea
> to the tomb's enduring shape. . . . But everything
> on earth is less than the high gods: mere stone
> can crumble even at a human's hands.
> His conceit is the whim of a fool.
>> (Fragment 387)

And again:

> For all things reach at last
> one sickening void,
> our shining virtues and our shining wealth.
>> (Fragment 356)

These judgments may seem harsh, cynical, and, for a man who earns great sums of money by composing threnodies and funeral inscriptions, rather hypocritical. What is the function of poetry, then, and what is the nature of immortality for Simonides?

> For those who are dead at Thermopylae,
> splendid the luck and bright the doom.
> An altar is their tomb; in place of keening,

remembrance, and in place of grief, our praise.
Their shroud nor rot nor time
that masters all will eat or fade.
The grave of valiant men is now the dwelling
of Greece's glory. Kind Leonidas
bears witness to my word, for he bequeaths us
undying bravery, and undying fame.

     (Fragment 362)

But if graves are ploughed under and sepulchres crumble, if poems are lost, where is the immortality? What is it that art does? It plants immortality, which is a spiritual thing, in the human heart, which is a spiritual thing. When the mind and heart ponder what that bravery was and so aspire to their own bravery, the old bravery continues its life in the eternal now which it and the poetry that communicates it help the minds and hearts of coming generations to desire and to renew. In this dialectical lyric and its particular vision of the eternal now, nothing that was of value perishes—indeed, everything that was truly of value not only lives but also engenders life and sustains it. When the metaphors of dialectical lyric have persuaded the human being to reconsider *for himself* what it is that his life is for, have involved in this process of consideration all his body and soul, all his thoughts and will and memory and feelings, then, independently of time and space, immortality has truly been attained and the incantations of poetry have achieved their end.

It is becoming fashionable to discount the ancient gossip about vehement rivalries between Pindar and Simonides (together with his nephew, Bacchylides), but when we compare the temperaments of the two poets, it is easy enough to see why and how such gossip should have originated and flourished. Where Simonides had developed a dialectical mode of lyricism in order to close with and to master the complexities that multiplied as archaic Greece was dying and classical Greece was coming into existence, Pindar recovered what was always surely the original function and meaning of lyric poethood (*vates*—"seer," "bard," "shaman," "prophet"), and so successful was this rethinking and reformulating of the vanished ideal that it is fair to say that in a sense Pindar invented the vatic personality. While his other great contemporaries, poets and nonpoets alike, were rushing forward to the enlightenment, while communities were being transformed into states and states into empires, while verse was giving way to prose and faith was giving way to reason, Pindar was becoming Orpheus. It is easy enough (has always been easy enough) to view Pindar's decision as conservative, even as reactionary, but such a judgment fails of truth miserably because it explains neither his enormous success during his lifetime nor his uncontested preeminence among the lyric poets of the West.

For Pindar (and, presumably, for those who were eager to witness the performance of his poems) the destructuring of the ancient legends was a foolish, impious, and self-destructive pastime. Where other intellectuals saw the hope of liberation from the shadows of mystery and ignorance, Pindar saw arrogance, a childish tampering with powerful and inexplicable secrets that neither could nor should be investigated, a frivolous and fatal effort to say the ineffable. Even the tragedians who were contemporary with him (even perhaps Aeschylus) may have seemed to him, for all their piety, more concerned at last to explain the workings of the venerable emblems, to decode and expose them, than to represent their grandeur, to renew them by affirming their force and primacy. Pindar's chief weapon against this tendency to destructure legend, to deny its truth, was, paradoxically, the art of silence:

> My spirit prompts me to proclaim
> That glory comes to Theron and his clan
> From the bright riders, Kastor and his Twin,
> Because of all mankind most eagerly
> They welcome them unto the festive table
> And guard with pious mind
> The secrets of the high and blessed gods.
> (*Olympian* 3.68ff.)

The legends are evoked and pondered briefly at a reverential distance; they are displayed almost as sacred tokens of a mystery that cannot be and must not be met directly. Like his audience, Pindar is content to recall the legend and to allow it to inspire his heart and his voice with faith in its meanings, in the secret nourishment that it furnishes his life and his art; but the evocation (the recollection and incantation) resolutely avoids analysis of the legend. Some things cannot be said, and this deliberate religious silence, that of Theron and his clan and of Pindar himself, strengthened by music and dance, which also suggest and evoke rather than reveal and explain, invites the Dioscuri, Castor and Pollux, to be present at the victory song, to sustain it and to eternize it.

In *Olympian* 1, the legend of Pelops is selected to illumine the victory song for King Hieron because of its political and historical relevance to this particular victor. But the scandalous aspects of the myth (that Pelops was offered by his father as a meal to the gods, that greedy Demeter actually devoured one of his shoulders, thus necessitating an ivory replacement for it) are scornfully rejected. Rationalist mythologists may rummage through this rubbish in their search for false clues to unreal problems, but Pindar has no time to waste in this fashion. "It is proper for men to say of the gods what is true and good [*kala*]: less, then, is their guilt" (lines 55ff.). Instead, he invents (or refurbishes) a counterlegend about the long disappearance of Pelops (not dead, having been devoured at the divine meal, then restored to life; rather, abducted by the amorous Poseidon, an honor similar to that bestowed by Zeus on Ganymede) which ennobles Pelops and his legend but does not seek to unravel its intricacies or to probe it to its core. And even when the fabric of the legend is so closely woven that it cannot be changed, when no variant can redeem its apparent ugliness, Pindar sternly refuses to venture where human reason is manifestly inadequate, and he fiercely rebukes the gossipmongering rationalists who will have "truth" at any price. In *Nemean* 5, he admits that the house of Aeacus, whose legend is crucial to the victory song he composes, has sometimes found itself involved in sordid, dishonorable (and mysterious) actions, but he will not make use of them in his poem:

> I refrain from disclosing
> Their unwarranted risks,
> How they fled from this fabled island,
> What god it was drove them from the land of vines.
> No, I take here my stand:
> Bare truth does not always find what it aims at,
> And often silence is man's best art.
>   (lines 25ff.)

"Bare truth," the prize that enlightened rationalism seeks for, tends often to obscure what it craves to understand. The true illumination that both Pindar's song and its hearers need is provided by the mystery of legend, which Pindaric silence (his piety, his discretion, his wisdom) at once guards and presents. All this may seem nothing more than the strategy of the obscurantist, but in reading Pindar, it is important to remember that Pindar holds this position in complete good faith (it is far more than a mere poetic strategy, the figure of thought: *praeteritio*—"a deliberate omission, passing over") and that his unique sublimities have much of their strength from his unique silence and from his challenge to rationalism and to fashion; for although Pindar's silence did not, of course, win its immediate contest with the flowering enlightenment in Greece, it helped guarantee both the beauty and the permanence of his art.

Traveling throughout the Greek world for over half a century, composing, performing, teaching song and dance, he was the poet of communities that had entered the fifth century reluctantly and wanted desperately to return to the sixth century the more they experienced of "modern times." These communities revered him, vied for his services, not because he entertained them, flattered them, and solaced them. They revered him because he did for them what he claimed he could do for them: he revealed to them, he brought them into contact with, the invisible real world of past and future on which the visible real world of their present, their existence, depended for its vitality and its truth. If we are tempted to think that both this poet and his audience were deluded in taking seriously the vatic personality that had by this time, in so far as it otherwise survived at all, dwindled into formulaic images and literary conventions, we need to think our way out of the purely literary lyric that Horace perfected and bequeathed to the Renaissance and turn our attention to one of the nineteenth century's most extraordinary poetic geniuses, Arthur Rimbaud:

> Right now I'm busy messing myself up as completely as I can. You want to know why? Because I want to be a poet, that is to say, I'm straining to turn myself into a *seer*. You won't have the faintest notion of what I'm talking about, and there's no possible way for me to explain it to you.[40]

Pindar really believed that he saw the gods and eternity, and he thought that his words and music and dances connected the communities he visited with what he saw. In other words, he believed in his own magic, and if we do not understand that he was heart-whole in this belief in his own magic and in the order of being that his magic served to render visible, accessible, and intelligible, his poetry will seem to us not only confused and monotonous but also silly and perhaps even crazy. The difference between Pindar and a Hölderlin or a Rimbaud is that Pindar's audiences believed in his magic because they experienced it, performed it, were gathered into the circle of its stillness as they heard and watched the present made eternal. But Hölderlin and Rimbaud had no audience until they were dead and had become the objects of cults that had and have nothing to do with their magic and little to do with their poems.

The figure of Orpheus in modern times manifests itself as pathetic illusion, but Pindar, by the force of his belief and (not least) by the power and purity of his art, made the figure of Orpheus, while he lived, a triumphant reality. Just as modern Europe was beginning to take shape, as science was beginning to find its objects of study and its tools, as everything that Pindar and his communities valued was disappearing before the advance of the new humanism, Pindar the seer found a way to reconstruct the old mandala and gathered his tribes into it to celebrate the old, abiding perfections, to exorcise time, the evil, and to partake of the rhythm of being. I am not, of course, claiming that after Pindar this miracle never again occurred, for wherever there is great choral lyric one aspect or another of this miracle is to be found. But very much of the purity and the power of Pindar's songs comes from this poet's sharing with his audience the metaphors that they performed and re-created together. The lyrics of Pindar are, no less than those of Hölderlin, "continuous metaphors of a feeling," but this feeling is both the poet's own feeling and the feeling he evokes in and shares with the community whose *vates* ("seer") he is. This condition is the ideal condition that any choral poet wants, and it is the condition of writing choral that all Greek choral poets before Pindar in some degree enjoyed and that all European choral poets after Pindar have tried, in various ways and with varying degrees of success, to fabricate. But it was the genius, perhaps combined with the luck of timing, of Pindar that gave this essential choral experience its most permanent and most perfect form.

In the moment of this performance, the past and the future are gathered into this "now" by this poet whose art summons us into the presence of the divine that created us and sustains us: we are safe in the rhythm of the cosmos that is outside us and inside us:

And therefore, racked in my heart though I am,
I dare to summon the gold muses
Since we are loosed from tremendous sorrows—
Let us not fail to find us abundant crowns,
Do not nourish your anguish:
We have escaped unpersuadable evils,
Weak though we are after labor,
Let us scatter and share what there is of sweetness,
For the stone of Tantalus that threatened,
Some god has averted it from us. . . .
Yet, deceitful time,
Arching above us, beyond us,
Makes crooked the steps that we take;
Yet if men hold to their freedom,
Even this sickness is not past cure—
It is the human task
To foster rightful hope.
            (*Isthmian* 8.5–16)

Pindar grieves for the political humiliations of his native city, Thebes; his audience, citizens of Aigina, grieve for family and friends lost in the war against Persia, and in particular for Nikokles, uncle of Kleandros, the victorious young athlete whom this poem celebrates. The legend of Achilles, descendent of the goddess Aigina, mirrors the greatness, the triumph and the death of Nikokles; and from this remembered and performed rhythm of birth, life, and death, there emerges a complex paradigm of sorrow, near despair, courage, and faith that issues finally in a simple, finely wrought feeling for which the entire performed poem is a continuous, unparaphrasable metaphor:

Now the chariot of the muses hastens
To exalt the boxer Nikokles.
Honor him who, in the Isthmian valley,
Gathered the Dorian parsley crown,
When he scattered with unerring fist
Those who contended with him.
His memory his cousin does not stain,
And for Kleandros, then,
Let one of his companions plait

A supple wreath of myrtle—
For even before this, the contests at Megara
And the youths of Epidaurus have hailed his victories.
A man of breeding can fairly praise him:
He did not squander the vigor of his youth,
Nor did he leave it untested by bright deeds.

    (*Isthmian* 8.65–78)

Achilles a champion, and Nikokles a champion also; now the nephew Kleandros preserves the integrity. Mastered by the solace of the story and its rhythm, the different griefs of Pindar and of his chorus and audience are merged,[41] the discordant emotions, relief and anxiety, joy in triumph and despair over death, without being weakened or lost, find an exact interdependence, become a new feeling, a feeling that is shaped. Treacherous time (*dolios aion*)[42] has twisted the road of life (*helisson biou poron*), it has brought disgrace to Thebes and Pindar, and it has come near to destroying Greece and Aigina as it has destroyed Achilles and Nikokles. But time, the enemy, is vanquished by memory and feeling, which catch hold of the rhythm of being with the aid of the muses. When we remember the old courage and the old victories, when we see them renewed in the present generation, and when we reenact them (*to kai nun pherei logon*, "And it is right now also") in order to feel them more intensely and thereby more precisely, we have moved (again, and temporarily—that is part of the rhythm) from the disorder of our hearts into beauty that endures. I and the world, we and the world: the endless complexities of this dichotomy, the anxieties of identity, the profundity of our ignorance and helplessness—all of this disorder and confusion, all this painful complexity, is finally gathered into the simplicity of feeling shaped as continuous, musical metaphor.

It is, paradoxically perhaps, the violence and the complexity of the feelings that the poet shares with his chorus and his audience that make possible this concentration, this simplicity, and this dynamic calm. More than other choral lyricists whom we know anything of, Pindar understood the difficulties and complexities of the choral situation and made them the instruments of lyrical feeling in its most subtle and most powerful manifestation—at that point in the lyrical spectrum where communal, ceremonial, and religious emotion marries with private, individual emotion. It is not a question of other, later lyric poets having less genius than Pindar. It is rather that Pindar had the perfect lyrical movement and knew what to do with it. For if it is pointless to wonder whether earlier choral poets were less or more gifted than Pindar, it is perhaps worth suggesting that Pindar, as the enlightenment began its flowering and the art of tragedy kept gathering splendor and momentum, sensed that he might be the last *vates* and that his art form might perish. If that is the case, it would not be unreasonable to suppose that he worked all the harder for the victory he achieved.

We have seen, in the delicacy and power of his handling of the challenge of rationalism to legend and to the idea of victory itself, one facet of Pindar's idea of lyric. No less crucial to his theory and practice of lyric are his sense of lyric form (form, movement; *not* structure) and his solution to the problem of how a lyric poem, a danced lyric poem, unfolds in his listeners' minds as it unfolds before their eyes. He formulates this problem in a way that will be very common as the theory of rhetoric develops in the century after his death, but his particular formulation is, so far as I can judge, peculiar to him:

> From the gods there have come to me,
> O Melissos,
> Each way I turn a thousand paths of song,
> For by your victories you furnish me
> Abundant ornament, abundant themes.
> (*Isthmian* 4.1ff.)

Homer had admitted himself unable to describe (remember) the vast, intricate gathering of the Greek armies as they moved against Troy[43] without the help of the muses. Later poets would frequently complain that they could not sing what they thought and felt (so powerful and subtle the emotions, so profound and extraordinary the thoughts). This device has earned the technical name of *aporia* ("helplessness," "difficulty in movement, of finding a path") and denotes the poet's (or orator's) clever admission that his skill is not equal to his task, that his material is so rich and so overwhelming that mere human resources are not sufficient. This technique, properly managed, secures the attention, and perhaps the esteem, of the audience, and it also allows the speaker to triumph over his predicament because, of course, he immediately proceeds to accomplish what he had announced was impossible of accomplishment.

Pindar does not stoop to this strategy. The god (the muse) is always with him, otherwise there would be no song at all, and this is scarcely worth his mentioning (see *Olympian* 11.8ff.). His problem is not that he has too much to say (and therefore cannot say it without divine help—he *has* divine help), nor that what he has to say is beyond human speech (if it were, he would, as we have seen, not bother to try). His problem is to *choose* what to say *by means of his art*, to select, from all the possible things that might be said on a given occasion, the central thing, the perfect thing; then, having made this choice, his problem is how to arrange the movements of his poem (and his dance) in such a way that this central, perfect thing achieves its proper radiance. Rhetorically speaking, this is the province of invention, of finding out, precisely, what to say (out of all the things that could be said) and of finding how to say it (out of all the possible ways of saying it). This may, at first, sound rather simple-minded, but it is not. Anyone who has written anything knows that composing (as against, say, expressing) is chiefly a process of discovery and then of refining that discovery, of arranging those refinements so as to ensure the discovery its exact setting, the precise prominence that it requires.

For Pindar the process and the standards of discovery are as complex as they are austere. Perfection alone will suffice, and he speaks (*Olympian* 13.93f., *Nemean* 9.55, toward the end of these poems) of hitting the target at its center. So, there are many paths to choose from (as in the verses quoted above), but there is only one path that will take him and his audience to the poem's center, and that path must be found—or there is no poem. (Both these images, the bull's-eye and the right road, utterly conventional by the time he takes them up, Pindar converts into emblems of his own poetic, and so transforms them brilliantly.) It is, then, something magical (his art and his god—it is difficult, at this level, to distinguish them, but he would be outraged if the god were made a mere metaphor for his art) that directs the aim of the missile, that points out the right road:

> The customs of such song
> And the Hours in their eager speeding
> Forbid me to rehearse these endless tales,
> And I am led, as by a sorcerer's spell,
> To choose the emblem of the waxing moon.
>   (*Nemean* 4.53ff.)

Among the bewildering richness and variety, one thing only can represent all the abundance, and his art searches after it patiently, isolates it, snares it, and enshrines it. To distill simplicity from the baffling complexity, this is the high art that is beyond blame:

> If you utter what is fitting,
> Twisting many strands to a single strand,
> Rare, then, the censure from the lips of men.
> (*Pythian* 1.158ff.)

At the poem's core, radiating from it through every part of it, is the single thing, the unique decorum, the discovered perfection.

But Pindar's insistence on, his obsession with, the discovery of the essence of his material and its truest form is only half of his solution to the composition of choral lyric. As important as the discovery is the search itself. For the poem is the search. To reveal the discovery without representing the search would be, in a sense, both vulgar (the rabbit from the hat) and aesthetically and intellectually dissatisfying:

> The sublime virtues abound with legends,
> But to take only part of the tale,
> To unfold it with intricate variations,
> This is to make a poem fit for cultured men.
> (*Pythian* 9.133ff.)

The simplicity that is to be distilled from multiplicity is the object of the search, but the aesthetic enjoyment, the excitement and the pleasant tension, the suspense as the search proceeds (think for a moment of what Aeschylus and Sophocles accomplish here in the rival genre)—these we experience because Pindar himself conducts us through the maze, the magnificent variety of his search for perfection. We see, we are brought into the presence of, the single strand, but we know and appreciate the simplicity and the perfection only because we have seen and shared the difficulty of discovering it. Pindar has gathered us into his search for form and matter in their perfection, and that is why we can see what he sees, the discovered perfection that is inextricably entwined with the poet's search for it. Here, and I think here only in Western lyric, we almost become part of the poet's sensibility, of the poet's creative act itself—because he *composes us* into his search and into his poem. The form of Pindar's victory songs, then, imitates (refigures) his process of composition, and near the secret of Pindar's theory of poetry is his willingness and his ability to share the excitement and the vitality of his creative moment with us: he allows us, he invites us, to become the dancers who become the dance. Most other lyric poems, even the greatest of them, leave us outside them looking into them. But in Pindar there is, again and again, a unique identity of matter and form, of poem and audience.

Simplicity, precision, form. I may seem to have overused these words in describing Pindaric sensibility and Pindaric artistry, but they are, I am convinced, the correct words for such a description. If the poems have often seemed complex, vague, and formless, it is chiefly because Pindaric critics have been looking in them for the kind of form to which they are accustomed in later European lyric and because they do not properly appreciate the function of Pindar's choral poetry. E. L. Bundy, who has taught us more about the modulations and transitions of Pindar's structure than any other critic of this century, insisted that the essential function of Pindar's *epinicia* ("victory songs") was to praise the victorious athlete and that every passage in the poem was "encomiastic" in the sense that each passage contributed in some way to the action of praising the victorious athlete.[44] Bundy's analysis of Pindar's form and function are specially useful in countering the old charges of formlessness and self-indulgent preciosity. But in correcting the errors of his predecessors, Bundy fell into not unsimilar errors in his determination to find purely rational patterns of thought and speech and a very narrowly defined purpose in a body of poetry that, by virtue of its overwhelming concern for music and eternity, transcends mere reason as it transcends mere pragmatism. Reason, prose, and sports are much concerned with beginnings, middles, and ends, with "linear unity," and it is proper for them to be so concerned. But lyric poetry, though it is not irrational, though, indeed, it despises reason at its cost, is never purely or essentially rational because it deals with realities (or illusions, as you will) that most good rationalists correctly proclaim to be beneath reason or beyond it. Lyric poetry in general and Pindar's lyrics in particular are not susceptible to very much in the way of linear analysis:

> It is impossible to travel "lineally" from start to finish of a Pindaric ode, dismissing what has been said the while, and not to

> miss most of what Pindar has to say, for . . . the coherence of Pindar's poems depends primarily upon the cross-references of one part of the poem to other parts. The unity thus created is formed by the aggregate of all passages, and the beginning is still very important at the end of the poem and, ultimately, the end is important at the beginning.[45]

Precisely said, for many reasons, not least of which is that Pindar's poetry is chiefly about eternity and our feelings about eternity, about the rhythm that is over and beneath our experience, about what we have come to feel and to think (but not to know) about ourselves and the world. It is our very limited human experience of this rhythm, of the mystery of this rhythm and of our fears and hopes regarding this mystery, that lyric poetry makes visible and forms. Beginnings and ends have little meaning and little use here. We are dealing, rather, with parabolas, helixes, crystals, with continuities of metaphors that shape feelings for which *there are no words* and which, therefore, cannot be paraphrased.[46]

Form, then, in Pindar's odes includes: (1) discussion of the victorious athlete, together with something about his particular achievement, his genealogy, his training, his hometown; (2) maxims (*sententiae*) that illustrate or adorn one or another of the poem's central moods, themes, ideas; (3) a *muthos* ("story") that magnifies the achievement of the poem's victor (and that also reminds the victor and everyone else involved in the celebration that these things are happening *sub specie aeternitatis*—"under the sign of eternity"); (4) some mention, brief or extended, shy or boastful, as need requires, of the poet's artistic gifts (and of his role as mediator between the eternal and the temporal, the seer who knows); and (5) a prayer or prayers to the gods and to the rhythm to bless the assembled celebrants (and to keep them from the arrogance that would occasion their losing their memory of the rhythm of being and would thereby lead them to their destruction).[47] But the ingredients of form do not, of course, create form. Pindar forms his poems by arranging these ingredients to suit the needs of the particular feeling he is trying to shape, the particular continuous metaphor he is attempting to summon up. Each of his poems crystallizes into a slightly different metaphor, and in each of them a slightly different cluster of feelings is being imagined and shaped, so his forms had to be as flexible as they were sturdy and precise. In some poems one element will be more emphasized than it is in another, none of them is really expendable, and none of them (except perhaps the *muthos*—"story"—that eternalizes the ephemeral victor) is clearly more nearly essential than the others; but one element that stands out in Pindar—and its prominence distinguishes him easily from Bacchylides and so far as we know from all other choral poets—is his passionate affirmation of the value and excellence of his artistry and his earnest and solemn claims for the holiness of poethood. When he prays to and praises gods, or warns and compliments men, or recounts the divine legends of *illud tempus* ("that time") that verify the truth of the present, or fashions maxims that will reflect and illumine the moods in question, we all listen to him and we listen to him carefully (if we listen at all) because the voice is unmistakably authentic. We believe—but not, obviously, as he and his audiences believed—what he says about gods and men, eternity and time, grace and doom, because he persuades us that he believes it—rather, lives it, hungers for it, for it and nothing else. He persuades us because he believes, no poet more, in himself, in his artistry, and in the beauty and goodness of the cosmos that his artistry serves.

The Genius of Greek Lyric

> A poem should not mean
> But be.[48]

That was an unfortunate way of phrasing it, but these verses seemed a cunning way of allowing the modernist romantic to eat his poem and seem to have it too. And so they became a kind of slogan for poetic independence from the tyrannies of society and of audience (but by this time the audience had begun to cease to exist). The poem, here, becomes a unique effusion, like amber or pearls, from a superior personality: passersby might stray into the temple of art to admire its beauties and powers, might gaze in astonishment and go reverently away, might "understand" the poem or not; but the poem remained in its absolute purity, beyond comprehension and, of course, beyond criticism. For those who could not quite swallow this, there was another version of poetic autonomy, another defense against the fatal (and nonexistent) crowds, most forcefully propounded by Eliot, in which the poet carefully "unselved" himself in order to submit to, and thereby enter into, the choice company of which the tradition was composed. Both these tactics reflect a complex response to the modern artist's alienation from society and audience, and they were, given the nature and the development of technological culture, perhaps inevitable. What matters here is that this condition of modern lyric is a central concern in modern poets, and we must have it clearly in mind if we want to understand what is of the essence for Greek lyric. When, in trying to describe Greek lyric, I emphasize its intimate concern with performance, its constant awareness of the lyrical and rhetorical triangle and pronominal form, I am aware that I may seem to be speaking of declamation, elocution, posture, and incantation—all the nightmare phantoms of classical rhetoric which the romantics labored so long and so vainly to exorcise. But those sad, bewildered neoclassical revenants have little to do with classics and nothing to do with rhetoric as it is.

What mattered in ancient rhetoric, and in the Greek lyric that I define as being rhetorical in its central strategy, was not the need to express something, but the desire, the choice, to conduct lyrical discourse. This desire and this choice imply that the poets believed that they had something valuable to say, something that other people might benefit from hearing, and believed also that it was up to them to say it in such a way that it was interesting, challenging, intelligible. In other words, the Greek lyricists knew that the burden of and responsibility for lyrical discourse was essentially theirs, and they respected the intelligence and the taste of their audiences sufficiently to believe that their listeners would adequately perform their own function in this process of discourse. The tendency of these poets to cast their songs in pronominal form arises from an attempt to dramatize, to incarnate, in the songs themselves, this reciprocity which must govern any genuine act of discourse.[49] The listener can identify either with the *ego* ("I") or with the *tu* ("you") of the song, or he can identify with both almost simultaneously: he becomes, for the duration of the song, and perhaps beyond it, part of the lyrical moment, part of the lyrical discourse of praise and blame that reveals that moment; witnessing this compressed, dramatic instant, listening to the words and the rhythms that illumine it, he is moved to ponder himself in relation to it. This process, in which the listener identifies himself with *all* that is sung, lyric shares, of course, with epic and with drama. What distinguishes lyric from epic and drama in this regard are the extreme compressions of the things that are imagined—inward motions of the soul that are revealed not through a series of actions (*ta dramata*), but through words alone—and the total concentration of the moment of private discourse, this speaker speaking to another, I and You, as if to thee alone. Greek lyric, then, is a peculiar fusion of the forms of epideictic oratory and of something like drama: that is, the dramatic—one is tempted to say, the Homeric—moment of rhetorical encounter, in which both poet and audience participate as they contemplate together the possible shapes of inward movements of the soul that they have felt or feel or may feel but cannot see or name or, in a full sense, know. For the purpose of containing, ordering, clarifying, this situation of discourse, the pronominal form, so far from being mere rhetorical artifice, is a natural, perhaps *the* natural form; for it re-creates, dramatizes, illumines, the ways in which we actually try to speak to each other; and it is, therefore, the natural way to hear ideal fictions that image feelings revealed by speech.

If this seems classicizing overstatement, I would invite the reader to recall that the last line of the last poem in Eliot's *Collected Poems* is: "These are private words addressed to you in public." The great theorist of impersonality and the great master of lyric monologue concludes this wonderful love poem, "A Dedication to My Wife," with a solution to a problem that had bedeviled him for five decades. A poem must both mean and be at once, it must embody the process of lyrical discourse, must describe and deliberate, even while it maintains its own integrities and guards its own aesthetic reserves. The claims of pure art and the responsibility for discourse are as ambivalent and as difficult as they are necessary; they are also antagonistic to each other, yet, at the same time, interdependent. The private and the public, the merely personal and the truly universal, resist one another, yes; but from that struggle comes lyric poetry, both monodic and choral, at its best. The genius of Greek lyric is to have seen the essential possible forms of the union between *ethopoeia* and rhetoric and then to have distilled these forms to their purest clarities. That, to our grief and to our delight, is what the fragments show.

But there remains the problem of didacticism. If the poet thinks he has something valuable to say, is he not arrogating to himself the role of teacher? Why should a lyric poet do something so banal, and, given the frequently unstable constitution of the lyric sensibility, how dare he do that? The answer to this question was well formulated by St. Augustine in his *De magistro*: in effect, we are all of us busy teaching each other all the time; instruction, like discourse, is a central law of human behavior. Whenever we open our mouths, we are in some fashion explaining something to someone; even when we ask a question, we are, paradoxically, teaching our ignorance. No good lyric poet undertakes to tell us what a given emotion or given cluster of emotions is or means; for that knowledge is beyond language and is very probably beyond reason. What a lyric poet does is to imagine for us a certain state of mind and soul and then to invite us into that imagined (re-created, refined), dynamic inwardness in order to let us contemplate for ourselves our own memories of our own inward motions of mind and soul. I think it was Auden who someplace says that a good poem makes us say, "Ah, so that's how I feel!" That is not quite a didactic way of looking at the purpose and effect of lyric, but it is not quite accurate either. What a good lyric enables and encourages us to say is: "Yes, I feel something like that, but that is not exactly how *I* feel." We refine our perceptions of what we feel and are both by seeing versions of feelings and identities outside us and by comparing those versions of feelings and people with what we find inside ourselves. In experiencing lyric poetry, then, in allowing our minds to become absorbed in the poet's ideal fictions, we see at once similarity and difference, and through lyric pleasure ("admiration": *thaumazein*),[50] we come to know, imperceptibly and uniquely, for ourselves, what we feel by contrasting it with the ideal fiction, with many ideal fictions; and—for the process is dialectical, reciprocal, unending—we come to understand the ideal lyric fictions by viewing them in the light of our personal memories which the fictions have illumined and refined; and, finally, we temper and correct the fictions with our memories and our own fictions, which is another step in knowing ourselves as we are and as we change.

It was once fashionable to suggest that the Greek lyricists discovered or invented the concept of the self.[51] That was not an absurd suggestion, but it was misguided. Long before selves began trying to record the fact or the nuances of selfhood, back in the irrecoverable, inconceivable strangeness of times and places without the means or the need for trying to make experience permanent by setting it down, there were people who had skins and names and selves, and all these people, like us, were worried and pleased by the gift of selfhood. A self without another self or selves to aggress or to admire or to solace might not—I doubt it—be truly a self; but, without doubt, when two or more selves come together, their near likenesses and their absolute distinctions combine to promote *knowledge* of identity, even as they engender the sense of community. What one does, has done, with that knowledge of identity is various and problematical. What the Greek lyricists did with it is a matter of ruined record. They emphasized both the likeness and the difference by dramatizing the process of discourse in respect of human emotion, by making the meaning of the self and its inwardnesses at once utterly private and utterly public—"See, hearer, this I am; this is also you and also not you." That inconclusive, wavering knowledge pleases us, is a peculiar epiphany of beauty and wisdom, and we learn from it in proportion as we are pleased by it. All lyric, any lyric, accomplishes this in some fashion. But Greek lyricists did it better than most other lyricists because the Greeks so worshipped language that they realized that they must not be controlled by it, that they must tame it or be enslaved by it. So they almost perfected the normal human capacity and need that we call rhetoric, and Greek lyric is part of that near perfection.

III

On the Absence of Ancient Lyric Theory

Cicero said that even if his lifetime were to be doubled
he would still not have time to waste on reading the
lyric poets. . . .

(Seneca, *Epistles* 49.5)

Though exacerbated by the new vogue for Alexandrian frivolity that
contributed its share to the irritations of his declining years, Cicero's
judgment is not unrepresentative of the received, established position toward lyric in the ancient world after the decline of the Greek
city-state. Some of this hostile indifference to lyric we may ascribe to
the misease with emotion that is common to schoolmasters, politi-
cians, and military men in any age, to their vague anxiety that the
young, and even the middle-aged and the elderly, may somewhere be
ignoring their duties or even be having fun. But more crucial to this
contempt for lyric poetry is the fact that the kind of lyrical poetry we
have just examined was not composed and performed with any real
vigor or success after the collapse of the civilization of classical
Greece. Even the surviving memorials to that poetry, having been
increasingly replaced by epic, drama, oratory, and popular philosophy in the schools,[1] became the private preserve of literary scholars
and of connoisseurs of poetry; and because of their difficulties and
what seemed their obscurities, the old lyrics were misunderstood, ignored, and finally all but abandoned by the common reader, who is,
after all, the final arbiter of what literature lives and does not live.
Hymns and victory songs, of course, continued to be esteemed for
their legends of law and order and for their unequivocal moral utterance and were therefore sharply distinguished from the immoral,

amoral poems that Cicero had consciously in mind when he dismissed lyric poetry from the attention of serious grownups. But even this moral, acceptable variety of lyric suffered a general neglect, for the moral functions it performed had been taken over by epic and by tragedy, high comedy, history, and oratory. As we shall see in the next chapter, the living lyric of this period did not deeply engage the serious attention of most ancient readers,[2] and even the frequent and amazing *tours de force* of Horace could not quite invest lyric poetry at Rome with anything like the dignity and the popularity it had enjoyed in Greece for well over two centuries.

If we take into consideration these attitudes to lyric poetry and keep in mind that by the time attempts to theorize about the nature of lyric began its composition and performance had all but ceased, we shall not be surprised when we discover how relatively unimpressive ancient theories of this most protean and complex literary genre seem to have been.[3] The ancients' efforts to grapple with the ideas of epic, tragedy, history, and oratory were as persistent as they were, in various ways at various times, successful; but lyric was curiously unsuited to the major categories of ancient literary theory. Ancient classical Greek lyric was, as we have seen, essentially concerned with worlds that were at once inner and shared, with the ceremonies and the habits of feeling of small, closed communities; it was musical and performed; and it transcended the morality of classical humanism as it transcended reason, logic, and rhetoric. The theorists of lyric lived in worlds where the social patterns that shaped and sustained Greek lyric were dying or dead, where the convictions about human nature and human destiny were radically different from the convictions that had informed Greek lyric and the communities that it had educated, solaced, and entertained. In ancient lyric theory, the dominant critical categories center on ideas of imitating the visible, outer world; on a rhetoric devoted to analyzing the structure and the effects of the spoken, as against the sung, word; on the strict moral functions of poetry (literature as the handmaiden, not the mother, of philosophy and politics); and on the autonomy both of artistic creation and of the enjoyment of art—at Alexandria and later at Rome the concept of art for art's sake naturally flourished in cosmopolitan societies which were too large and too complex to allow much scope for the older lyric poetry and its profound, eccentric commitment to *communitas*.[4]

I am not, of course, suggesting that ancient critics of lyric did not know far more facts about ancient lyric than its modern students, but it is clear that they interpreted the old lyrics and the idea of lyric according to their own critical categories and their own patterns of aesthetic enjoyment and that in so doing they tended to misinterpret the function and the nature of a kind of poetry that was essentially alien to their interests, their expectations, and their experience. This is, of course, a perennial, inescapable, necessary problem in literary criticism, but if we consider that ancient literary critics were less prone to err in theorizing about other major literary genres than they were when handling lyric, we may perhaps gain a better sense both of the peculiarities of Greek lyric poetry and the difficulties of lyric theory in general.

> There is one kind of poetry and fable which entirely consists of imitation: this is tragedy and comedy, and there's another kind consisting of the poet's own report—you find this particularly in dithyrambs; while the mixture of the two exists in epic and in many other places. . . .
> (*Republic* 3.394B–C)

> What shall we do then? Shall we admit all these patterns into the city, or one or the other unmixed, or the mixed one?
> If my vote is to prevail, the imitator of the good, unmixed.
> (*Republic* 3.397D)

In the passage quoted here from his attack on mimesis in general and the epic and tragedy in particular, Plato seems to be stating his approval of lyric poetry, but we quickly see that the only kind of lyric poetry he deigns to sanction is the most ancient, the most conservative, and the least lyrical form of lyric poetry: the other, later and richer, forms are utterly ignored as if they did not exist; and indeed in Plato's city of the soul they do not and must not. For Plato, as for Aristotle, the object of poetic mimesis is the human being and his behavior,[5] and if there must be mimesis in the city of the soul, it can only be an imitation of "the brave, the self-controlled, the righteous, the free" (3.395C) that promotes the growth toward goodness that is the goal of Platonic man. Pure imitation (tragedy and comedy, where the poet disappears into his creatures and thus apes them freely and irresponsibly) and mixed imitation (epic, where the poet mingles direct narrative with pure imitation) are inevitably drawn to imitate men and even gods in their passions, their weakness, and their degradation; and the result of such imitation—consider Emma Bovary leafing ruthlessly through her penny dreadfuls—is spiritual ruin, in which the illusory fruit of such imitation becomes the evil reality. The seductive power of such artifice first instills a desire for the illusions it imitates, then convinces that the intense, disgraceful illusions and passions are the only realities, that they alone are proper models for our lives. Only the poet who does not need to hide behind his personae because he has nothing to hide, who can tell his story straight because his story is straight [6] (*haple diegesis*—"pure, direct, simple narration") may be permitted to remain within the walls of the soul's city because only he is a good man imitating (or rather, pointing to) the good.

In his usual manner, Plato has taken a fundamental concept of Greek civilization—here, the concept of mimesis, the belief that reality can be understood by being re-created and reordered through metaphors, through imagination, by being sculpted, drawn, danced —and radically redefined it. For Plato the object of poetic mimesis is no longer humans and their behavior. And the agent of poetic mimesis is no longer any poet, whatever the mode of his narration, whatever his persona as a storyteller; it is always and only the good man telling his story about goodness candidly, without artifice:

> So when you find admirers of Homer saying that he educated Greece and that for human management and education one ought to take him up and learn his lesson and direct one's whole life on his principles, you must be kind and polite to them—they are as good as they are able to be—and concede that Homer is foremost and the most poetical of the tragic poets; but you must be clear in your mind that the only poetry admissible in our city is hymns to the gods and encomia to good men. If you accept the "sweetened Muse" in lyric or epic, pleasure and pain will be enthroned in your city instead of law and the principle which the community accepts in any given situation.
>
> (*Republic* 10.607A)

In this closing attack on "bad" mimesis and irresponsible, destructive poetry, the kinds of lyric poetry that Plato had carefully ignored in his earlier argument are banished from the city along with epic (tragedy and comedy have long since been bundled off); it is Pindar[7] and his holy predecessors who remain to foster the imitation that instills righteousness and prepares the soul for the journey into goodness and the really real.

This is not the place to argue the wisdom or folly of Plato's moral and ontological aesthetics. For our present purposes, it is enough to point out that in the course of his argument Plato succeeds in establishing the classic triad of genres (lyric, epic, and drama) that continues, even today, to exert a strong influence on generic theory and that he distinguishes among these genres by examining them in terms of their characteristic agents of mimesis. If he ignores Sappho, Anacreon, and Simonides in this discussion, it is perhaps because narrative lyric provides him with the clearest foil to the drama and the epic that he is anxious to reject; but it is also possible that neither he nor his audience would think of the various kinds of personal lyric as vehicles of stories. In any case, it is certain that whatever it was that Plato may have thought Sappho and Anacreon to be imitating, both the objects and the agents of this imitation could do the city of the soul no possible good and could do it endless harm. Such dismissal of this considerable portion of lyric poetry does not advance investigation of the idea of lyric very far, but in raising these issues about the nature of lyric in order to conduct his ethical debate, Plato nevertheless fastened on problems that are central to any discussion of lyric genre: the primacy of the object and the agent of mimesis, of story and of lyric voice, in discussions of lyric as a genre.

This Platonic formulation of generic distinctions in poetry is recalled and, of course, reformulated by Aristotle at the opening of his *Poetics*:

> Epic and tragic poetry, comedy and dithyrambic, and most music for the flute or lyre are all, generally considered, varieties of mimesis, differing from each other in three respects, the media, the objects, and the mode of mimesis.
>
> (1447a)

In addition to agent (mode) of mimesis, Aristotle also posits medium of mimesis (rhythm, harmony, verse) and object of mimesis (people performing actions: people as they are in life, or better or worse than they are in life) as elements to be considered when we are attempting to distinguish among genres, but he gives agent or mode of mimesis pride of place in his listing of generic differentiae, and much of what he goes on to say about Homer and tragedy turns on this final element:

> There is still a third difference, the mode in which one presents each of these objects. For one can represent the same objects in the same media
> 1. sometimes in narration and sometimes becoming someone else, as Homer does, or
> 2. speaking in one's own person without change, or
> 3. with all the people engaged in the mimesis actually doing things.
>
> (1448a)

At first glance, it might appear that Aristotle has done nothing more than rephrase Plato's description of the agents of mimesis and their particular genres (mixed agency, epic; pure narrative, lyric; pure imitation, drama), but Aristotle, for all his passion for both Homer and tragedy, at first seems to play no favorites with one of the three possible agents of mimesis: all are equally necessary, all are equally valid—in theory. In practice, Aristotle's bias in favor of drama requires that he prefer the mode of pure imitation of drama (not incorrectly, Aristotle recognizes Homer as a forerunner of dramatic sensibility and technique, and it is the dramatic Homer that he reveres). In drama the biologist discovers a concentration of plot and action, a unity, a tidiness, and an immanent intelligibility that neither pure nor mixed narrative can achieve. After his balanced and objective analysis and description of possible narrative agents, he tacitly opts for the supremacy of the narrative mode that Plato had specifically condemned, the pure imitation of drama, partly because it was natural to him (and perhaps fun for him) to disagree with Plato and partly because the controlled dynamism and the concrete lucidity of drama were as welcome to him as narrative sweep (when untempered by Homeric drama) was alien to him.

But why is lyric not even in the running here?[8] It is possible, of course, that in lost portions of the *Poetics* Aristotle did examine lyric in some detail and gave to it the appreciation that he lavishes on tragedy and grudgingly allows to epic. But when the superiority of tragedy over epic has been so elaborately and so cunningly demonstrated (1461a–1462b), it is unlikely that lyric could have garnered anything but the crumbs of his praise. Although it is idle to speculate about the reasons for Aristotle's prejudices here, it may yet be worthwhile to indulge in such speculation because what I take to be the possible prejudices of Aristotle against lyric suggest the real prejudices of later ancient literary critics who were inevitably influenced in some degree by his formulations and who also show only the faintest interest in the theory of lyric. What follows then, is sheer fiction, but I hope it may be useful fiction. First, as against Plato, Aristotle believes that mimesis is a way of learning about truth (1448b) and that poetry is a form of knowledge (1451b); therefore, though Aristotle is wholly lacking in Plato's rage for perfection and is everywhere charitable to natural aberrations from the ideal in space and time, he has his own hierarchies of moral grandeur, and it is not likely that Sappho, let alone Anacreon, would stand any chance against Homer or Sophocles in Aristotle's ordering of degrees of poetic truth. In his own way, Aristotle is as much a proponent of moral aesthetics as Plato, which is not strange because all ancient literary critics were, and wisely so, essentially moral in their aesthetic orientations.

Second, just as Aristotle may have found Sappho's "He is a god in my eyes" either frivolous or immoral or purely artistic (and therefore relatively deficient in valid general truth), so he may very well have failed to see that Sappho is in fact engaged in telling a story (in a lyric manner) whose plot and action (*muthos-praxis*—"story-action") are, in their own way, for all their brevity, as valid, as significant, as true as the story of Achilles and Hector and the story of Oedipus. In other words, judged by the categories of Aristotle's criticism, the object of Sappho's mimesis may seem, in comparison with Homer and Sophocles, so fragile as to appear almost insignificant. (It may also seem lacking in amplitude [1450b–1451b]: after Callimachus' defense of brevity, it will not be until the romantics in general and Edgar Allan Poe in particular that champions of the short personal lyric will dare, without qualification, to assert its superiority over epic and drama and "short" will become not only beautiful but also the only beautiful.)

One thing about the nature of poetry that moderns have steadily recognized and that ancients could not recognize is the significance, the importance, of the inner stories that personal lyric imitates. Aristotle, perhaps, did not see that Sappho also is imitating a human action, or he thought that the action she imitated (whether her own or that of an imagined person—"When I state myself," said Dickinson, "as the Representative of the Verse—it does not mean—me—but a supposed person")⁹ was too insignificant, too "merely personal," to be the vehicle of the *anagnorisis* ("recognition") and the *peripeteia* ("sudden change in fortune") that make manifest *hoia an genoito* ("what may be")—such things as may possibly occur any place, any time. But "He is a god in my eyes," fragile and ephemeral as the action it imitates might seem, catches and holds the light of things as they are, everywhere, always, as surely as does the *Iliad* or the *Antigone*. It differs from an epic or a tragedy in its dimensions and range; but it needs offer no apologies for its intensity or its profundity or its own moral grandeur. Aristotle's passion for order led him, it seems, to prefer the concentration of drama to the (to him) uncontrolled sprawl of epic; but, so far as one can judge, his earnestness precluded his appreciating both the earnestness and the concentration of personal lyric. It would not be until the romantics taught us that any inner story, precisely imitated (imagined), can reveal general truth that the real seriousness of lyric could be seen and understood. These hindrances to lyrical theory—exaggerated and misdirected emphasis on the morality of art and inability to grasp and appreciate the kinds of stories, that is, emotional actions, that lyric has to tell—exert their force throughout antiquity. They are both serious hindrances, but the more serious is the ancients' inability to make proper use of their favorite and precise aesthetic concept, mimesis, in their efforts to investigate the genre of lyric.

After Aristotle, the Alexandrian critics worked hard and well to define the forms and subgenres of lyric poetry, and this effort implies a theory of lyric that has not, unfortunately, come down to us. The beginnings of serious literary scholarship in Athens of the late fourth century B.C. might easily have been aborted or have dwindled into fruitless word games had the structure and dynamics of Alexander's empire not caused its diffusion throughout the new Greek world of the third century B.C. But it was at Alexandria, with the founding of the museum and its library, that the study of literature in the West came to its first flowering, for in gathering literary texts and scholars to edit and order them, the Ptolemies both assured the survival of the literature of classical Greece and promoted an atmosphere in which the work of sorting out and interpreting that literature could be vigorously and profitably pursued. To suppose, as it has sometimes been, that this endless chore of collecting manuscripts, sorting them, correcting them, cataloguing them, and arranging them was somehow dull and simple-minded is to fail in performing the act of historical imagination. Imagine all of English literature from Chaucer to Tennyson, long circulated in manuscripts indifferent and bad, suddenly dumped helter-skelter in your lap. The task that confronted the Alexandrian scholar-librarians was herculean, and they performed it for the benefit of all posterity magnificently, their imagination and ingenuity as ruthlessly tested as their erudition and industry.

None of the sorting and editing can have been easy, but lyric presented special problems. In its linguistic variety, its antiquity, its metrical difficulties, and its bewildering profusion of similar, sometimes nearly identical subgenres, lyric poetry required all the talent and all the tools of scholarship and criticism that the museum had been able to assemble. The immediate practical result of the long and arduous labor of editing Greek lyric of the archaic and classical ages was the survival of this poetry (much of it down through the life of Byzantium) in accurate and readable editions, but what matters here is that in performing this labor, the scholar-critics of Alexandria were forced to shape theoretical categories that remain invaluable to the study and enjoyment of lyric poetry. With Aristophanes of Byzantium we encounter the first serious and successful theorist of lyric genre in Western literature, for it is he, who, confronted with the jungle of the Pindaric corpus, invented the strategem of sorting them, not only on the basis of their musical modes or metrical schemes but also on the basis of their themes and concerns.[10]

Aristophanes arranged the Pindaric corpus into seventeen books: hymns and paeans in one book each; dithyrambs, processionals, maiden songs, and poems for dancing in two books each (with perhaps an added book for purely secular maiden songs); four books of victory songs; and a book each of encomia and threnoi.[11] It is not a question here of Aristophanes's having invented these terms and the categories they denote since at least some of them go all the way back to Homer and most likely precede him.[12] What Aristophanes did, what he had to do in order to make adequate use of these old, vague categories, was to study their formal properties, the meters,

the topoi and rhetorical stratagems, the formulae and themes that
were characteristic of them; on the basis of this study he was prepared to formulate descriptive definitions of the categories that were
superior both in precision and in flexibility to the traditional, uncertain definitions that he had inherited; and on the basis of his improved definitions he was able to assign the jumble of poems he had
confronted to their proper categories.

Beyond his immediate purpose—the ordering of chaotic bodies of
poetry, the making of intelligible, enjoyable collections—the method
he devised and refined had and continues to have major importance
for the theory and practice of the lyric genre. The idea behind Aristophanes's method (this is a modern inference for which we have no
hard evidence) is the idea of decorum, and the method itself is the
analysis of particular instances of decorum. The kinds of questions he
seems to have asked himself, both in devising and refining the method
itself and in applying it to the actual sorting poems into their proper
categories, would seem to have been something like this. What are
the essential elements in a paean? What is the natural (or conventional) order of these elements? What metrical or rhetorical patterns
tend to appear in the paean? What instruments accompanied it and
what were the conditions of its performance? What elements can
possibly be omitted from a paean without its ceasing to be a paean,
and what elements cannot under any circumstances be neglected or
altered? How does a paean differ from a dithyramb or a hymn?

The concept of decorum, its uses and its limitations, is so familiar
as to seem to us perhaps obvious, if not simple-minded. But to
ignore the realities of decorum in the study of literature is usually
to invite confusion and error. In concentrating on the contents of
lyric poems and the surfaces of their content, in systematically collecting and synthesizing his observations on the conventional and
formal appearance of lyric poems, Aristophanes made it possible for
later critics and common readers to see the substance of the poems
through their surfaces ("It is only shallow people," remarked Wilde,
"who do not judge by appearances"). Once it became habitual for
critics and readers to look for and recognize the conventional features in a poem that would tell them what kind of poem it was (and
the looking for and the recognizing quickly become almost auto-
matic and largely unconscious), it became easier to understand and

to enjoy the special artistry and the special sensibility—the origi- nality—of its poet. What are the usual, what are the suitable, things to say in a love poem? What sort of person is the proper person to say these things? Once a spectrum of conventions has been estab- lished and the reader's expectations have been properly defined, it is then possible to notice how a particular poet distorts conventions even as he makes use of them, defeats expectations even as he satis- fies them. Guided by an understanding of decorum (what is proper for a given kind of poem), we can respond accurately to wide vari- eties of feeling, to a given poet's new, unfamiliar attitudes toward his material—life, his chosen form, the conventions that obtain in that form. We can, in other words, hear precisely the distinctive voice of a particular poet because we hear it against, magnified by, the stan- dard patterns that he uses and transforms. But until that standard pattern is isolated and defined, the artifice and the integrity of the poet's voice in a given poem will not be available to the reader.

It goes without saying that Sappho's audience did not consciously consider what species of poem they were listening to when they watched and heard her perform it—because they did not need to. When conventions are living, when both poets and their listeners respond to poetic conventions they have grown up with as naturally as they breathe air or drink water, there is of course no need for crit- ics to distinguish among kinds of poems and to list the characteristic formal elements of different species of lyric.[13] In general, it is only when artistic conventions are dead or dying or when they have been so transformed as to be unrecognizable that critics want or are re- quired to attempt to recover them, to distinguish them, stabilize them, arrange them. There was, for example, very little effort to de- scribe and codify the formal conventions of modernist poetry until it began to be vaguely sensed that the great modernist poets had all disappeared and that the music of their epigones sounded not quite right; while the great modernists were writing, though there was plenty of propaganda, controversy, and explications, there was not and could not be much in the way of formal analysis. The living con- temporaries of the great modernists did not need to be instructed in conventions that they lived in and shared with their poets—they needed only to read the poetry, experience and enjoy it. We who live when modernism is exhausted can only experience and enjoy its poetry by trying to understand it, and to do this, we need all the help we can get from critics who can recover and describe its formal conventions, its special hybrid genres, and the sensibilities that created them.

Aristophanes of Byzantium and the readers he helped lived in a world of books rather than of performed poems, in a world where music had become, for the most part, separated from poetry and where the occasions for and the function of the old lyric poetry had either disappeared or had been altered beyond recognition. Thus, as the circumstances in which old lyric poetry was experienced changed, as its conventions became unintelligible or blurred through the passage of time and the hybridization of genres and subgenres, the services of Aristophanes and his successors became indispensable to ancient readers, who, without these scholar-critics, would have had neither adequate texts nor notions of literary convention and generic forms that were and are necessary for enjoyable reading of these poems. But it was not merely readers of the postclassical age who were indebted to the Alexandrian critics. All lyric poets in the classical tradition of Europe, whether they are directly or indirectly in that tradition, whether they are consciously or unconsciously influenced by it, depend on Aristophanes and his school for their understanding of the possibilities of lyric poetry, of its various kinds, and of the various voices and combinations of voices that are suitable to its various kinds. It goes without saying that good lyricists could grasp the generic forms and the voices they need by direct imitation of their predecessors, by the intuitions proper to their talents, without the help of critics. But the fact is that they seldom do this, that they "find their own voices," their particular attitudes toward their materials and their artistry within the tradition of lyrical categories that critics (many of whom are poets) redefine after each of the poetry's major renewals.[14] What Aristophanes found and sanctioned—it was not exactly what he intended to find and the way I define his discovery is not the way he would have defined it—was the range of voices, styles, and attitudes that are appropriate to the varieties of lyric poetry; and he found this spectrum of lyric voices by studying the outward forms of classical lyric poems.

It was the poet-critic who was to serve as the essential link in the chain of Western lyrical tradition who saw and acknowledged the

prime importance of this Alexandrian theory of lyric genre. In discussing the importance of metrical decorum and metrical tradition,
Horace turns from epic, elegiacs, and iambics to lyric poetry and
remarks:

> To praise the gods and the children of gods,
> to honor the triumphant boxer,
> to tell of young lovers and their sufferings,
> to commend the solace of wine—
> these offices the Muse conferred upon the lyre.
> If I am unable or unwilling
> to preserve the distinctive patterns,
> the special shades of the several genres,
> why should I expect to be hailed as poet?
> (Art of Poetry, lines 83–88)

Though "the distinctive patterns" and "special shades"[15] refer to
epic and the other genres mentioned before lyric, it is possible that
Horace discusses lyric last not only because it has become his own
special preserve and the source of his greatest pride but also because
the "shifts and shades" of lyric poetry needed far more care in their
analysis than the other, larger and simpler genres.[16] In its metrical
variety, in its subtle differences in content, function and form, and,
above all, in its varieties and combinations of voices, the practice as
well as the theory of lyric poetry had benefited and would continue
to benefit from Aristophanes's analysis of lyric content, from his emphasis on the crucial importance of lyric categories.

The successors of Aristophanes continued to be engaged in refining the lyrical categories that he established, but so far as we can tell
from the meagre and often obscure information that has survived,
their interest in these categories and their manner of dealing with
them gradually shifted direction and focus. If the résumé of Proclus's
work on lyric by the Byzantine Photius can be trusted,[17] it would
seem that some time soon after the beginning of the Christian era,
lyrical theory has completely abandoned (or taken as resolved) the
question of the essential nature of lyric, has come to treat the musical nature of ancient Greek lyric as something approaching antiquarian curiosity, and has begun to busy itself primarily with rhetori-

cal analysis of lyric and with definition of the purely secular, purely literary varieties of poetry that had replaced ancient lyric in Hellenistic literature. Given the overwhelming importance of rhetoric in education (throughout this period and until the end of antiquity), combined with the failure of music in poetry, this change—one is tempted to say, this trivialization—of emphasis is natural enough, indeed, is all but inevitable, but it betokens not only the death of ancient lyric but also, incredibly, a lack of any awareness that lyric had died. As we shall see in the next chapter, the lyric spirit had, of course, survived, had emigrated into and hidden itself in other kinds of poetry, but Greek lyric, this musical, ontological, social, performed poetry, had vanished as a living art.

Proclus, apparently, divided lyric poetry into four major categories: (1) lyrics addressed to the gods, (2) lyrics addressed to men, (3) lyrics addressed to both gods and men (a confusing, uncertain category), and (4) verse for occasions (*prospiptousai peristaseis*). Proclus himself protested that this final category should not properly be classed with the others, which are traditional.[18] That he finally and grudgingly does admit this category is an index to its extreme popularity in late Hellenistic times, and to the fact that this occasional verse had almost completely replaced the older lyric forms.[19] Religious poetry continued to be written (and the old religious poetry continued to be performed) for cults and festivals; and royal personages and wealthy men continued to commission celebrations of themselves, but the remnants of this poetry show why it perished rapidly. Love songs, dirges, victory celebrations, semiphilosophical drinking songs, marriage songs, the poems that comprise Proclus's second category, tend to find themselves transformed into elegiac epigram. Since there was in fact little real, or at least little good, lyric poetry during the centuries in which Proclus's sources were theorizing, it is no wonder that the lyric categories were expanded (padded out) to include prosaic doodling in metrical disguise that concerns itself with impressions of travelers, advice to friends in epistolary form, suggestions about farming, musings on Life, and reflections on destiny—Polonius poetasting.

But why did Polonius take to writing verse? How did he learn to do it? And why did he think anyone would be interested if he attempted to subject his earnest ponderings to the discipline of verse?—because he had been to school and there learned to read poetry rhetorically, as had the readers he wrote for. Reading poetry for its rhetoric and for its moral platitudes was, of course, no worse than reading it for its ironies and ambiguities or for its criticism of life or for any other modern reductive function of poetry we might recall here—indeed, to read poetry for its rhetoric is hardly the worst way to read poetry. Nor was much harm done by the little rhetoricians who grew up to be soldiers, businessmen, teachers, and government officials and who scribbled verselets in their spare time on subjects dear to their hearts—money, connections, prospects, status. The harm was— well, but there was no harm. These poets and their readers were apparently content with this versifying, and the lyric spirit, while waiting its reincarnations into Horace, into Latin and Greek Christian hymns, and into the songs of Provence and Sicily, masqueraded as epic, as epigram, as pastoral. It is a world of rhetoricians, professional and amateur, active and passive, that unites to produce the categories of Proclus, in which occasional verse, prosaic thoughts woven into mechanical verse and mechanical rhetoric, hobnobs with Pindaric *epinicia* ("victory songs") and Sapphic *erotica* ("love songs"). A strange poetic world—emptied of the lyric spirit, filled with busy poets with their dull, correct rhythms, their rhetorical commonplaces and their commonplace notions—a million miles from the passions and paradoxes of great lyric poetry; yet if it is boring, it is civilized, and if it is safe, complacent, tidy, it is not wholly unattractive. There are worse poetic worlds than this.

Nor, moreover, were its virtues merely negative or neutral. Schoolmasters and the students who were obsessed with rhetoric and occasional verse perfected the discipline of poetic rhetoric that in the hands of Horace, Joachim du Bellay, and Ben Jonson would kindle into incomparable glories. Francis Cairns has reminded us, indeed has retaught us, that each of the varieties of lyric (he calls them genres)

> can be thought of as having a set of primary or logically necessary elements which in combination distinguish that genre from every other genre. For example, the primary elements of the propemtikon are in these terms someone departing, another person bidding him farewell, and a relationship of affection between the two, plus an appropriate setting. . . . As well

as containing the primary elements of its genre every generic example contains some secondary elements (topoi). These topoi are the smallest divisions of the material of any genre useful for analytical purposes. Their usefulness lies in the fact that they are the commonplaces which recur in different forms in different examples of the same genre. They help, in combination with the primary elements, to identify a generic example. But the primary elements are the only final arbiters of generic identity since any particular individual topos (secondary element) can be found in several different genres.[20]

The poet who inherited and submitted himself to the strict yet flexible system of these primary and secondary elements was possessed of an enormous poetic freedom, the freedom to use and to alter the system that he preserved. Poetic rhetoric, at least by the beginning of the Christian era, was the common, living poetic language just as oratorical rhetoric was the common language of history and moral philosophy as well as of the forum and the courtroom.

In a very real sense, it was his reader's mastery of poetic rhetoric that assured the poet his complete poetic freedom. And if the modern reader shudders as he glances through Cairns's invaluable discussion of this poetic rhetoric, if he pities the ancients who troubled themselves with the endless, ugly jargon that denotes varieties of lyric poems and who learned by heart the lists of decorous clichés (topoi) that structured these lyric poems—*tant pis pour lui* ("that is his problem")—and the problem of the contemporary poets he reads. The lyrical theorists of later and late antiquity completed the work begun by Aristophanes of Byzantium by systematically subdividing the varieties of lyric, by rigorously defining the elements of lyrical poetry, and by collecting, distinguishing, sorting out the commonplaces and the combinations of commonplaces that are typical of particular kinds of lyric poems.[21] Much of the poetry that grew out of and depended on this theory of lyrical poetry was evidently (and, naturally) not very good, but largely because of the work and genius of Horace, it is this rhetorical theory of lyric poetry that dominates European poetry from the late Middle Ages until very recent times, and it is this rhetorical tradition that is largely responsible for Petrarch's, Herbert's, Goethe's, and Valéry's having been able to do with lyric poetry what they could do with it. In this sense, the patient labors of Aristophanes and his followers were and remain crucial to lyric and the idea of lyric.

Not the least surprising thing about lyric theory in antiquity is that one of the greatest lyricists, himself a literary theorist of the first rank, did not bother to theorize formally about the idea of lyric. Horace's theory of lyric is implicit, of course, in his lyric composition, that careful, systematic re-creation of as much of ancient Greek lyric as a Roman poet, writing in Latin in the second half of the first century B.C., could succeed in re-creating. Still, it is puzzling that this poet who had given so much of his time and talent to reviving the dead genre, transplanting it into a culture and language that were alien to it, should refrain from a precise and extended statement of his theory of lyric. Perhaps he eschewed such a statement because he found, at last, that it was unnecessary—his poems, in which the old Greek voices spoke again, in another language, in the modern world, needed neither explanation nor defense. Perhaps that is what he thought, but he did defend them, rankled apparently by their tepid reception outside the charmed circle of the best people, the happy few who recognized his lyric genius and his lyric achievement. *Epistles* 1.19 is a ferocious answer to the stupid critics and semiliterate readers who had no notion of Greek lyric and could therefore have no notion of how hard his task had been or how brilliantly, how completely, he had performed it: "I have set my footprints in open country / where none before me dared venture" (lines 21–22). That is a favorite topos among both Greek and Roman Alexandrians, but the next statement, which introduces his claim to have imported Archilochus and Alcaeus into Roman literature undamaged and (perhaps) improved, has none of the ironic modesty, almost the coyness, of similar claims elsewhere (see particularly *Odes* 2.20 and 3.30): "He who trusts himself will rule the swarm" (lines 22–23). The poet who has confidence in his own powers, the poet with guts, is the "king" bee who dominates the hive. He had dared much and won everything. If he seems merely an imitator (lines 26–31), he must seem so only to the uneducated who misunderstand tradition and do not see that Sappho and Alcaeus had imitated Archilochus even as Horace has imitated all three. But especially Alcaeus:

His verse forms, attempted by none before,
I, the Latin lyricist, have given the world.
It pleases me to be read by the eyes,
to be held in the hands,
of the happy few.
      (lines 33–34)

Latinus fidicen, "*the* Latin lyricist"! It is more than a boast, more than
a challenge: it is a full-voiced, ruthless statement of fact, a fact that
the *ingratus lector* (the "thankless reader," the Philistines, the stupid
public) cannot begin to grasp. It is the eyes of the happy few (*inge-
nuis oculis*) that will read his poems, and it is their hands that will
hold the book.

Yet if the ignorant herd cannot appreciate the blessed miracle of a
Horace in their midst, an emperor can:

The poet is usually a lazy, a terrible soldier.
Yet if you'll admit
that greatness can be served by what is humble—
he has his uses to the City.
      (*Epistles* 2.1.124–25

The ironic humility returns as he addresses Augustus in one of his
greatest, perhaps one of his last, poems. The Latin lyricist serves his
community even if it cannot appreciate who he is and what he is
doing for it:

The poet shapes the child's stammering mouth,
diverts his ear from vulgar speech,
then forms his heart with cordial lessons,
redeeming it from harshness, from envy and rage.
He sings of good deeds and he furnishes
those flowering years with famous models,
he comforts the poor and the sick.
Where could the unmarried girl or the pure young man
discover a teacher of their prayers,
had the muse not sent them a sacred poet?
Their chorus begs his assistance,
then, feeling the divine presence,
persuading with the prayer he taught,

it asks for rain from heaven,
it wards off plague and banishes war,
it wins peace for the city and rich harvest.
The heavenly gods and the gods below
yield to its incantation.
(*Epistles* 2.1.126–38

Musa dedit fidibus ("the Muse gave to the lyre") (AP 83) recalls *vatem ni Musa dedisset* ("had the muse not sent"). Though Horace seems to slight lyric poetry in his theoretical criticism, here, in his most subtle and most powerful defense of poetry, he places lyric even above epic and tragedy. A poet of many voices, Horace deliberately avoids mention of his favorite voices (Archilochus, Alcaeus, Anacreon, Simonides) in this passage in order to elevate lyric poetry by focusing on its most exalted figure—the vatic Pindar. The satirist, the epicurean dialectical poet, and the dandified hedonist are temporarily and ironically sequestered because this is no moment for the paradoxes, the ironies, and the eccentric orbits that this configuration of voices recalls. What is needed here is the shaman, the figure of Pindar, "to purify the language of the tribe," to preside over the city's *paideia* ("education"), to define and to instill *sophrosyne* ("prudence"), to recall the grand origins of courage and morality, to evoke eternity (*praesentia numina*), and to win divine blessings for the community. The image of the chorus recalls Horace's own *Carmen Saeculare*, and this image is, in the modern Rome of Horace and Augustus, as anachronistic as that poem and its performance had been. Yet it is the image that Horace wants and needs here, for since the question he is asking in this poem is, "What are the uses of poetry?" and since the answer he gives Augustus is, "Not primarily, not really, to immortalize emperors," he does well to exclude from his definition of lyric all varieties of lyric except the one that manifests clearly the most ancient and most vital lyrical form and function. By this strategem he answers Augustus with a fair amount of tact, and he also reminds the vulgar throng of their ignorance of the essence of lyric poetry, a long vanished, long dead art that he had succeeded in resuscitating almost single-handedly. Himself an ironic Pindarist, a spoiled shaman-turned-epicurean humanist, he ironically and sincerely recalls, defines eloquently and for good in the classical tradition, the religious origin, the religious function, and the religious power of lyric poetry. Having put away his feathers and his drum, having relapsed once more into Simonidean humanism and modern times, he had still the taste and the judgment to praise his betters— the forgotten authentic *vates* ("seer") with whom the evocation of eternal moments had begun. This is not perhaps a theory of lyric, but it is good to find Horace in his humility reminding a world that had lost all memory of great lyric what the idea of great lyric must be.

 # IV

In the Birdcage of the Muses:
Ancient Literary Lyric

Where the Sea Is Remembered: Callimachus and Meleager

Though lyric poetry continued to be composed and performed after Pindar, what remains to us of the lyric poetry written in Greek after 450 B.C. and what we know of it secondhand suggest that the genre had become so enfeebled, partly by heavy competition from rival genres, that it could not continue to flourish.[1] In the fourth century, the rise of literary philosophy, of new comedy, of history, and of oratory precluded whatever recovery lyric might otherwise have made, for these new genres usurped many of the functions that lyric had once shared with or had itself usurped from other ancient genres. The great theorist of the idea of prose, Isocrates, speaks for great writers of his century when, pretending to complain of the advantages that poets have over writers of prose, he arrogates to himself and his fellow prose artists the functions and the glory of poetry:

> The poets compose all their works with meter and rhythm, while the orators do not share in any of these advantages; and these lend such charm that even though the poets may be deficient in style and thoughts, yet by the very spell of their rhythm and harmony they bewitch their listeners. The power of poetry

may be understood from this consideration; if one should retain the words and ideas of poems which are held in high esteem, but do away with the meter, they will appear far inferior to the opinion we now have of them. Nevertheless, although poetry has advantages so great, we must not shirk the task, but must make the effort and see if it will be possible in prose to eulogize good men in no worse fashion than their encomiasts do who employ song and verse.

(*Evagoras* 10–11)

Isocrates is himself busy, of course, inventing new harmonies and rhythms, and he is not shy about filching from the poets all of their tricks and ornaments that he can lay his hands on.[2] But he is correct in seeing (though, naturally, he does not say it here) that the music is gone. And gone with it are the inner worlds, the inner dramas and stories, the exultations and intensities that the music had magnified and confirmed.

When the lyrical sensibility and the idea of lyric resurface again in the third century B.C., the world it encounters is radically different from the world in which it had flourished over a century before.[3] In Alexandria and the other centers of poetry where lyric would begin its new life, music was to become a symbol, an emblem, of the poetry from which it had been divorced, and verse, now spoken not sung, was experienced not by members of communities but by groups of educated readers.[4] But though the medium of his mimesis has altered immensely with the failure of music, though his audience also has changed completely, the lyric poet himself, together with his function and the object of his mimesis, remains recognizably himself for all the vast transformations that he and his world have endured since his apparent extinction. Since Hellenistic poetry had, until very recently, a pretty bad reputation and since there may seem a certain terminological inconsistency in applying the term *lyric* to a body of poetry that lacks the music, performance, and intensity that we have seen to be the hallmarks of archaic and classical Greek lyric, it would be useful to examine the circumstances in which Alexandrians wrote the poetry that I am now calling lyrical and to refute, so far as may be done, accusations of frivolity and artificiality that are frequently brought against this poetry.[5]

For the purposes of polemic, let us carefully overstate these accusations. Taking Callimachus as an emblem of the new lyricism (for in addition to his having done much to invent it, he is, in Greek literature, perhaps its most subtle and most dynamic exponent), we will describe the circumstances of his poethood in this fashion. He lived comfortably, safely, and productively in the greatest city (Alexandria) that the Western world had ever known; it had the first real library and university, a delightful climate, a superb cosmopolitan atmosphere, wide, clear boulevards, the finest in modern plumbing, a vigorous economy, and a relatively stable political system—absolute, hereditary monarchy. The heirs of Alexander, here and even elsewhere, had found a way of bringing order into human society and had made the safety and happiness of the deserving the *summum bonum* of human existence. Of course, one continued to read and to adore the old tragedies of Athens and the old epics that Athens, Sparta, and Corinth had so treasured. But for all their power and their manifest poetic greatness, there was something almost droll about those ancient poets: illiterate princes fighting over cattle, armor, and women, killing each other when they should have been out pacifying the savages; a crazy princess getting herself smothered ignominiously for the sake of unwritten laws; another crazy princess ready to kill her mother and the king or die trying—all in the name of some bewildering notion of justice. Everywhere in those pages, in the dramas, the epics, and even in the lyrics, this shrill, incessant quibbling over the meaning of freedom, this childlike, irritating debate, never conducted according to logical procedures, over destiny and responsibility and doom—well, it was all quite hopeless. Beautiful as the language was, precious and fascinating though the effort might be to say the ineffable and think the unthinkable, these people and their grand illusions were—what other term for it?—underprivileged. The magnificent, silly past had vanished because it was finally unsuited to the business of living; in some curious way, the great dead were not very clever, and the fact that they were unable to retain their world is the clearest evidence of their incompetence. Today, we are, if we are not really more wise, luckier than they were.

So much for overstatement. Beneath this smugness there is not only an apparent contempt for the barbaric past but also a genuine admiration for it, a sorrowing envy of it and its hazards and freedoms, which is intensified by deep anxieties about the present and the future. The modernist, any vital modernist, despises the past and cherishes it, loves and fears it. If one lives and works in a superb modern university that is lavishly funded by an omnipotent and uniformly benevolent emperor, what does one write about? The answer is, clearly: *what* one writes about is far less important than *how well* one writes. For such a sensibility as this, the objects of mimesis of less fortunate writers are bound to seem a sad by-product of their misfortune, even as the perfection of one's own style and the consummate refinements of one's own technique might well seem to outsiders merely the offshoots of one's own great good luck. And if such outsiders, having looked at this pure and perfect art, should decide that it was wholly artificial, that it lacked any vestige of power or commitment, that it was sterile, suspiciously delicate, narcissistic, overripe? Well, what is there to say to a barbarian? And if one's life is in fact meaningless and if existence is pointless, if the emperor should fall from his parade horse or choke on a fishbone and the bad times rush back, sweep through the boulevards, burn down the library? Idle, foolish, neurotic thoughts. There is no danger here, and even if there were, it would somehow be unreal, for even if one's life should prove to be pointless, one's art is not.

So much is, in a way, true of the Alexandrian poet's vanity, self-satisfaction, slender intellectual means, poverty of courage. But that is not the whole picture because his poems and the moods that they inform survive with a luster and an intensity that are all their own. As the boundaries of the Greek world widened, the sense of self diminished. The idea of heroism vanished or became grandiloquent, grotesque, funny; the emotions that were shaped in these poems seem to be completely untempered by any trace of hope or courage, seem dangerously meager in self-respect. And it is this absence of true heroic gesture, this utter distrust of freedom and volition, this despair over purpose in life, that makes this poetry, in its own way, in a new way for Greek poetry, genuinely lyrical. The world had become too wide, and the distinctions, the clarities of music, of community, and even of doom, had disappeared, leaving behind them that ominous, immense distance that one of the most romantic and most classical, not to say, best, of modern lyricists would precisely describe: "I, a stranger and afraid."[6] Parallels between Alexandrian and modern times may sometimes be careless, and there may seem to be too many of them, but there is every reason for trying to draw them.

All the dread and distances are fully masked under the cool perfections of Callimachus's lyric epigrams:

> I detest the grandeur of oral saga,
>   it vexes me to stroll
>   streets where the mindless millions bumble;
> Nor have I much tolerance for
>   those who are sexually liberated;
> To drink
>   from the public drinking fountain is
>   beneath a gentleman:
> Everything vulgar offends me.
> Lysanias, you are
>   extraordinarily handsome,
>   yes.
> Yet before Echo can reshape the phrase,
> I hear another voice that says:
>   He's somebody else's.
>
>   (Epigram 30)

Artistic and erotic values are exquisitely fused here. The dandy rejects
what is not worth knowing because to attempt securing it would be
dangerous, would remind him of other, more painful losses, of more
serious hazards. This is the spirit of Anacreon, but more deeply ironized and more ironically controlled. The distance between life and art
has immeasurably widened, and the ancient gaiety, the exuberance
and measured self-esteem that mark Anacreon have been swallowed
up into the sad, paradoxical isolations of the metropolis and its world
empires. This poet is a connoisseur who must take no chances, not in
writing the spare, flawless lyrics, not in courting (seriously) the wonderful Lysanias, who is dismissed with a witty jibe, with a suave gesture of renunciation: My poems are pure, my lovers must be similarly
pure. But that narrowness, both of art and of passion, has all the
defects of its virtue. There can be no gambling for happiness, or even
for a flash of bliss, because the odds against success are so extreme,
because the hazards are ubiquitous and powerful. The older lyric poets
knew all this, of course, but either they did not know it quite well
enough, or they had resources that we moderns lack—trust in life,
some mysterious faith, now utterly dissipated, that made possible the

passion and the affirmations we cannot lay hold of. Better, then, to cultivate nuance and precision. And what that means is that the center of these severely polished emotions is a delicate, radiant futility that finds its proper forms in these poems. Love, in these poems, almost ceases to be love. It becomes a striving for an imaginary voluptuousness, sure to be thwarted because life cannot rival art. Not simple hunger for sexual gratification, not passion that maddens and destroys, certainly not a desire, a pure desire, for the happiness of the beloved—the erotic has rather become, like art itself, a game in the mind, a diversion, a matrix of poetic occasions. [7]

For art does matter, is real. If passion exposes us to the dangerous, sinister world of emotions of which our experience is meager, uncertain, frightening, at least poetry and friendship sometimes allow the comfort and the steady, moderate pleasure that are within our grasp and that do not betray:

> When someone mentioned
>   that you, Herakleitos, were dead,
> Quick tears obscured my eyes as I recalled
> How often our conversations
>   had seen the sun to sleep.
> You, friend from Halicarnassus,
> Are vanished from us now time out of mind,
> But your nightingales, they endure, they thrive—
> The Lord of Hell who seizes all that is,
>   his hands your songs elude.
>   (Epigram 2)

Is poetry, then, immortal? Strictly speaking, no. But the spirit that informs good poetry and the living voice that is shadowed in it, these manage, in a way, to ward off oblivion for a while, and who should know this better than the poet-librarian? Thereby poems achieve something that we might well be tempted to call deathlessness. There is a slight melancholy even in this poem, but a combination of two emotions that were very powerful in Callimachus, passion for friendship and passion for literature, succeeds in tempering the melancholy, in fighting free of the characteristic impulse to close with a perfectly formed gesture of resignation. The beauty and even the power of art may be gently affirmed though life itself may not partake in that affirmation. When Callimachus goes, the conversations about art, all memory of them, go, like the sun, to oblivion—but not quite; they survive, pure and unperishing, in these brief, exactly crafted lyrical inscriptions. Kings have their walls carved with records of their glory. Poets have their quatrains into whose inviolable excellence the entire life has been compressed.

It is a charming, bewildering irony that the lyric sensibility should be reborn in the scholarly librarian whom necessity impelled to invent the card catalogue. Perhaps, in the history of Western poetry, there are monsters stranger than the man who devised and executed the *Pinakes* (lists of the library's collections, summaries of the individual works), who also found time for hundreds of essays on antiquarian, paraliterary topics, who composed fragile, erudite hymns to the vanishing gods and droll satiric dialogues. But Callimachus, though he seems like a fabrication of Borges's, though it is paradoxical that a new, pure lyricism rose out of all this sorting and ordering of other men's poems, was able to revive lyricism, to make it new, because as tradition passed before him and took form as it was divided into its categories in the *Pinakes*, he understood the history and the conventions of lyric in a way that no poet before him had been in a position to understand it. Callimachus is, in the realm of lyric, an ideal example of Eliot's individual talent both because the death of lyric in the century previous to his own gives him a necessary distance and objectivity for his work and because he achieves an intimate experience of the dead, a complete experience of the tradition, that is not, strictly speaking, possible in any essentially oral tradition.

It is with Callimachus that lyric poetry becomes literary, and if that means, to some degree, that it becomes oblique, learned, derivative; if in this poetry passion and belief and affirmation are no longer, cannot be, central; if so much is true—still the virtues of these defects are to be found in the increased elegance of syntax and in the increased concentration and definition of feeling that the poems of Callimachus and his followers show. These temperaments are much less robust, much less willing to risk their small safeties for the slim chances at joy than were the poets whom they echo and redesign, and their poetic worlds have grown smaller in proportion as Alexander's empire and the heavens of Alexandrian astronomy have expanded. Where the aged Alcman had cried, wittily, blithely:

Girls, with your voices of soft honey,
my legs buckle beneath me,
O catch me up!
If I could be transformed—
O, could I become
the easy kingfisher bird that swoops
across the blossoming foam,
comrade of the halycons,
those sacred indigo couriers of Spring!

    (Fragment 26)

Callimachus takes this universal emblem of poetic freedom and
poetic power and models it to an image of pathos that resists all
comfort:

Who could you be,
    poor shipwrecked, alien man?
Leontichos came upon you here,
    a corpse washed up on the bare strand,
and sheltered you within this grave—
weeping all the while for his own fragile life,
for he too has no share in ease,
    but like a gull
he wanders endlessly the wide salt wave.

    (Epigram 59)

Pity for the victim, self-pity, pity for all creatures and for all being.
The art seeks to hide what the pity is for, to deflect our vision to a
near-solace that will be almost acceptable; but the art cannot hide
the dread occasioned by meaningless freedom, meaningless dying,
meaningless living. Instead, it confronts the dread and shapes a metaphor for this feeling in all its confusion and complexity of fear,
compassion, anger, and despair. The old music it may lack, but it
makes up for this defect with its compression, its purity of selected
detail, its austere voice, with a new verbal music. The shape of the
universal feeling is uttered from the disorder of the particular feeling;
the universal pity is not abstract, artificial, and the subjectivity is
not eccentric.

   Leontichos and his seagull move away from the immensities of
freedom toward the small, complex, ordered works of "dispassion-

ate" voices, of narrow griefs and joys, and of books. They are not free, these poets and their poems; they do not even ponder freedom wistfully because they bear the burden of tradition and because the object of their mimesis is no longer the human spirit in the exultations of its self-discovery and its growth but the human spirit in its increased sense of limitation and vulnerability. Not identical with, but connected to, the world of books that now begins to dominate ancient poetry is the world of pathos that now begins to dominate not merely ancient poetry but ancient art and ancient philosophy as well. Tradition and its grandeurs belong to the past that is secured in books and libraries; the present is informed by its sense of human limitations, of a human bondage that both a sense of the great past and a materialistic, uneasy optimism foster and magnify. Small wonder that the authentic lyric of this period of antiquity, down to Horace and for the most part including Horace, will grow from vague intuitions of desolation; that it will find its characteristic and appropriate tones and moods in forms where anxiety masquerades as frivolity and where an artistry that proclaims the autonomy of art evades, or tries to evade, the powerful but now ambiguous claims of morality and mortality.

As the lyrical epigram evolves,[8] after Callimachus has given it its essential shape, though the fiction of the dispassionate or sophisticated voice never wholly disappears, the sense of pathos and the feeling of defenselessness become more emphatic. Meleager, the next great voice in this new tradition, continues the elegance and some of the learning that are central to this lyrical experience, but in him the educated dandy has become less surely poised, more given to whimsy, is constantly subject to brittle elations and feeble depressions. Where Callimachus was an unwilling victim of hopeless love and of thwarted or imagined eroticism, where his protests against mortality had been as bitter as they were ironically graceful, with Meleager there is something like pleasure in defeat, in his vulnerability and helplessness; being victimized by inscrutable powers has all but become a poetic way of life. The dandy is now passing from ironic narcissism to genuine solipsism:

> At 12 o'clock in the afternoon
>   in the middle of the street—
> Alexis.

Summer had all but brought the fruit
   to its perilous end:
   & the summer sun & that boy's look
did their work on me.
   Night hid the sun.
   Your face consumes my dreams.
Others feel sleep as feathered rest;
   mine but in flame refigures
   your image lit in me.[9]
      (Poem 15)

Reality and the realities of the sunlit world outside him have been
swallowed up into personal sufferings or, to put it more precisely,
have been devoured by erotic illusions. What are now real are the
omnipotence of the illusion and his painful, pleasant submission to
it and to his humiliation. The comfort and solace that others find
in sleep are contemptible; the enslaved lover, whether he feels giddy
as he stands in the sweltering noon street and sees Alexis in the flesh
or dreams of Alexis in the actual night, knows a glory of sickness
that the healthy cannot know, and finds splendid identity in the annihilation of his being by the irresistible force of this destructive
beauty.

   The older poets had known the power and the terror of eroticism
and had fought it or tried to escape it, but for Meleager the danger
and the consummation of the danger are welcome, are a kind of
salvation:

Sweet, by Arcadian Pan
   the music that you make
Zenophile/sweet
   (by Pan)
the Lydian lyre
   when you strike it.
Where shall I go?
   With Cupids fluttering
about me/ the air
   stifled with longing.
What words shall I speak?
   Who looks only for your beauty

> who looks for your song
>   for your body moving,
> where all things flame
>   I, who burn.
>   (Poem 34)

Poi se phugo? ti lego?—*phlegomai*—"Where shall I go (to flee you)?" "What words shall I speak?" "I am consumed with fire." This hopeless, helpless mood is, of course, common enough in lovers (both poetic and actual), but in Meleager the mood is constant, unvaried, except, perhaps, by degrees of flippancy, for in many of the poems—for example, the charming poem to the messenger mosquito (Poem 38)—the fragile eroticism melts into pretty conceit and nothing more. In these poems, the lyric first-person I has been reduced to a permanent victim of passions that it cannot master, cannot understand, cannot fashion into metaphors that will reveal and share the shape of human emotions. Instead, lovely pictures and graceful similes are made to substitute for emotions and their lyric metaphors. The extended cry of hurt desire is fancifully muffled; the force of the emotion is evaded in a langorous, opaque *Stimmungsmusik* ("mood music"):

> Love in silence shall
> its levy of tears
> draw from the eyes, ears
> fill with clamour,
> familiar impress
> takes (already)
> the heart,
> darkness & light
> powerless both
> this charm to unwind:
> Those wings, my Cupids
> so strong in urging love
> so weak now
> at the time of separation.
>   (Poem 1)

The sweet Cupids and their delicate fluttering are, once again, the cause of his malaise and, through the poem that they inform, its remedy and solace. Love itself, the object of love, the struggles of love, are too difficult, too painful to be confronted. But images, memories of love, reduced to charming music, transformed to unreality—these can do no harm. The pathetic mood and the languid, exquisite sensibility that contain and nurture this mood—it is for them that the poem exists, and for them alone. Life is a fretful dream that can be controlled by the narcotic delusions of poetry.

Even when Meleager turns from a personal I to what appears to be a more objective mimesis, the emphasis remains on sickened pleasure and frustrated purpose:

> What hand unloosed Clearista's zone
>   at the bride-night, in her bride-room?
> Death in the guise of the bridegroom.
> Evening, flutes & clasping hands
>   clamour at the bridal door.
> At dawn the funeral wail. No more
> the Hymen song. The very lights
>   that lit the bridal bed
> light now Clearista's journey to the dead.
>   (Poem 55)

The poem is ordinary enough in its theme and even in its selection of detail; what is morbid are the studied understatement and the unspoken assumption that the marriage with death is somehow an acceptable substitute for the marriage that death deprived the young bride of—indeed, that for all its sadness, this marriage is somehow perhaps preferable to the earthly marriage that has failed to happen. What these gentle ironies and watercolor tones inform is a sentimental evasion of the fact of death (and perhaps a fear of the life which the successful marriage would represent). Clearista descends into hell with a kind of poignant, subdued magnificence; who she is and what her life and death mean merge into a pathos that is at once decorous and somehow enviable—because she has avoided commonplace destiny and commonplace suffering. Her vulnerability and doom, our grief at what she misses and what she finds, are in fact being celebrated in this poem; we are asked to, persuaded to, enjoy her failure and our own failures.

As we shall see in the next chapter, from the late Euripides, down through Virgil's sad shepherds and his lost ladies, to the disembodied lyrical heroes of Senecan tragedy, it is this vision of human spirit in

its willingness to surrender to mysterious powers beyond it, in its ca-
pitulations to the incomprehensible and overwhelming assaults of
inner and outer worlds that will increasingly become a central subject for the lyrical imagination, when, in the absence of a strong,
living lyric tradition, pathos gradually invades and sometimes ab-
sorbs even nonlyrical genres.

The Sparrow and Nemesis: Catullus

Strange that this hysterical, foul-mouthed young man should
have become, since the fourteenth century, when his *oeuvre* was recovered from oblivion, one of the special lyric darlings of Europe.
All the world loves, or did love, a lover, yes—but *this* lover, with his
sulks and posturings, his tantrums and arrogance, his uncontrollable
scurrility? Translations, even recent translations that avail themselves of the current fashion for unconstrained license, cannot quite
re-create the sputtering, crackling vehemence of his obscenities.
Even Martial, when barely a hundred years after Catullus he tried to
reproduce this phenomenon in the same language, ended usually
with little more than pale, soft porn; nor, so far as I know, has any
other poet in the European tradition seriously challenged Catullus in
this particular area. Catullus's supremacy here is best explained perhaps by the quality of his music and of his syntax, the way in which
this violence is compressed, is pressed, into exquisite patterns, transformed into pure objects without losing any of its wild, reeking im-
purities. His admirers, of whom I am one, may object that there is
much more to Catullus than four-letter words deftly arranged, that
there is also tenderness and exultation and something not unlike innocence. All this I grant, but the obscenity is somehow central to
Catullus's art, and so it is with the obscenity that we begin:

> Your most recent acquisition, Flavius,
> must be as unattractive as (doubtless) she is unacceptable
> or you would surely have told us about her.
> You are wrapped up with a whore to end all whores
> and ashamed to confess it.
>   You do not spend bachelor nights.
> Your divan, reeking of Syrian unguents,
> draped with bouquets & blossoms, etc. proclaims it.

the pillows & bedclothes indented in several places,
a ceaseless jolting & straining of the framework
the shaky accompaniment to your sex parade.
Without more discretion your silence is pointless.
Attenuated thighs betray your preoccupation.
Whoever, whatever she is, good or bad, tell us, my friend—
Catullus will lift the two of you & your love-acts into the
     heavens
in the happiest of his hendecasyllables.[10]
     (Poem 6)

Poor silly Flavius, his whore is *illepidum atque inelegans* ("lacking all charm, all elegance"). And he has therefore wisely decided not to introduce her around, will not confide to his closest friends about his mania, his problem. But Flavius's shyness cannot hinder Catullus from performing the offices of a friend. Catullus imagines what Flavius's bed, mute in vain, cries out (*nequiquam tacitum cubile clamat*, 7) and so immortalizes the squalor *lepido versu*, in "elegant verse." The *lepido* ("charm") of the final verse echoes, with devastating finality, the *illepidae* ("charmlessness") of the second verse. *Coup de main*: for all poetic eternity Flavius writhes with his oversexed (*febriculosi*) companion on the squealing mattress. If a perfect poem can be called minor, this is a minor poem, but its frivolity matters much less than its perfection; for erotic vitality (Flavius's, anybody's) has been neatly caught by the speaker's ironic, solicitous courtesy. Catullus is not attacking Flavius but, as is customary with male bonding, roughly congratulating him; the poem, with its suave distancing, is a small hymn to carnality in the guise of satiric censure. The experience of robust sexuality, evoked by the picture of the bed and the outcome of these encounters (*latera ecfutata*: "flanks ruined through copulation"), adroitly magnified by the pretense of malice and envy, here finds form that answers its vigor perfectly. But the word that is crucial to this process of evocative formation is *lepos*—"elegance," the precise framing, the precise choosing, the discrimination that makes all the difference between art and raw, unintelligible sensation, between adequate refinement and inchoate impressions and expressions, between artistic discourse and speechless emotion.

This adjective, *lepidus*, is prominent in the introductory poem of Catullus's *Passer* (*The Sparrow*)[11] and its noun, *lepos*, reappears in the penultimate poem, 50, of the collection. *Cui dono lepidum, novum libellum / arida modo pumice expolitum. . . .?* "To whom do I give this elegant, new little book, its rough edges just now smoothed with dry pumice?" (1.1–2). It is a new elegant book, ready for market, its appearance fresh and clear. What is inside it, of course, is also elegant and new—and polished with the dry pumice of disciplined, high art. New discipline, new finish. Not exactly new, in fact, for it is as old as Callimachus but new to Rome, this flawless artistry, incarnate in a collection of *nugae* ("trifles") poems about adultery and the gay life, about gutter politics and gutter love, about poetic politics and poetic ambitions, about the beginnings of vanished innocence and of abiding corruption.

We like the book, we love it, because it breathes life, a rich, untidy, troublesome plenitude and complexity. But we love the book and its author not only for their élan but also for the stern resolve of the poet who ordered this louche and enjoyable mess. We do not know whether Flavius actually existed or not, and, when we are reading, that is, listening to, this poem, we hardly care if he existed or not. His existence or nonexistence is irrelevant to what matters for us: the life of the poem. What orders that life and sustains it, as Catullus emphatically insists at the poem's witty closure, is *lepos* ("elegance"): Flavius and his bed survive by virtue of Catullus's elegance. If this is so, poetry does not, as the soberer *littérateurs*, Cicero among them, suppose, have any special affinity with the world historical destinies and their heroes; it is just as much attracted to this randy bed or Egnatius's maddeningly white teeth (Poem 37) or a missing napkin (Poem 12), any sight or sound or smell that somehow sets this music and its pictures in motion, that wants, demands, a frame and a form.

But what kind of mind is it that cares whether white teeth and stolen napkins, low bars and riggish ladies, find their ideal fictions? A frivolous mind, apparently. Catullus is not interested in refuting that sort of accusation; indeed, he glories in it:

> The other day we spent,
> Calvus, at a loose end
> flexing our poetics.
> Delectable twin poets,
> swapping verses, testing
> form & cadence, fishing

for images in wine
& wit. I left you late,
came home burning with
your brilliance, your invention.
Restless, I could not eat,
nor think of sleep. Under
my eyelids you appeared
& talked. I twitched, feverishly,
looked for morning . . . at last,
debilitated, limbs
awry across the bed
I made this poem of
my ardour & for our
gaiety, Calvus . . . Don't
look peremptory, or
contemn my apple. Think.
The Goddess is ill-bred,
exacts her hubris-meed:
lure not her venom.
                    (Poem 50)

An idle day, a squandered day; a day well squandered on wine and
vague erotic stirrings, on laughter and on art. Here, in the penultimate poem of his first and, in his lifetime, only collection, the
dandy's battle cry is sounded. Let the elderly and the middle-aged,
the soldiers and merchants and, as they like to call themselves, the
statesmen, indulge themselves in *negotium* (in "business") in the earnest and boring real world. We, my dear fellow (*ocelle*), who live the
life of the mind, or rather, of the mind and the heart and the nerves,
have better things to do. "I left you late, / came home still burning
with / your brilliance, your invention." That gets near the heart of
atque illinc abii tuo lepore / incensus Licini, facetiisque, except that
"brilliance" cannot capture the immensity and the lightness of *lepos*
("charm"): Calvus's outer elegance and, more crucial, his inner elegance, the sensibility, the balance and harmony that move him and
permit him to search after the adequate shapes for sensation, for perception, for experience, for emotion, however trivial, however "un-
important." *Tuo lepore incensus*: this kindred capacity for elegance
becomes almost a physical passion, a moment of high eroticism, as
Catullus tosses on his bed throughout the night, remembering that

lepos, pondering it, responding to it, finally shaping it into the *don du poème*, a kind of love poem that celebrates his union with Calvus, their good rivalry in art, their shared passion for artistry. With charming irony, this poem about the love of art becomes a threatening seduction poem. Catullus wants this encounter repeated, demands that his gift be accepted, insists that what he feels for Calvus be reciprocated. Otherwise, if Calvus proves unkind, Nemesis will inevitably take care of him. This erotic metaphor neatly emphasizes the total commitment to art that Catullus here affirms; for art demands of the artist what love demands of the lover—total, complete devotion.[12]

This is a Callimachean principle and is therefore not "new" with Catullus. But Callimachus did not have to choose between art and life, between culture and ancestral duties. For the traditional, conventional Roman, art might serve life directly by teaching it truths, or indirectly by diverting it when it was weary, but art as an end, as a way of life, was unthinkable. Yet for a Roman of Catullus's generation who had been seduced by Callimachean *lepos*, life tended to be, when it was not merely a boring, exhausting illusion, essentially the material which art shaped and illumined. Callimachus knew that books, the written word, can, in a sense, replace the life that they clarify and transform, and this he taught to Catullus and his friends;[13] but Callimachus had not to face the resistance to art, to books as supreme value, that traditional Roman culture offered this radically aesthetic world view. Catullus and his friends were forced to close with that resistance, as, in other, and in many ways more effective ways, their immediate successors, the generation of Virgil, would have to close with it. It is this resistance, this fine tension, that nourishes the great Calvus poem and that inspired much of the content and all of the form of *The Sparrow*. The young dandy makes an obscene gesture to his elders and proclaims his liberation from the rotten, stupid past: *l'art pour l'art*. Frivolous? Not really. To make this gesture and to confess this doctrine is to perform a moral act; it is to criticize life as it has usually and clumsily been lived in the past, and at the same time to offer new modes of seeing and doing, new concepts of the human person and the human condition. The frivolity, then, the gusto for what is trivial and un-Roman in human life, including its random lubricities, is a necessary and enjoyable pose. Beneath this pose, calling it into being, is a sense of identity and of life as passionate as the art that informs it is rigorous. In Catullus's *Sparrow*, artistic discourse, a process of reflection that is at once sensual and intellectual, is made new for Rome in the written book, in the meticulous, formal shaping of emotions and of language by language.

I have been emphasizing *lepos* because that is the first emphasis that *The Sparrow* demands. But it is not the only emphasis that this book and its poet require. If we no longer consider the Catullan corpus a reliable record of his life in the fifties B.C., if we tend now to be chiefly concerned with the study of his treatment of traditional literary themes and of rhetorical modes, that is to say, with the formal aspects of his poetic, it does not follow that these poems in no way reflect Catullus's experience or his life. I assume that the figure of Lesbia is something more than a composite of Catullus's erotic entanglements with women; I doubt that the affair was of long duration and doubt, too, that it was ever very serious on her side; and I do not doubt that Catullus embroidered this brief encounter with all the fervor, pleasure, and skill that masochism is capable of. Lesbia, then, like other persons in *The Sparrow* and in the elegiac poems, was very probably actual, and she also was and is beautifully imagined. She, like the other images of Catullus's world, partakes of literary convention, but she also partakes of the times and places that Catullus moved in and through. For no less astonishing than the force of *The Sparrow*'s shaping *lepos* are the force and vividness of the real *and* imaginary world that it deepens and unfolds; and it is as hard to think that this entire world was invented *ex nihilo* ("from nothing") by literary convention as it is to think that Catullus's actual experiences would have their present power and clarity had they not endured the alembic of his imagination. Which experiences were actual and reimagined and which were totally invented we cannot now know, will never know probably, and it does not matter in the least.

Lepos aside, what gives most pleasure in these poems is their profusion of sensation, that and Catullus's indomitable panache as he struggles to enclose that richness and that jumble within the limits of artistic clarity. But clarity cannot quite contain this remarkable frenzy. For all the superb control that *The Sparrow* and the elegiac poems show, the frenzy keeps bursting through its frames, back into the delight of its disorders and its turbulent appetite for seeing and feeling. Clarity struggles, and wins, and loses: that is the rhythm of *The Sparrow*—not the defeat of art by life or the victory of art over life, but a peculiar dynamic stasis of these strange incompatibles: the kaleidoscopic world and the imprudent young man who keeps plunging zestfully back into its hazards and mysteries, the still art and the poet who shapes that art and is in turn shaped by it. What mediates between life and art is the astonishing fusion of crazy young man and severe, mature poet.

Is this new to lyric, this centrality of the actual person who happens to be a poet? Is that the secret of this vitality, of this overwhelming sense of a genuine life, a recognizable world? Some have thought so, but we need to recall that *The Sparrow* is merely the first book of ancient monody that has reached us (almost) intact. If we had Archilochus or Alcaeus, Ibycus or Anacreon, if we had—but that would be, probably, another, subtler kind of world—Sappho, the chances are that our sense of Catullus's wild energies and our admiration for his evocation of life as it was lived by himself and his contemporaries would be considerably altered, that we would see his achievement in another, better perspective. Lacking that perspective, remembering that it is not unlikely that the collected poems of Archilochus would offer us a similar, perhaps more dazzling, sense of a life lived and a world known and mastered, we should probably look beyond the personal emphasis of Catullus's poems for the secret of their vitality.

Or rather we should look not beyond this poetic personality, this configuration of real aspects of a self reimagined into richer unities, but deeper into it. For Catullus, like any great lyricist, does not simply look into his heart and out on a world that surrounds him and then set down, like a superior kind of journalist, what strikes his eye. This peculiar lyrical process of unfolding and distinguishing, of contrasting, of reforming, and reunifying, what is felt within and felt from without, *Erlebnis und Erfahrung*, requires that the poet perceive and then imagine—"understand" is too coarse a notion here—the central conflicts inside and outside him that move him to undertake this singular, difficult task of making songs, in part, out of his existence. This process and this task will have been no different in kind for Catullus than they were for Archilochus; what is different is that we have, in the whole corpus of Catullus, this process and this effort entire whereas for Archilochus we do not. Furthermore, in the Catullan corpus, not in *The Sparrow*, but in the long narrative poems and in some of the elegiacs that I consider to be late poems, we sense an urgency about selfhood, part Alexandrian pathos, part Roman anxiety, that is hard to posit for Archilochus or for any of the Greek monodists.

There are doubtless several layers to this Catullan pathos and anxiety, and to approach them and distinguish them we must venture into the forbidden territories of psychocriticism and historicity; we must move outside *The Sparrow* into the elegiacs, which, so far as we know, Catullus did not live to form into a volume; and we must briefly look forward to what will be discussed at more length in the next chapter, the subjective, symbolist narratives.

To put it briefly, Catullus sees himself, at the core of himself, as the victim of the world and the victim of himself. This overwhelming sense of alienation and of hopeless vulnerability, which is almost hidden in *The Sparrow*, enhances its hilarity and energies in retrospect; so when we turn to the narratives and the elegiacs, the zest and swagger of *The Sparrow* foil and heighten the powerful feelings of impotence and isolation that find their full unfolding in these poems, which I believe to have been written just before their poet died. In poem 11 of *The Sparrow*, one of the latest of the polymetrics and a delicate adumbration of the final despair, romantic frustration and defeat, carefully ironized in delicate self-mockery, can still be bantered with and finally dismissed. In the magnificent opening of this poem, epic geography and momentous current events universalize and augment the private agony; then the mood shifts, and the poem fragments into a malicious lampoon on the wicked, nearly fatal seductress:

> . . . whatever Fate has in store for me,
> equally ready for anything,
> I send Lesbia this valediction,
>   succinctly discourteous:
>
> live with your three hundred lovers,
> open your legs to them all (simultaneously)
> lovelessly dragging the guts out of each of them
>   each time you do it,

blind to the love that I had for you
once, and that you, tart, wantonly crushed
as the passing plough-blade slashes the flower
    at the field's edge.
        (Poem 11)

She was only, is only, an ordinary whore, as it has turned out; the
dazzling, sordid affair had been after all only a tempest in a chamber
pot. Still, there are clear poignant echoes of Sappho here, and
echoes, too, of Meleager's wistful pangs: Catullus becomes a sweet
flower destroyed by the eternal feminine in the worst female mood.
For all that, in terms of the progression and momentum that Catullus designed when arranging *The Sparrow*, this blossom in the dust
survives, and the sardonic swashbuckler returns in the following
poems to the business of irritating his elders, criticizing Roman life,
bellowing out his loves and his hates, seeing the city, wallowing in it
and composing his exquisite poems.

Melancholy, then, has almost no place in *The Sparrow*, for "the
creature has a purpose, and his eyes are bright with it." The poet is
too filled with a sense of his gifts, with fascination for his materials
(the world, himself, his delight in the world and himself) to notice
what rumbles beneath his boisterous enthusiasms and discontents.
Nevertheless, in the last stanza of *The Sparrow*'s last poem (which is
a re-creation of Sappho's "I think that man is like a god," which defines the Lesbia figure as the poem's central inspiration and which
acts as Catullus's *sphragis* or "seal"),[14] there is a sudden fading of the
zest that has suffused this volume, and there is also a peculiar fore-
shadowing of the moods that will inform most of the long poems and
the Lesbia epigrams which Catullus lived to write but not to collect
into a new volume:

    otium, Catulle, tibi molestum est:
    otio exsultas nimiumque gestis:
    otium et reges prius et beatas
        perdidit urbes.

    Leisure, idleness, Catullus, has become bothersome to you; be-
    cause of your idleness, you're always dashing about, you're al-
    ways too much in the swing: before now, idleness has destroyed
    kings and wealthy cities.
        (Poem 51)

Did this final stanza, appended to the Sappho translation, appear in the original edition of *The Sparrow*, or is it a later addition? I choose, with no very great confidence, the second possibility. As we have seen earlier in poem 50, which precedes this poem, *otium* is part of the cultural revolution these young dandies are trying to effect. For Cicero and his friends, *otium* means "wicked idleness," "self-indulgence," "calculated lethargy"; for Catullus and Calvus and all the expensive, lucky people, it means "freedom," the chance to acquire pure *lepos* ("charm"). Who is wrong here? Both and neither.

Catullus, the rich young provincial from Verona, came to see that perhaps he had got out of his depth, that perhaps he was wasting— had wasted?—his life. *The Sparrow* shows only the barest inkling of this hesitation, this fear; but the uncollected poems, except for the elegiac elaborations of the old scurrility, show little else; and we cannot help but read both *The Sparrow* and the posthumous poems in this light. Let us risk a treacherous analogy. Calvus and Catullus, these youthful mandarins, giggling into their goblets and their notebooks, belonged to a lost generation and were pleased at first to be lost since being lost meant being free. But a little less than a decade after the publication of *The Sparrow*, Calvus died a political death; Catullus had, apparently, simply died. It was a luckless group of people. Ticida, Cornifucius, Cinna, all the young Callimacheans, died in the early forties B.C., ground up in the death rattle of the ruining republic. They had all of them wanted a new poetry, Callimachean *lepos* in Roman poetry and in Roman culture; some of them also wanted a new society, a new world. Perhaps they did not quite know what they wanted, which, given the immense confusion of the *Welt-wende* ("world change") they endured, is hardly an accusation. They did not get much, if anything, of what they wanted. They had ideas, ideals, guts, illusions, high spirits, and bad luck. This Catullus perceived, and his presentiments of failure shape the poems after and outside *The Sparrow*. Bright young people floundering in the system, floundering outside the system—that, disguised by his exuberant disdain of old values, is part of Catullus's world that always enchants us, seems to us so vivid and fresh, so resonant and enduring. Catullus and his friends circled the glamorous, deadly edges of political delusions and political catastrophe; but for Catullus, these outer hazards answered a premonition of inner losses, became a metaphor for wrong roads taken, chances missed, time squandered.[15]

For if the outer world was exciting, dangerous, ridiculous, problematic, fascinating, the inner world became increasingly unstable
and frightening. The game of love had been at first a game like any
other game, to be played with vast energy, to be enjoyed, to be won
or lost as the chances were won or lost. This game, however, turned
out to be different from the other games: the stakes were much
higher, and its gambits, on either side, tampered with precious values that had been, at first, ignored or taken for granted; and these
gambits tampered, too, with levels of the soul that could not safely
be tampered with: the figure of Lesbia comes to symbolize these dangers and the defeat they eventually effected. For reasons I shall try to
explain in the next chapter, the meaning of the Lesbia figure and its
ruinous victories over the poet take on their purest power when
Catullus lyricizes narrative. In the elegiac epigrams, where Catullus
begins trying to deal with this fragmentation of reality directly, what
we witness, are invited to witness, is the poet's struggle to deal with
the defeat of the self, to save something from the erotic wreck, from
all the wrecks.

The deepening of this struggle can perhaps be best seen by comparing Poem 8 from *The Sparrow* with the most elaborate of the epigrams, Poem 76:

> Break off
>   fallen Catullus
>   time to cut losses,
> bright days shone once,
>   you followed a girl
>   here and there
> loved as no other
>   perhaps
>   shall be loved,
> then was the time
>   of love's *insouciance*,
>   your lust as her will
> matching.
>   Bright days shone
>   on both of you.
> Now,
>   a woman is unwilling.
>   Follow suit

weak as you are
    no chasing of mirages
        no fallen love.
a clean break
    hard against the past.
        Not again, Lesbia.
No more.
    Catullus is clear.
        He won't miss you.
He won't crave it.
    It is cold.
        But you will whine.
You are ruined.
    What will your life be?
        Who will "visit" your room?
Who uncover that beauty?
    Whom will you love?
        Whose girl will you be?
Whom kiss?
    Whose lips bite?
        Enough. Break.
Catullus.
    Against the past.
      (Poem 8)

If evocations of past kindness shed
ease in the mind of one of rectitude,
of bond inviolate, who never in abuse of God
led men intentionally to harm,
such, as life lasts, must in Catullus shed
effect of joy from disregarded love.
For what by man can well in act or word
be done to others has by me been done
sunk in the credit of an unregarding heart.
Why protract this pain? why not resist
yourself in mind; from this point inclining
yourself back, breaking this fallen love
counter to what the gods desire of men?
Hard suddenly to lose love of long use,
hard precondition of your sanity

regained. Possible or not, this last
conquest is for you to make, Catullus.
May the pitying gods who bring
help to the needy at the point of death
look towards me and, if my life were clean,
tear this malign pest out from my body
where, a paralysis, it creeps from limb to limb
driving all former laughter from the heart.
I do not now expect—or want—my love returned,
nor cry to the moon for Lesbia to be chaste:
only that the gods cure me of this disease
and, as I once was whole, make me now whole again.
                    (Poem 76)

Lesbia is, in fact, not mentioned in either of these poems, but the
translator has not, I think, exceeded his license in evoking the figure
of Lesbia in his renderings. For what is in question here is more than
the aftermath of a single affair or of several affairs; what matters here
is a state of mind, a withering of soul, for which the figure of Lesbia
has become a sinister token. In the first poem, with its familiar cir-
cular pattern, the speaker's effort is to change his life, to persevere in
renunciation, to survive and walk away. He argues with himself, attempts to curse her; then, suddenly—for in attempting to curse her
he succeeds only in refiguring her power over him—he breaks off
with a stumbling, unpersuasive reaffirmation of his resolve. We sense
that he will most certainly, tomorrow or the next day, turn up on her
doorstep. The poem is serious in its meditations on erotic crisis, and
its imagination of fury—humiliation, helpless desire, and anger at
self for self's impotence of will—is superbly controlled. Yet the
poem does not, and does not try to, close with everything that the
poet fears from his love and from himself. The poem is chiefly concerned with the woman's awesome hold on him and, more particularly, with his vanity, his endangered self-esteem. He does not like
realizing how little he is his own man, and neither does he like the
idea of losing her, of losing the identity as lover that their union,
however brief, fragile, and bitter, has conferred on him. But he has
not asked himself the hardest questions: who am I? for what do I
want to survive this ruin, to what will I walk away from this ruin?
   In Poem 76 he begins formulating these questions, and he finds

that he cannot answer them satisfactorily. Once again the poem begins and ends with the same concept, *pietas* ("piety"), which is among the most resonant and untranslatable words in the Latin language. *Pietas* connotes a kind of spiritual integrity that is grounded in the individual's sure recognition of his place in the order of things. In learning his responsibilities to his family, his city, his gods, and to all humankind, the individual learns also something of the eternal, universal truths that govern all reality. In meeting his responsibilities as son and brother, as husband and father, as citizen, as worshipper, as human being, in so revering the mysterious truths that shape his existence, the individual learns to know and honor himself, understands the value of his life, and therein finds both his identity and his happiness. This was the core of Roman life, and we are astonished, I think, to find Catullus suddenly talking in this way. The sophisticated madcap had preached *otium* ("leisure") with frivolous, inexhaustible ingenuity. The afternoons with Calvus, the nights with Lesbia—not to mention those with Juventius—what had they to do with *pietas*?

Nothing whatever, but it is not that Catullus, those Catulluses, who speak this poem. This person, who feels himself sick unto death and who here lays claim to some share in his ancestral *pietas*, has been asking himself the questions that *The Sparrow* poet would or could not ask himself. And in the process of asking these questions, he has discovered what his life is for—too late, almost too late. He wants to live, and beyond that, he wants heart-wholeness. It is not that the speaker really imagines himself to be innocent, to have been the innocent victim of the figure of Lesbia and of the world; it is rather that, in his extreme affliction, he realizes that *pietas* and "the bond inviolate" (*fides*), the values of his childhood, are and always were his real values. The language of this poem is crabbed, tentative, wavering, not a new language for the man but a new language for the poet: a forgotten language, slowly remembered, desperately pieced together.[16]

He had left the *longueurs* of his childhood and of Verona behind him, had come to Rome for fun and for fame: to become a great socialite, a great poet, and a great lover. In the painful process, he became a great poet. This wisdom and the customs of his ancestors might be shrugged off, and *pietas* might be packed away for a later time, but some part of him did not approve of what the conscious, fashionable, clever young man was doing, was trying to do. This secret part of the poet has no share in *The Sparrow*, not even in Poem 8, where its impulses have not yet discovered their full powers. In the narrative poems and in the personal elegiacs, this old, new voice begins to usurp the poetry. In the process of this usurpation of modernist poetry by the ancestral voice, what was merely troublesome in Poem 8 becomes, in Poem 76, a disease that has devoured the personality; and in the course of this disease the figure of Lesbia has been transformed into the figure of Nemesis,[17] who was frivolously and ominously invoked at the end of the Calvus poem. In the later poems, frivolity now vanished, Nemesis manifests herself as the unpersuadable punishment that must—so the unconscious, fiercely illogical logic now works—hunt down the mocker of *pietas*, the man who dishonors his cultural traditions and their mysterious truths and himself.[18]

This is a very great neurotic poet, almost in the modern mode. To write about oneself and one's life, that was not new; but to write about inner conflicts and divisions, about the fragmentations of self that could be barely glimpsed, never truly understood; to try to grasp these opaque inward alienations and to dramatize the attempts to grasp them—that was, very probably, new for lyric poetry. These poems were still written to be recited, to be read aloud, and there is still, even in the poems to the self, a sense of public discourse, almost of performance; but there is also what seems a new inwardness here, in the transition from *The Sparrow* to the posthumous poems, which is proper to poems meant to be collected in a book, which is proper to literary lyric.

This is not autobiographical poetry in the strict sense of the phrase; rather, it is a kind of spiritual autobiography, at a very profound level, in which the conscious poet undertakes to probe the unconscious springs of his life and of his art, to try to master what is invisible and essentially unknowable in himself. It is worth remarking, perhaps, that Poem 76 is almost wholly lacking in imagery, consists almost entirely of abstract nouns and pure deliberation; and this is Catullus's most complex, most fully achieved, and most powerful short poem. How much direct influence it was to have on later literary lyric I shall not pretend to know or guess, but the major strategies of Petrarch and of Shakespeare are already present here in clear outline. The monodist has now discovered that beneath the singing, writing self there are many selves, many wills, and it is his task to identify and to distinguish them, then to attempt to reconcile and to unite them. Catullus does not, did not live to, succeed in doing that, and this incompletion, this sense of large, vital ambitions left unfulfilled, is also part of his charm. But it was enough, and more, to make a beginning.

In the Deserts of the Heart: Horace

Horace's *Odes* 1–3 is one of the most astonishing books in Western literature; given the extraordinary odds against its having been written, this book should not have come into existence. The obstacles to its composition that Horace's genius and ambition confronted and overcame were, not necessarily in order of difficulty: (1) the technical problems of imitating, or, rather, re-creating, Greek lyric meters in the Latin language; (2) the antipathy of the Latin language and the Latin temperament to the themes and the conventions of Greek lyric; (3) the indifference of Horace's age to the idea of lyric, which goes a long way toward explaining the initial reception of the book (embarrassed irritation);[19] and (4) the magnitude of the task that Horace had set himself—nothing less than to re-create the spirit of Greek lyric in its entirety. Compared with these external handicaps, Horace's merely personal difficulties as a lyric poet may be quickly reviewed and passed by. Though he had begun his poetic career as a satirist and was always in some sense to remain one, the satiric temperament ended by enriching his lyricism rather than by distorting it or overwhelming it. And though he apparently began his serious lyrical compositions when he was in his mid-thirties[20] (the first collection of odes did not appear until he was forty-one), at an age when most lyricists have begun to feel the spring running dry and have shifted to counterfeit forms or wholly new genres, Horace turned even this disadvantage to his advantage. Indeed, as we shall see, the achievement of the *Odes* is everywhere a matter of the defect transformed to the virtue. At the core of Horace's poetry is the perennial wisdom to which Cicero gives memorable shape: "We don't need to work nearly so hard at cultivating the virtues that are natural to us as we do at overcoming our handicaps and at escaping our inborn flaws."[21]

Horace displays his technical virtuosity in prosody by placing twelve poems in twelve different meters at the beginning of Book 1, and the sheer skill that this variety requires is uniformly sustained throughout the first three books of the *Odes* and does not weaken in the fourth book, which was published some ten years after the appearance of the first collection. Well might he hint (it was his favorite boast) that the ingenuity and the patience that were required for this feat, the transplantation of Greek stanzaic meters into Latin, went far beyond the limited experiments of the Roman tragedians and Catullus, even as they were to go beyond the shy imitations of his few successors in lyric: Bassus,[22] Seneca, Statius, Boethius. To begin with, Latin lacks the abundance of short syllables that allows classical Greek verse its extraordinary flexibility. This deficiency, bad enough in the relatively simple meters (iambic trimeter, hexameter, elegiac couplet) becomes desperate even in the regular stanzaic lyric meters that Horace mastered (he did not, could not, attempt Pindar's much freer choral meters, which required verbal resources that Horace's genius could not supply and a stronger musical tradition for poetry than the Roman dramatists had been able to create).[23] If it seems that metrical difficulties are being exaggerated here, for, after all, Renaissance and post-Renaissance Latinists composed fluently in some of these meters, it is worth remembering that ancient Latin poets, even after Horace had shown what to do and how to go about doing it, restricted their imitations to a relatively small group of the easier meters; furthermore, no Roman lyricist with the possible exception of Bassus, whose work is not extant, attempted to repeat the scale, much less the variety, of Horace's *Odes*.[24] It goes without saying that Horace's entire success and the infuriating aura of ease that attends it may have dissuaded later writers from doing badly with endless effort what Horace had done superbly. But the triumph and the sense of facility, like the random success of ambitious Renaissance poets, mask both the magnitude of Horace's undertaking and the passionate craftmanship that earned the success of his undertaking. Few poets have worked harder to ensure their escape from facility (and that, without losing spontaneity), from facility that enslaves talent, and no poet has seen more clearly the quality and the degree of freedom that difficult song confers or struggled harder to earn it, to be worthy of it, to possess it. It is certainly too much to say that Horace, having begun as a satirist, became—almost accidentally—a lyric poet because he was attracted to the high challenge that the technical problems of Latin lyrical meters posed—there were doubtless other attractions, and some corner of the satirist's heart must have been lyrical before the time when, without ceasing to be a satirist, he transformed himself into a lyricist. Nevertheless, since as he himself constantly claimed, much of his genius was a genius for versification, it is perhaps at least worth considering that one of the things that initially set Horace to designing Latin equivalents for Greek music was the enchanting impossibility of the task.

Nor were Horace's problems with versification his only technical problems. Where Greek proliferates distinctions and nuances in its vocabulary with baffling fecundity, Latin—particularly after the campaign in the age of Caesar and Cicero to purify the language and expel its "primitive" luxuriance—tends to be rather intolerant even of necessary subtleties, aims for an immediate, superficial clarity in the connotations of its words, and frequently pays too high a price for its austere intelligibility—these extreme compressions discourage exact perception and sharply limit freedom of verbal and conceptual experiment. Though the poetry of Samuel Johnson and many of his contemporaries might seem to offer a familiar parallel to such severe restraint, it is actually to classical French poetry and above all to Racine that we must go to find anything in modern times that is really similar to this obsession with economy of diction, this belief that the resonance and the emphasis that are achieved through condensation of meaning count for more in the description and investigation of realities than wealth of shade and delicacy of tone. A narrow range of diction, then, seriously limited the choice of vowel patterns (long and short) that were necessary to the quantitative lyrical meters Horace was writing in; and of the words that remained after the unofficial academies had completed their winnowings, many would not fit the complicated metrical patterns Horace was adapting from Greek lyric for Latin use.

No less formidable to Horace's lyric goals than the problem of diction were the problems of Latin's fairly strict word order and its limited range of sentence structure. Again, compared with Greek, Latin shows a fondness for regularity in phrasing; and mostly because of its emphasis on the verb as a means of ordering the sentence, because of its underdeveloped participial system, and because of its great love of and dependence on relative clauses, the variety of sentence structure is relatively narrow. These multiple difficulties had, of course, troubled Latin poets for two centuries before the Augustan poets, following and perfecting the example given them by the previous generation of poets, succeeded in solving them. What Virgil, the elegists, and Horace did to help gain flexibility for their phrasing and an impression of variety for their sentence structure was to perfect the use of hyperbaton, that is, they disrupted, deliberately and systematically, the normal order of words in their verses.[25] This stylistic device had always been available, in theory at least, to Latin poets, but it is the Augustan poets who see its extraordinary efficacy in overcoming problems of meter and style in Latin verse. They avail themselves of it whenever their material and the level of style their material requires permit them to do so, and none of the Augustans, not even Virgil, uses it as effectively as does Horace in the *Odes*. In adapting radical hyperbaton as a normal stylistic mode, Horace was able to solve, avoid, or mitigate the verbal difficulties that stood between him and the accomplishing of his lyrical ambitions. By rearranging the normal patterns of phrasing, he was able to confer unusual flexibility on his sentence structures, and he was also able to make maximum use of available words by fitting them, as occasion demanded, into metrical patterns from which normal word order would have tended to exclude them.

Yet even after these matters of meter and style had been successfully dealt with, there remained one last impediment to Latin lyric that could not be surmounted, even by Horace's genius and patience—yet, in a sense, it was surmounted. The absence of music: there was no adequate poetic musical tradition that could be borrowed to assist this new Latin lyric, and the surviving (debased) Greek musical tradition was of no use either. Horace confronts this challenge in two ways. Lacking music, he supplies an overwhelmingly persuasive illusion of music for these spoken poems. The literary lyric constantly recalls its musical heritage in its settings, themes, and images; and so persistent and so tactful is the fiction of music that we come, without even knowing it, to acknowledge the power of the fiction (some have even been led to believe, and that passionately, in the reality of the music).[26] Horace sings, the Greek courtesans who are invited to the picnics and suppers also sing,[27] and these invented songs and singers are as credible as the food, the wine, the laughter, the flirtations, and the innocent, infectious, ideal pleasure of these most famous and enduring of literary parties. After Horace, this perfection of the fiction of music will henceforth be available to literary lyric whenever music (the singer and his instrument, and the audience for his live performance) has disappeared from European poetry.

Crucial to this fiction of music and performance is Horace's constant use of a formal addressee for his poem (see Chapter 1 above). Again and again, the You to whom Horace's poem is spoken serves as a metaphor for the readers of the poem. Following the example of Callimachus and Catullus, Horace adapts to his needs and strongly emphasizes the pronominal form of Greek monody. By thus recapturing some of the *hic et nunc* ("here and now") of Greek lyric, he manages to suggest some of the feeling of music and of performance *on paper*. Any lyric poet, and particularly a writer of literary lyric, dispenses with the sense of this place and this moment to his peril. It is a mistake Horace never made. Horace is present to us because he makes sure, through his metaphoric second-person pronouns, that we are present to him.

But in addition to creating the illusions of music and of performance by imagining himself a singer with an occasion and an audience for his song, Horace recalls the vanished essence of Greek performed poetry in a more subtle and more powerful way. A lyric poem in Latin written for the page, though intended to be read aloud (and the poems were usually read aloud, even by solitary readers), might become so essentially visual because of the reader's effort to handle the hyperbata and because of his unfamiliarity with these "new" meters, that its acoustic elements became subordinate to, finally dissolved into, its images. It is, I think, partly as an effort to overcome a possible victory of the static picture over dynamic song that Horace develops his own version of the characteristic movement—not structure—of Greek lyric. By mingling styles and shifting moods, by employing frequent ellipses and understatement, by working his images into patterns of dialectical modulations,[28] by sometimes closing his poems with a vivid and haunting image that does not quite gather the themes and moods of its poem into unity but rather suggests continuities and reverberations outside its limits,

Horace presents us, in the Greek manner, not so much with a finished artifact, an artistic object, as with pictures that speak and pictures that move. Thus, if the exquisitely shaped stanzas and the epigrammatic patterns of words often give us the impression of mosaics or of "well-wrought urns," if the habits of compression and austere control seem directed only to the creation of a motionless, timeless order that cannot be altered, the sound of the poems, their unusually free and powerful motion through space and through time, offer us not structure but dynamic patterns, not mosaics, but kaleidoscopes. Horace can, of course, achieve something like the unpersuadable stillness that Ben Jonson designs again and again ("Would'st thou hear, what man can say / In a little? Reader, stay" or "Though beauty be the mark of praise"),[29] but he seldom allows himself or us the solace or the enchantment of closed forms, and his music frequently breaks through the limits of closed form, past structure, past harmony even, into another flux, another vision. In *Odes* 4.1, his ironic erotic swan song, he promises to attain "the dimension of stillness":

> Wars long suspended, Venus, now
>   Again you threaten. Spare me, I pray you, I pray—
> I am not what I was when good
>   Cinara ruled my heart. O rabid mother of
> Delightful Cupids, try no more
>   To force a man whose will these fifty years have steeled
> To assume your delicate yoke—
>   Go where the suave young men entreat your expertise—

and in the course of the poem he attains it (or seems to), but only in order to abandon it:

> Neither woman nor boy can please,
>   Nor any gaudy hope of love that's mutual,
> Nor sharing wine with my friends,
>   Nor gladdening my hair with garlands of fresh bloom.
> Why, then, Ligurinus, why
>   Do these infrequent tears dishonor my resolve,
> And why should this eloquent mouth
>   Grow stupid in its speech and falter and be dumb?
> Throughout the long night and its dreams,

Now I embrace you, and now after you I speed,
Swift as you sprint the fields,
Now, o fiend, as you glide swift through impalpable waves.

The poems are, of course, beautifully, intricately contained within
their forms when we look at them and their designs. But simultaneously, when we listen to them, the designs begin to shift, their
limits dissolve, and the words and music restore the elemental *con-
cordia discors* ("discordant concord") from which they arise. This
unity of stillness and motion is doubtless characteristic of much great
poetry, but few poets exploit this antinomy as frequently or as flawlessly as Horace does, and I think it was the absence of music that
induced Horace to develop a poetic in which his pictures were at
once at rest and in motion, in which the distinction between stillness and dynamism was radically defined, even as the coinherence of
rest and motion was re-created for both the eyes and the ears.

Horace succeeded, then, despite all obstacles, in making the old,
foreign lyric new and native. But he could not create, as he obviously wished to create, an audience for his new lyrics, for his literary
lyric. Several factors would seem to have contributed to this failure.
Audiences of literature, who delight in transforming writers into intimate acquaintances, tend to be hurt when their poets (their pets,
their personal property) begin to behave eccentrically. Horace the
suave satirist had utterly disappeared—or so it seemed—to be replaced by an arrogant, affected stranger. (The satirist, of course, had
not vanished, but it would take considerable patience and experience to recover him in the bewildering novelty of his new styles and
sounds.) Worse, in addition to overestimating his audience's capacity for loyalty, Horace seems also to have overestimated their capacity for learning to master the conventions and the premises of this
new literary lyric; and he seems to have underestimated the real difficulties those conventions and premises posed for his intended
readers. The happy few were immediately persuaded to expend the
energy necessary to experience the *Odes*, and they quickly acknowledged the greatness of these poems; in succeeding generations there
were always devoted readers for the *Odes*, and their beauty and the
arduous artistic triumph they represented assured their high, their
uncontested, place among the classics of Latin poetry. But the com-

mon reader, and indeed most uncommon readers, were not part of Horace's audience and would not be until Renaissance readers, for whom the conventions of literary lyric were second nature, transformed Horace into a "popular" classic at long last.[30]

But the contemporary audience for whom Horace began writing lyric could not adapt their taste to the demanding intricacy of his new poetry. They had, of course, or thought they had, some sense of what lyric was and what it should be, but their notion of lyric matter and manner was very far from the peculiar, the unique, fusion of Greek elegance and Roman gravity that Horace had invented for them. For serious lyric they had, and it was quite good enough, the traditional songs of tyrants slain and barbarians subdued (plodding, earnest, complacently old-fashioned ballads) which they sang at their drinking bouts;[31] for lighter entertainment, they had the traditional Greek frivolities, authentically performed by frivolous yet professional Greeklings. Both the uncomplicated patriotism and uncomplicated levity, in addition to being as familiar to Horace's contemporaries as the small poetry of daily life (naenia—"charms," "dirges," "lullabies"; archaic hymns for archaic festivals), were musical whereas Horace's paradoxical re-creation of Callimachus's invention, lyric without music, was radically literary, was difficult and obscure. The old patriotic ballads were, in their way, as accessible as the popular songs, could be immediately and even freshly enjoyed, had been tested by the centuries and survived into modern times, as pleasant and intelligible as the vituperations and eroticisms of Catullus or the wry sensualities of Philodemus. But these songs without music, as baffling in their sound as they were in their meaning, though they were often contemporary in theme and image, were steeped in a foreign antiquity. Little, if any, concession was made by the poet to the audience he was trying to win.

Trying to win? or trying to educate, to reform? There is frequent condescension in the poet's attitude, which, like his growing contempt for the semiliterate poetasters and the illiterate mob, is more than mere convention. Horace is, at times, almost messianic, and the salvation he brings when this mood is upon him is that of art, of good breeding, of taste and judgment. In the Odes, as earlier in the Satires and later in the Epistles, one thing that Horace is telling his contemporaries is that they are not refined, that they are in some sense lacking in authentic humanity, that the language of the tribe must be purified. It is not a message that this or any audience wants much to hear (unless they imagine themselves as among the refined to whom the message is not addressed).

As Cicero, at the end of his life, had undertaken to distill what was best and most necessary (as it seemed to him) in the heritage of classical humanism, so Horace undertook to condense the spirit and the artistry of Greek lyric. In part, this desire in both men to sum up their respective traditions arose from their extraordinary ambitions and, doubtless, from some envy of Greek achievement, but Cicero and Horace were also motivated by intuitions of a change in culture, a transition from one world to another, and they were anxious to preserve what they felt must be preserved of the grand past in Latin for Romans: for Cicero, the ethical wisdom both Greek and Roman, from Socrates to Cicero's day and the habit of intellectual humility that had always fascinated him; for Horace, the extreme beauty of form that Greek lyric had achieved and the moral beauty of old Rome, two splendors he sought to fuse in contemporary settings and contemporary moods. Eventually, both writers accomplished what they had set out to do and accomplished it more brilliantly than either would have dared to dream, but initially the success of Cicero was more evident than that of Horace. For Horace was attempting something rather more difficult than what Cicero had attempted. The Alexandrian artist wanted to address the Roman people; he wished to be for Rome what Pindar and Simonides had been for Thebes, Sicily, and Aegina; and while doing this, he wanted also to continue to perfect his difficult art and to protect his privacy and his integrity. He wanted too much, but, though he did not live to know it, he got all that he wanted.

Callimachus had apparently been content to have as his audience a small circle of hand-picked connoisseurs. Horace had tried to be content with a handful of fellow mandarins, found that he could not be so content, then found that he must be. The support of Augustus, most notable in his commissioning of the *Carmen Saeculare*, may have expanded the audience somewhat, but whatever it was that Roman readers and the age demanded, it was not Horace's lyrics. [32] Other Augustan poets whose art was rooted in Alexandria found immense favor with Augustan readers, even as Horace had done with his *Satires* and was to do with his *Epistles*: Virgil, by re-creating the long dormant tradition begun by Naevius and Ennius in a poem which, for all its remarkable transformations of epic form and epic meaning, was nevertheless accessible to his contemporaries; the love elegists, by merging Alexandrian epigram with the motifs and figures of Roman comedy to create a brilliantly complex yet immediately intelligible form of narrative poetry and psychological description. But Horace's use of Roman poetic tradition was even more elaborate and more original than Virgil's, for he was determined to unify the Roman moral tradition with the Greek lyrical tradition in its entirety. Small wonder, then, that his contemporaries should have been baffled and felt rejected by the *Odes*, in which, all by itself, the individual talent of Horace masters the Greek lyric tradition, recapitulates its essence, preserves it, and transforms it.

Modern lyric poets tend to be obsessively concerned in their poetry about the name and nature of poetry and about the meaning of their poethoods. Poetry is, of course, a natural subject for poetry and a natural concern for poets, and all the Roman Callimacheans of the Augustan age wrote poetry about poetry, but in Horace this gesture has extraordinary prominence. Given the grandeur of Horace's ambitions and the obstacles to his achieving them, this obsession is natural enough; yet even when we have allowed for it, the emphasis still seems extraordinary, and it deserves investigation.

With the exception of the opening of Book 4, each of Horace's four books of lyrics opens and closes with a poem that either directly or indirectly speaks to the question of the poet's fame or the poet's craft. *Odes* 1.1, 2.20, and 3.30 take the poet's fame and immortality as their central theme (poetic fame in general, Horace's fame in particular). *Odes* 1.38, 2.1, 3.1, and 4.15 examine some aspect of Horace's craft or of his problems as a writer of lyric. The first group in which Horace celebrates his achievement (adumbrating it in 1.1, celebrating it with grand wit in 2.20 and 3.30) are not unsubtle poems, but they are straightforward in their handling of their essential themes. In the second group, however, the poetic meditations are, in varying degrees, oblique. *Ode* 1.38, on its surface, is a slight, dandified fragment of pastoral, in which a charming, self-conscious epicurean, very pleased with himself, casually confesses his sensual creed:

Boy, I detest Persian elaborations,
And garlands twined with linden bark displease me—
Stop ferreting through desolate places
    For the final roses.
Contrive nothing to beautify the myrtle's
Easy simplicity, for the plain myrtle
Shames neither you the slave nor me the master,
    Who drink under shadows.

Read as a statement about his poetry, what the poem signifies is one of Horace's essential poetic methods—the exertion masked by smooth, clear surfaces, the passion for decorum presented with understatement, the rejection of false ambition by a poet crazed by (true) ambition, the absolute demand for pure beauty and pure form ironically dismissed. A rather similar irony informs 2.1 in which Horace warns Asinius Pollio of the dangers of writing about recent and current events, then writes a harrowing vision of the civil war, one of the greatest of his serious poems, and closes with a rejection of grand themes and an affirmation of the frivolity he constantly claims to favor. In 3.1, the prelude to the superb series usually called the *Roman Odes*, Horace wryly dons the robes of Pindar (which elsewhere he constantly tells us are too big for him):

I loathe and ever shun the impious mobs.
Keep holy silence. Hymns never heard before
    I who am the muses' priest shall sing
    To blameless maidens and to fearless boys.

And in 3.15, after a conventional *recusatio* ("refusal") in which he complains to Apollo that he is not fit to poetize Augustan wars and Augustan grandeur, he distills the Augustan achievement into seven flawless stanzas whose careful imagery and smoothly tempered style and content Simonides would not be ashamed of. It is true that it was the fashion for Augustan poets to open and close their books with statements about the individual volume and about the poet's attitude to his art, and this fashion seems to have been influenced by Alexandrian practice. But Horace's use of the convention, at once emphatic and subtle, shows something more than elegant refinements of a convention. He continually draws attention to his craft and his artifacts because, in a way that goes beyond the other Augustans, his book is a sort of spectrum of lyric voices; and in selecting and arranging these voices, he is performing a critical, indeed an almost scholarly, act as well as a poetic one.

What kind of lyric poet is it who collects and orders the great lyric voices of the past, who exhibits the tradition he has patiently recovered and analyzed? Isn't this degree of self-consciousness almost the last thing we would expect from a lyricist? In a way, Horace only does here what all artists and even all lyricists have to do to find their own styles, their own voices. Each poet begins by modeling his voice and gestures on voices and gestures that he admires, that excite his love and envy—I want to be like that, I can be like that, I can rival and surpass that. But this process of finding one's personal voice is easier, or at least seems rather more natural, when the tradition in which one is trying to work is a living tradition, when it is a living voice, representative of the entire tradition, that inspires, challenges, and encourages. When the tradition is dead or dormant, the process of experimentation, of testing one's own personality against the spectrum of possibilities, is much harder. Horace collects the ancient, alien voices because there are no immediate predecessors for him in the tradition of Latin poetry except Catullus and his circle; he, of course, makes good use of Catullus and the other neoterics, but their range was too narrow for his powerful and complex personality, for the range of things he had to say, and for his ambitions as a writer. It is by patient study of the dead, foreign tradition, which will have included the critical theories implicit in the texts in which Horace read and studied the Greek lyric canon, that Horace succeeded in reviving that tradition in his own mind, ears, and heart; and it is from this tradition, which his own efforts had caused to live again, that he began to choose the elements from which he would invent his own lyric voice.

Before *Odes* 1–3 began to take shape, he had experimented in the *Epodes* with the voices of Archilochus. This was a satirical manner that suited, or seemed to suit, his temperament; in Archilochus he found a harshness that matched, or seemed to match, something in his own soul; and, finally, Archilochus's meters, though demanding, did not always require the fiction of music. But the experiment was not entirely successful. For where Archilochus was—and remained—ferocious, great-hearted, many-minded, and outrageously witty, where his barbs stuck, Horace in the *Epodes* tends to sound petulant rather than terrifying, barks and does not quite bite. It was a good beginning because it taught him a great deal about the kind of poetry that he wanted to write, about how hard he would have to work in order to be able to write that verse, and because it taught him something about his own consciousness—he learned that he was not really like Archilochus, that he would have to search for the kinds of selves he was or could become. An adequate beginning, but only a beginning.

Versions of Anacreon came easily, perhaps too easily (and, having a grander beast in view, I deliberately minimize here Horace's cordial, carnal charm). The light, mocking sensuality, the suggestion of intelligence deliberately squandered in the sheer pleasure of laziness, the clear eye for the shapes and colors of the world, these were qualities that Horace could readily identify with, appropriate, modulate, and alter as he needed them. Moreover, the suave weariness and worldliness suited the times. For a man who had tried, without much success or distinction, to play a part in current events, who found himself on the wrong side, then found himself out of a political career, the general sense of *otium* ("leisure," but it also means "laziness") that settled on Rome after the defeat of Antony and Cleopatra was a welcome, pleasant excuse for dabbling with life, dabbling with verse. The voice and gestures of Anacreon, delicately combined with the voices and gestures of the Alexandrians, become an extremely suitable disguise for a man who takes both life and verse very seriously, so seriously in fact that he wishes to disguise that seriousness. The studied frivolity and the bantering self-deprecation of Horace's reshaping of Anacreon's voice become standard features in the *Odes* partly because there was some part of Horace that really meant to say, "Life is boring, I am boring," and partly because the irony of this disguise provides him with a useful foil for other voices in the *Odes* that are, in their various ways, truly serious. Hence the frequent and charming invitations to other amiable, distracted souls to help the trivial poet waste some useless time in vaguely innocent, vaguely amusing ways. (I'm growing old, you're growing old, everybody's growing old. What does it matter because what does it mean? Who knows, who cares!) This mood is flawlessly captured—again and again—and these poems about trivial desperation are impressive and important not least because this is a persistent human experience that is very hard to imagine accurately; but in Horace's recrea-

tion of his (and our) consciousness of futility the chief function of
this fusion of Anacreonic and Alexandrian voices is to help define
clearly parts of the soul that are resourceful, that are not enslaved to
circumstances and obsession.

Horace borrows Sappho's most famous meter with a great success, but the poet herself he cannot, of course, borrow. A woman's
voice, for one thing, would be of little use to him in the kinds of
poems that he writes, and this woman's voice, even if it could be
borrowed, would be of absolutely no use to him. But Alcaeus could
be kidnapped and was. In *Ode* 2.13 a rotten tree in the famous garden has fallen and almost bashed its master's brains out. Horace re-
proves the tree severely and remarks:

> . . . how near I came to beholding in person
> The Dark Queen's empire and Aeacus judging
> And the blest in their distinct abodes
>   And Sappho chiding in Aeolic song
> Her compatriot maidens for their disdain,
> And you, more resonant, with golden plectrum,
>   Alcaeus, singing toils of the sea,
>   Evil toils of exile, and toils of war.
> Though the shadows in wonder listen as each
> Tells fables worthy of hallowed silence, yet
>   Quicker the thick crowds of dead devour
>   Tales of battles and of tyrants banished.

It is perhaps a little sexist, this demotion of Sappho, but the accent
on Alcaeus's resonance is reasonable enough. This was the less subtle mind, and his feelings were less exquisite—but, yes, plenty of
resonance (which is one of the main reasons why the Alcaic stanza
predominates in the *Odes*). Also, in place of subtle inwardness, Alcaeus offered strong petulance and uncomplicated self-esteem and
was, therefore, very suitable for some of what Horace had found out
about himself and the world. Last, but not least, the themes that
had helped to shape this particular temperament and its voice and
gestures were ideal for Horace's needs: battles, politics, exile, civil
war. When Horace touches on—for he seldom confronts it directly—the terror of politics, the style and metaphors of Alcaeus are
very useful to him: the sense of being down but not quite out, the
sense of losing not really gamely but not ignominiously; acerbic com-

mon sense, adequate courage, a capacity for energetic resignation in the face of political muddles and other current events. In short, Alcaeus gives him as much in the way of a bitter style as occasions demand and as his own temperament can properly handle.

Pindar in his pure state Horace did not need, and Pindar he could not have handled had there been any use for heroic sublimities. For one thing, it would have been difficult, if not impossible, to borrow the style and the gestures without the sounds of Pindar, and even Horace's command of Latin and his metrical genius could not transplant those sounds (Pindar himself had needed the musical instruments and the dancers). Fortunately, there was no need for Pindar (as Horace saw very clearly, though others, apparently did not),[33] for the age, however tumultuous and forceful, was neither heroic nor sublime. A bureaucrat of genius had finally managed to seize power and to keep it, and he had succeeded in tidying up a bad century's legacy of uncommonly ugly messes. Not everyone was entirely satisfied with this solution; some were actually disgruntled; and in some quarters restiveness grew as the harmony and prosperity continued. But for the most part Romans and non-Romans were reasonably content with being both modern and safe, and such people did not need Pindaric magnificence. They and their emperor needed (but did not get) poets who could praise a stable economy, tranquility inside and outside their borders, a dependable food supply. Horace did not help here much—only Virgil tried, with half his heart—except on the occasions when he was induced to write an archaic hymn for choral presentation and, in Book 4 of the *Odes*, some ironic victory songs (4.4, 4.14). Even in the series of poems (the *Roman Odes*) in which Pindaric magnificence is promised, it is Simonidean dialectic that is delivered:

> And mighty Caesar, when he has settled in
> Towns his legions weary of warfare, seeking
>   Rest for himself at last, you Muses
>   In your still grotto refresh and hearten.
> Gentle advice you give and joy in giving,
> O Kindly Ones! We know how the unrighteous
>   Titans and all of their bestial throngs
>   Under the plunging lightning vanished. . . .
>   (3.4.37–44)

The myths of the Roman odes are about the splendid past when un-common virtues, courage and integrity the highest among them, were the ideal toward which the norm strove constantly, and they are also about what happens when these virtues degenerate (*cor-ruptio optimi pessima*) as the exercise of power becomes the end of governing rather than one of its means. The highest praise that the Simonidean poet can offer the ruler of the civilized world, its bright-est and best (*sapientissimus et unus*—"the wisest and the only"), as Tacitus, with clean malice, will call a later incumbent of this post,[34] is that he actually pays attention to the counsels of wisdom. That, too, is Pindaric, but in the absence of the unironic splendor that Pindar created as a background for this message, the praise that Horace offers Augustus consists more in warning than in lauda-tion—it shifts into something drier, harsher—into wary congratula-tions: Yes, you are doing extremely well, better than we had a right to expect of any man—because you have unusual prudence, because you are restrained from outrage by remembering the dangers that hedge you round.

Paradoxically, then, the real absence of Pindar from Horace's rep-ertoire of voices is as crucial to the success of his re-creation of Greek lyric and to his shaping of his own essential voice as is the Anacreonic-Alexandrian foil. This absence of Pindar precisely de-fines the integration of lyrical voices that Horace makes his own. It is for this reason that the figure of Pindar is evoked again and again in the *Odes*, ironically, wittily, but never in mockery. "I am not Pin-dar," Horace keeps reminding us (most brilliantly in 4.2 with its se-rious and loving adaptation of Pindar's best manner and its careful, proud example of Horace's own best manner at its close) "because I am Horace, whom you need to tell you who you are; if I could some-how transform myself into Pindar, I could only lie to you about your-selves—which I would not do, even if I could." The ironic, com-monsensical, Simonidean craftsman wants always to be measured against Pindar, not out of some ridiculous idea that this comparison would somehow elevate him beyond this greatest of masters but be-cause he wants himself and his audience and the world they share to be seen in their proper proportions. Only in rare moments (we shall look at these presently) is Horace heart-whole; for the most part he is various, human, at times even silly—an actual human being and anything but a seer. It is in order to express this spectrum of selves and this variability of strength and weakness, this immense richness of sensibility, that Horace carefully cultivates his diversity of voices. If anything stands at the center of this whirling pattern of selves as a poetic principle (Epicurus, as we shall see, centers the life), if there is one voice that dominates this rich configuration—with Pindar at one end of the spectrum and Anacreon at the other—it is the voice of Simonides, with its healthy, moderate skepticism and its love of the physical world and awe at the mystery of being, that can adequately mediate among the diverse aspects of Horace's chosen voices, even as it mediates among, but does not arbitrarily order, the flux and tumults of the human consciousness and its perceptions. But it is the memory of Pindar's wisdom—remembered but incapable of being revived—that foils perfectly the wisdom of Simonides and the vitality and the limitations of the authentic, unheroic world that Horace in his several moods sees and illumines.

Here, and here only, in ancient poetry can we see how theory of lyric transformed the practice of lyric and the genre itself. Since Horace chose to write lyric and since he had no native tradition to learn from, he found it necessary to master both the poetry and the commentary on that poetry of an alien, long-vanished culture. To this study he added the more recent traditions of Callimachus and his followers, including his Latin followers, in the generation before him. This massive re-creation of a dead tradition entailed a great labor and great difficulty, but it conferred great freedom. In a way that Pound might have envied had he been able to consider the matter, Horace was usually free to choose his poetic selves, his poetic self. The burden of tradition, which he patiently searched out and assembled, allowed him to be himself because it allowed him to create himself, and the paradox of his enormous burden-turned-freedom yielded itself to Horace because he had no choice but to remake the tradition by mastering it. Few other lyricists in the West have had such an opportunity perhaps, but no other lyricist has used his chances so expertly; certainly no other lyricist has possessed the idea of his genre so completely.

To do what? Splendid equipment, and splendid discipline and freedom, but what did he do with it? Or, to put it in terms of the old-fashioned banality that we are constantly being warned against, what are his poems about? What does he use his lyricism for? One way of avoiding interpretation would be to say that the poems are, in the comforting modern manner, about poetry, that the voices exist to sing of themselves. In a way, as we have seen, Horace's poetry is about his own poetry and about poetry in general. But at its moral— no, I will risk calling it—its religious core, it is about what the self-regarding poetry also sees: freedom, escape from the deficiencies and limitations that gradually become vices; escape, too, from delusions of splendor (*fuge magna*—"flee great things").[35] This poetry is, then, a poetry of disenchantment, and in a sense, it is counterlyrical, like the poetry of Herbert, say, or the best of Browning and of Auden,[36] for the feelings for which it finds continuous metaphors are very often designed as negative paradigms, as examples or evocations of feelings we should try to fight free of; and what is praised is usually a cleansed soul at rest (not a dead soul, not a sterile soul; and even this repose shimmers with desire, with questioning).

The most constant and most fluid symbol of this freedom is Horace's Sabine farm, that is, his version of Epicurus's garden and of his own art.[37] Readers sometimes seem to feel that this garden is essentially a symbol of his art, that even the freedom to flee vice and enact virtue is itself a symbol of the art. But though this is clearly an accurate reading of both the *Odes* and the *Epistles*, it is no less accurate to say that both the garden and the art are symbols of Horace's inner spiritual world. Though these symbols, the garden and the song, are so frequently paired that they seem at last almost indistinguishable, of the two, the garden is the more resonant metaphor for the spiritual reality that Horace reveals in the poems, which deal not with the dangers to freedom but with the excellence and the beauty of freedom itself. In *Ode* 1.17, one of the most famous and most beautiful of these poems, Horace issues an invitation to Tyndaris, a woman who interests him, to come for a visit to the safe, pastoral paradise he has designed both for himself and for his friends and lovers—for the poem is, among other things, a delicately ironic seduction poem. The safety of this special pastoral world is formally presided over by Faunus, the Roman Pan, and the animals in this garden enjoy their lives in prelapsarian immunity from the enemies that would threaten them in the disordered natural world. But what actually govern the paradise Tyndaris is being coaxed to are Horace's art and his spiritual dedication:

The high gods guard me for my pure devotion,
My craftsmanship delights them: here for you from
    The kindly horn's plenty will spill forth
    The ripeness and the splendor of the fields.

Pietas ("devotion") and *Musa* ("poetry") are both aspects of the ordered personality that accounts for the integrity and the invulnera-
bility of his garden, but this is more than an artificial paradise
(though it is certainly that too): it is a spiritual landscape (*vera
vita*—the "true life")[38] that self-discipline and careful habits of virtue, both artistic and spiritual, have called into existence and now
sustain. The artistic discipline and the moral discipline coinhere to
form a world that can both delight Tyndaris and protect her:

In this sheltered place you'll shun the Dogstar's blaze;
Here, as you touch the lyre's light strings, you'll sing of
    Penelope and lucid Circe,
    How they contended for the same man's love.
And here, hidden safe in shadow, you may sip
Wine from Lesbos, not dreading each moment that
    Semele's child and Mars will tangle,
    Wrecking the party; nor need you worry
That Cyrus, always jealous, will cause a scene,
Will offer you force (who can least repel it),
    Snatching from your hair the wreath twined there,
    Rending the sheen of your innocent gown.

The invitation, as Tyndaris knows perfectly well, is cleverly
framed to ensure her acceptance. Music—which she will provide,
thus delicately flattering her—wine, lovely countryside, a light bit
of romance with a charming gentleman who knows both how and
when to keep his hands to himself, escape from the rotten Cyrus and
all the rottenness he tokens—how could she in fact resist? It is a
marvel of polish and of subtle articulations and modulations, and it
imagines the gaiety and the humility of this peculiar world exactly.
But it is more than a fantasy of refined flirtation and lilting, casual
song, and it is more than an artificial paradise that artistry has evoked
for the duration of the song and the fantasy. What this poem is
founded on, what its polish hides, is what all of Horace's poetry and

all Horace's life is founded on: *virtus est vitium fugere et sapientia prima / stultitia caruisse* ("to be virtuous is to shun vice, and the beginning of our wisdom is to have escaped our own stupidity").[39] Cyrus, the Dogstar, and the poisonous vipers are within as well as without, and these inner dangers to our moral natures and to our freedom must be fled as swiftly as we would flee their physical counterparts which symbolize them. The garden of art and morality, or perhaps we should say, the garden of moral art, is a place of refuge, both from the hazards of the great world and from the dangers of our own hearts.

Does this make him sound like some kind of prig? make him sound rather smug? It shouldn't. The satirist, who also knew how to satirize himself without being morbid about it, never yielded to the calm gardener. The *Odes* are shot through with laughter (and not all of it pleasant), with petulant lechery, with petty irritability and real malice, with furtive, exhausting obsessions. He gathers himself and all of us into his richly meditated, richly harmonized group portrait. He never forgot (as he reminds us in *Epistles* 1.1.106–08) that "the sage is a king among kings, and preeminently sane—except when he is bitten by a flu virus"; nor (in *Epistles* 1.1.10–19) did he forget that he was not beyond the reach of mere velleities—always various, always flawed, always human. There is also throughout these poems considerable melancholy, and at times there are even dreadful intimations of despair. He understood the dark places of the heart (and recalled them even near the end—*Ode* 4.7 is fierce in its irremediable grieving, and all the more so for its somber modulations and understatement), and if he does not capitulate to his dread, he never allows himself to forget it. It is not, then, strange that he should be proud of having won some control over this disorder of his moods, that he should have learned to feel some joy in the partial mastery of his moods, having been, like most humans, so frequently their helpless victim.

What he was fighting free of can be seen in a more serious poem than the one we have just looked at. Indeed, it is almost a tragic poem that stands next to the last one in *Odes* 1–3 and thereby strongly emphasizes the peculiar blend of somber brooding and celebration that constantly moves through the entire collection. In the Great Maecenas Ode (3.29), as it is commonly called, Maecenas,

Horace's best friend and for a long while one of Augustus's most
trusted advisers,[40] is being invited[41] to visit the garden, but the tone
of the invitation is deeply urgent and the sense of hazard is intense:

> Abandon then that revolting abundance,
> Those buildings soaring into the heaven's haze,
>> Cease gaping at the stunning fortune,
>> The smog and the money and the clatter of Rome.
>> (9–13)

Outer events, nagging worries about the state of the nation, are—it
is not too strong a way of putting it—destroying Maecenas. If he
could visit, even for a short time (but preferably forever), the pastoral world that Horace again evokes in this poem, then he too
might find sanity and freedom. The poem, then, is an invitation, an
exhortation to a beloved friend, but it is also the statement—perhaps Horace's most solemn statement—of a man who has reached
his chosen destination:

>> . . . he is master of himself
> And leads a happy life who has learned to say
>> Each twilight, "I have lived—tomorrow
>> Let God fill heaven with storms or sunlight,
> What's past He will not unmake. . . ."
>> (41–46)

At a time when political freedom seems to be—and is—jeopardized
and when a variety of artificial paradises seem to offer false remedies
to real diseases (and who should know this better than Maecenas?),
Horace asserts calmly, here as elsewhere, that the true paradise of
real freedom is within the individual human being: *Caelum non ani-
mum mutant qui trans mare currunt*—"they change their scene, not
their hearts who rush across the sea."[42] This is a lesson that his father might have taught him, but he learned it as well from Lucretius
and Epicurus and himself.[43] The various false escapes to the various
artificial paradises are dissected and then placed on display in the
satirical lyrics, and rarely have secular answers to spiritual problems
been so subtly and so utterly destroyed. But in the Great Maecenas
Ode the stakes are too high for satire because Maecenas is endangered. In no other poem is Horace so vehement or so memorable in

his affirmation of what true, possible freedom consists in or in his warning about the things that menace our freedom—most desperately, ourselves.

This heightened sense of the outer dangers, the real evils, and the ersatz solutions that make it easier for us to betray ourselves into spiritual slavery seems to have grown even as the lyric genius grew and fulfilled itself. The freedom won for the verse and the freedom won for the soul are interdependent, and it is not therefore strange that Horace's sense of poetic solitude—despite our sense of his gregariousness, which the wide acquaintance addressed in the poems evokes, few poets write better or more passionately of solitude[44]—should keep pace with his equally fervent sense of social and spiritual solitude. By the time he comes to write the first book of *Epistles* (begun shortly after the publication of *Odes* 1–3), he has pretty much left Rome for good, has come to the farm and its garden not on a visit but to stay. The deliverance from the illusions of society and from his own illusions had made possible the true independence he had longed for and fought for; but it had also shown him what he had not quite been able or willing to see: that a poet who is separated from his intended audience is a lyric poet in a very paradoxical way, that lyricism requires real performance in a real community. Nevertheless, until he had learned this truth about lyric genre, he had busied himself with the perfection of literary lyric; and by virtue of his patience, genius, and integrity, he had learned to write lyrical poetry as though an audience for it existed. And when the *Odes* were published and he seemed to have done as much with the genre as he could do in the society he lived in, he perfected the solitude of his garden and invented a genre of his own, spiritual autobiography.

In the first poem of the first book of *Epistles*, once more addressed to Maecenas, he apologizes for the end of his lyricism rather as he would apologize to Venus for his erotic decline: *non eadem est aetas, non mens*, ("my years are catching up with me, my temperament has altered"), and he therefore now busies himself with occupations suitable to his years and frame of mind: *nunc itaque et versus et cetera ludicra pono*, ("therefore I now lay aside my verselets and my other toys").[45] It is sometimes thought that these words and the poem from which they come were written when Horace was still smarting from what he took to be a less warm reception than he thought his lyrics deserved. There may be something to that, yet it may also be the case that he needed a new form by means of which to examine the nature and the limits of the freedom he had battled to win, not so much now for his art as for his spiritual freedom itself.

The self had found its integration and its repose. There was no longer any need for the spectrum of identities or the metaphors that re-create the emotions, the shiftings of inwardness. The poetry of the *Epistles* becomes, in a sense, "prosaic," rather in the manner of the *Satires*, and a single voice re-creates a self that has finally become single and an inwardness that has finally discovered its proper stillness. How had this come about? How indeed? The mock philosopher mocks the philosophers suavely and unmercifully. *How* has this come about? —Oh, I don't know. Just by surviving maybe. By not reading philosophy very seriously. By learning to be my own man. By learning that I'm free in some ways, not free in others. By not conceptualizing too much. By reflecting on how strange and impossible and fascinating it all is. By living a life.

No need here for finding sounds and pictures and discourse for the viewless passions and their coruscations; no need here for fashioning lyrical identities in whom the lyrical dramas of selfhood may be played. Portly, sometimes a little grumpy, mostly fairly cheerful, always amazing, the creature interrupts his sunbath to smile out at us: yes, life is mostly very good and reality is very real. And so he breaks his lyric staff.

There was, however, to be one further book of lyrics (and they are not at all inferior to his earlier one), and there was even to be, at long last, and against all expectations, a choral poem and a choral performance. But for the most part, the rest of his life would be devoted to quietly meditating the nature of his art, of his solitude, and of his freedom. The dialectic of lyric had achieved its essential goal: the discordant concord had reached its proper balance; the paradise, the praise of possible freedom, the assent to the limits of freedom had been fashioned from the outer and the inner desolations.

V

The Figure of Ariadne: Some Lyric Mongrels and Lyric Monologue

The major lyric hybrid (*hibrida, hubris*—"unnatural," "lawless") lies far outside the scope of this book. When, to use Nietzsche's elegant fantasy, Dionysus mingles with Apollo, when choral lyric and drama unite to create Greek tragedy and Aristophanic comedy, a new kind of lyric comes into existence, which, subordinate to dramatic purposes and energies, is related to the entity we examine in this book only in certain of its outer manifestations. The choruses of tragedy and of comedy are, of course, lyric poems, and, in the usual way, they imagine human emotion, shape it, and deepen it to clarity, but in drama the lyric exists to serve dramatic ends. Not until Euripides, when the dramatic forms themselves are changing under his hands, when tragedy becomes almost comic, when comedy begins to approach tragedy, and when, beyond this tragicomical reversal, drama is lyricized, does the dramatic moment yield to, almost become a foil for, the lyric moment. But in most of Aeschylus and, powerful lyricist that he is, in all of Sophocles, lyric that remembers the past and intimates the future has one special function: to frame, intensely, vividly, the limits of the present dramatic moment, to provide an emotional resonance that allows the intellectual conflicts represented by *ta dramata*—humankind in its moral and spiritual dilemmas and choices—to be adequately, that is to say, dialectically, experienced.[1]

146

The key word here is "choices." It is perhaps not too much to say that, like Homer before them, Aeschylus and Sophocles are primarily interested in the mystery of human volitions, in the struggle of human beings to master their ignorance, their limitations, and their destructive impulses and so to win through to the destiny they want, or to try to escape the fate that closes upon them. (The same concern, seen from the other side of the mirror, informs the incomparable comedies of Aristophanes, where the strangeness, the absurdity of human volitions, the complexity of human conditions and of human shifts and stratagems, are seen as being ridiculously miserable and ridiculously sublime.) This double vision, man as spiritual hero and man as irrelevant dream, was grounded in a vital faith in the cosmos that Homer and Pindar share, and whose tensions Aeschylus and Sophocles dramatize. With Euripides, this faith begins to disintegrate, is replaced by an insuperable pathos whose intimations of an unintelligible cosmos leave little margin for human volition or for its choices. Gradually, the figures in Euripidean drama move from struggle with self and with world to a habit of succumbing to incomprehensible destiny: that is, to fortune and to happenstance, which are sometimes, at the close of the *Orestes*, for example, seen as demonic. By this process, the figures of Euripides are transformed from agents of dramatic conflicts to vessels of lyric meditation: they feel stimuli from without and from within and contemplate their effect and, vaguely, their source. Euripides becomes increasingly fond of choosing a dramatic—or rather, pathetic—moment in which his creatures are trapped by circumstances that render volition all but useless—they may long nostalgically for vanished good, they may express hope for deliverance, they may bewail their situation, but they cannot try to fight free of the mechanism that contains them.

The exiled and the vanquished: the world of Euripides is not unlike the world that Baudelaire offers here:

> Andromaque, des bras d'un grand époux tombée,
> Vil bétail, sous la main du superbe Pyrrhus,
> Auprès d'un tombeau vide en extase courbée;
> Veuve d'Hector, hélas! et femme d'Hélénus!
>
> Je pense à la négresse, amaigrie et phtisique,
> Piétinant dans la boue, et cherchant, l'oeil hagard,

Les cocotiers absents de la superbe Afrique
Derrière la muraille immense du brouillard;

A quiconque a perdu ce qui ne se retrouve
Jamais! jamais! à ceux qui s'abreuvent de pleurs
Et tettent la Douleur comme une bonne louve!
Aux maigres orphelins séchant comme des fleurs!

Ainsi dans la forêt où mon esprit s'exile
Un vieux Souvenir sonne à plein souffle du cor!
Je pense aux matelots oubliés dans une île,
Aux captifs, aux vaincus! . . . A biens d'autres encor![2]

Andromache, slipped from the embrace of her tall husband,
now become the worthless chattel of the arrogant Pyrrhus,
stands bent in an ecstacy of grief before an empty tomb—she,
widow of Hector, alas, and wife of Helenus!

I think of the black girl, gaunt, consumptive, tramping through
the mud, searching with wild eyes for the missing cocoanut
palms of her splendid Africa behind the endless wall of fog;

I think of everyone who has lost what can never, never be
found again, of those who gulp their tears greedily, who suckle
on Grief as at the teats of a kind she-wolf, of haggard orphans
who wither like flowers!

So, in the forest where my soul is exiled, an old memory sounds
its shrill horn. And I think of sailors forgotten on some desert
island, I think of prisoners and of the defeated—and of many
others as well!

The literary *donnée* of Baudelaire's poem which answers its formal
donnée (the pathetic swan escaped from the menagerie) is Virgil's
Andromache, who, in turn was borrowed, as was much of Virgil's
poetic, from Euripides. In the theater of Euripides, conflict gives way
to isolations and troubled inwardness, and his chief vehicle for discourse is what amounts to monologue, even when it appears to be
part of a dialogue, which sometimes simply usurps lyric meters and
which is very suitably enhanced by, but not counterpointed by, the
play's choral lyrics. In effect, the central Euripidean character often
blends into the chorus, or the chorus fuses with or becomes the cen-

tral character. In its reformation of dramatic modes and in its emphasis on pathos, the lyric monologue that Euripides shaped for antiquity shows striking similarities to the modern lyric monologue, which is its distant and indirect heir and which was to become, in many ways, the most powerful of modern solo lyric forms.[3]

As lyric is the most elusive of generic forms, so is it the most protean, the most unstable of generic impulses. When the lyric poet casts his poem in the first-person singular (personal or fictive), in lyric meter, the integrity of lyric form and lyric impulse remains intact. But when the lyric poet undertakes to write drama, he does not necessarily become a dramatist, nor, when he undertakes to write a novel, does he necessarily become a novelist. What tends to happen in either case is that drama and novel become lyricized: the invaded genre endures some degree of mutation when lyric purposes usurp its form and ignore its customary objects of mimesis; and the lyric impulse itself, either diminished or uncannily nourished by its imposture, is also transformed. The novel is less prone to such possession than the drama probably because, since its natural mode is the anonymous, distanced narrator, it offers considerable resistance to lyric intrusions and temperings.[4] Even Virgil, the supreme master of lyrical disguises, has some difficulty in working against normal narrative styles, in lyricizing epic; it is in Books 2 and 3 of his epic, where Aeneas narrates, that is, re-creates his feelings about, the fall of Troy and his subsequent wanderings, that Virgil's lyric impulses are untrammeled. In the modern novel, Ernest Hemingway, a lyric poet if ever there was one, triumphs in *A Farewell to Arms* by allowing the first-person mode to absorb characters, landscapes, and story into his powerful, compulsive inwardness.[5] John Keats, whose "The Eve of St Agnes" is an adumbration of symbolist poetry, found it possible to lyricize narrative by relentlessly dissolving his figures and his story into his imaginations of emotion: in this poem the outer world and the "characters" become vivid shadows which, in the authentic symbolist mode, reveal, or rather suggest, invisible realities, the emotions and states of mind that pulse behind them.[6] But, on the whole, except in the ballad, which is an extremely successful lyric hybrid, narrative tends to be fairly secure against lyrical aggression. So-called lyrical novels, which often thrive on the sentimental, that is, on the inchoate impressions and frustrations of their readers and so make them complicit in the illusion of composition, tend to be bad novels. (The greatest achievements in the modern lyrical novel are, of course, the novels of Virginia Woolf: *Mrs. Dalloway*, *To the Lighthouse*, *The Waves*, *Between the Acts*; but this splendid success depends not a little on Woolf's having always kept the *social* concerns that are of the essence for the novel firmly in mind.)

But the case with drama is very different. We may complain about Euripides, we may even, with Nietzsche, and his other detractors, decide to blame him for the ruin of tragedy, but we cannot deny him the highest genius. If we happen to feel that pure tragedy is Aeschylean or Sophoclean or both, we cannot pretend that in writing his late plays Euripides did not create a new and major subgenre, that of lyric drama. His success in effecting this transformation arises, in part, from the ease with which drama accommodates the first-person singular. The same ambiguity that invites us, but does not permit us, to reconstruct the minds and feelings of a Sophocles or a Shakespeare by selecting bits and pieces of what they imagine their dramatis personae as saying also invites a lyric dramatist to use his dramatis personae as a vehicle for lyric meditation. The figures in these lyrical dramas no longer enact intellectual or ethical conflict; instead, they betoken motions of the soul and the dynamics of inwardness. Nor is it merely lyric invaders who make use of this ambiguity in dramatic form. Another generic impulse, to which the first-person singular is natural, that of the preacher-satirist, is also tempted to usurp dramatic modes for its own purposes. Yet the plays of George Bernard Shaw, as against the plays of most other *philosophes* who have tried to kidnap the theater, are not (always) merely lectures and diatribes in careless disguise; at their best they are, like the dramas of Euripides, genuine hybrids, not fatuous monsters. As we feel and know the conflicts in Shavian drama, even as we sense that they do not exist in their own right for their own purposes, so, in Euripides, we contemplate and participate in something like the older, genuine struggles of volition and the dilemma of intellectual conflict that are proper to tragedy, even as we know ourselves overwhelmed by lyric powers.

But this balance, or illusion of balance, between lyric and drama is rare, is, one is tempted to say, unique to Euripides. In Seneca, whose plays may very well have been intended for performance and may very well have been performed, lyric impulse, liberated by Euripidean example, overwhelms dramatic form to a degree Euripides never dreamed of. Indeed, the vestiges of dramaturgy that remain in Seneca's tragedy seem almost intended as ironic pointers to the absence of drama, of tragedy; it is as though the lyric impulse were intent on celebrating its triumph by emphasizing the failure and the hopelessness of intellectual conflict and of the dramatic modes that properly represent it. Seneca's Medea is not a desperate woman torn by intellectual and ethical doubts, driven to choose between one fatality and another; she is a state of mind, self-exulting, self-punishing, self-annihilating, and her voice and the voices of the phantoms who try to question or comfort her, vague images of a world she has almost forgotten, reverberate from a vast depth of consciousness that is endlessly distant from the place and time in which she has her physical presence, the wavering illusion of her physical presence. In this play, and in Seneca's other tragedies, the object of mimesis is the motions of the soul, and whatever dramatic conflicts or echoes of dramatic conflicts are allowed entry into these lyrical imaginings exist only to frame and to augment them. This is not to say that Seneca's plays lack power, for their power, their lyrical power, is enormous; nor is it to say that these plays cannot be performed, for in the last few decades we have seen that they can be performed, that they are, as the Elizabethans knew, extraordinarily compelling theatrical experiences: but dramas they are not quite, and tragedies they certainly are not. Their power and their fascination depend in large measure on our uneasiness with and pleasure in this generic disruption and on the intensity, and paradoxically, the strange purity which this disruption affords Seneca's lyricism.

Dialogue in Senecan tragedy tends to disappear into monologue. This is hardly a problem for him since without dramatic conflict, dialogue is at once irrelevant and, strictly speaking, impossible. In any case, the life of Senecan tragedy is in its monologues, with their hammer-and-tongs rhetoric, their surreal hyperboles, their constant momentum, a building toward conflagration, explosion, disintegration. Who knows why this style, this lyrical *maniera* ("mannerism"), precisely suited the Elizabethan temper? Even Shakespeare did not completely outgrow his taste for it, though he, almost alone, managed to countervail the tendency to random dramaturgy which this style seems to encourage. In the other major tragedians, from Chris-

topher Marlowe and Thomas Kyd to John Webster and Cyril Tourneur, the struggle to write tragedy, valiantly conducted, ends usually
in the triumph of lyrical melodrama and, more important for our
purposes, in the most abundant flowering of lyrical monologue in
Western literature.

I am not arguing that Elizabethan tragedy is purple patches stitched
carelessly together or that these plays did not provide, in their own
lucky times, good theatrical entertainment. What these playwrights
wanted, what, apparently, their audiences wanted, was a rich welter
of *frissons*; beyond that, beneath the gorgeous shiverings, there was a
fascination with the mystery of emotions, the motions of the soul at
fiercest pressure, the possibility of which lyric monologue confers
abundantly. Even when Elizabethan characters seem almost to be
conversing or arguing with one another, even when the dramatic demand for dialogue seems about to be honored, suddenly one of the
characters soars off into lyric flight, talking now no longer to other
characters and talking not so much to himself as to some other self,
to a vast darkness of unreality, some black, wordless place both inside him and outside him, neither inside nor outside him:

> . . . That I may hang him, and then cut him down,
> Then cut him up, and with my soul's beams search
> The cranks and caverns of his brain, and study
> The errant wilderness of a woman's face;
> Where men cannot get out, for all the comets
> That have been lighted at it; though they know
> That adders lie a-sunning in their smiles,
> That basilisks drink their poison from their eyes,
> And no way there to coast out to their hearts;
> Yet still they wander there, and are not stayed
> Till they be fetter'd, nor secure before
> All cares devour them, nor in human consort,
> Till they embrace within their wife's two breasts
> All Pelion and Cythaeron with their beasts.
> Why write you not?[7]

With this question to his wife, Montserry, in George Chapman's
Bussy d'Ambois, breaks off the jagged music of his "lyric of sexual
disgust"[8] and returns, as it were, to the dramatic moment: his tortur-

ing of his wife with a view to having her write a letter of assignation which will lure Bussy to his death. But the action of this play exists for the sake of these lyrical moments: the sudden, violent implosions of dark language and its darker thoughts. What interests Chapman, and what interested most of his fellow tragedians, are the unconscious and irrational places of the human spirit—that and the clotted speech and feverish music which can help us glimpse but cannot reveal this awesome disorder. Not before or after has the English language (or perhaps any language) been so ingenious, so fertile—by virtue of its efforts to imagine the hidden soul and its hidden lives.

The romantic recovery of the "other" Elizabethans, together with the romantic obsession with Hamlet (the lonely neurotic and his lyrical monologues, not the play), emblems an attempt to find a way of writing solo lyric that will evade the growing sense of depersonalization that I have sketched in my first chapter. From the Coleridge of "Kubla Khan" and "The Ancient Mariner" and Thomas Beddoes to Tennyson, the attraction of lyric monologue was as intense as its advantages were manifest: here was a way for the threatened I to speak without seeming to speak; here was a way to escape the relentless pressures of radical individualism and the contradictory burdens of modern selfhood, without abandoning the privileges of discourse; here, in short, was the ideal mode for the glories and misadventures of modern inwardness.[9] During this period and beyond it, poets continued, of course, to write solo lyrics that were, in some sense, personal both in their form and in their content. But the courage of a Baudelaire was the exception to the rule. *He* might mutter his irritations or scream his anger, might discourse wildly and morosely on his kinky dreams and vile regrets, might weep and whine and rage, but that kind of behavior was in rather bad taste, was embarrassing, was self-indulgent. If one wanted purest intensity, wanted to visit and to contemplate the darker, the darkest, places of the heart without seeming to have done so personally, it was best to search for a mask: *larvatus prodeo* ("I go forth masked"). Which was precisely what those extravagant Elizabethans, those hardened, shameless villains, those bewildered lost ladies and young men—most of them Italian, naturally—gave with a lavish hand. At the death rattle of romanticism—but the patient was to revive and is still hearty—Eliot updated Tennyson and Mallarmé and gave his official approval, both in his essays on the Elizabethans and in his own poetry, of the preeminence of lyric monologue. But before we look at this vanished orthodoxy, we should go back to the Roman versions of lyric monologue.

We left Catullus with his *Sparrow* published, his personal elegiacs well into their composition, and his narratives in some state of progress. Nemesis had been summoned to make a brief appearance as part of a giddy joke in the Calvus poem: she decided to stay and preside over the remaining poems. Aside from the late elegiac epigrams, these poems are longish, designed, one guesses, in part to display Catullus's virtuosity in controlling the current fashion of Callimachean *techne* ("art"). They do not fail of this aim. The wedding songs, the Attis, the Peleus-Thetis, the re-creation of the Berenice, the long elegiac monologue—all are superbly crafted and might well have won a small nod from the master himself. What might have puzzled Callimachus are the not-so-distant rumblings behind these technical masterpieces. Nemesis is angry. But that anger and the emotions that it evokes in Catullus are hidden, or almost hidden, in the symbolist inventions, the narrative evasions and lyric monologues, that shape these poems.

What unites the three poems we are about to look at is their profound sense of isolation, the speakers' feelings of having cut themselves off from their authentic places in the world, of having somehow traded a true self for a false one, of having allowed themselves to become trapped in a dark, irremediable mode of being in which their humanity becomes problematic. Catullus's Poem 63 is a treatment of the Attis legend which ignores its central elements.[10] In place of the Phrygian shepherd who becomes Cybele's lover, betrays her with a nymph and is then forced, after madness and self-emasculation, to become her priest, Catullus offers a young Greek who flees his homeland for reasons that are not specified, who arrives in Phrygia, emasculates himself, and immediately begins his ecstatic worship of the goddess. Exhausted by the frenzies of his ritual initiation, he falls into a deep sleep, then wakes to the horror of what he has done and what he has become:

> At once, shedding the night's tranquility, Attis
> relives the pictures of her heart, freed from the maelstrom,
> unclouded, recognizes the rootless place where she has come,

her thoughts turned inside out, goes headlong back
to the beach, where she cries to Attica she has lost
forever . . . looks over the brutal water
that stares back at her through her tears. . . .
". . . have I stripped myself of my patrimony
friends, goods, kin?
                     Are these ungreek landscapes
my new life-home?". . .
Once the flower of the athletes,
                     Once the pride of the young wrestlers,
My doors and thresholds were warm with friends.
The house full of blossoms greeting
the morning separations from the lover's couch.
And now, I, but part 'I.'" [11]
       (lines 44–49, 55–59, 64–69)

Ego mei pars: "I, a part of myself." Cybele, having heard this lamentation, this betrayal, immediately sends her lions to hunt down the
disobedient votary and chase her back into the sacred wood. The
poem ends with an apotropaic prayer, in which the poet asks to be
spared from sharing the fate of Attis (at one level of the poem, perhaps its deepest, the prayer is to Nemesis):

Great Cybele, Mother Goddess, Berecynthian Queen,
avert your fury from Catullus's house,
goad others to your actions,
others trap in the snarl of fury.

dea, magna dea, Cybebe, dea domina Dindymi,
procul a mea tuos sit furor omnis, era, domo:
alios age incitatos, alios age rabidos.
       (lines 91–93)

Attis's monologue is framed by narrative: between the action that
gives rise to it and its immediate and enduring effect, between the
madness that drove Attis to become one of Cybele's eunuch priests
and the madness that will continue to possess him as long as he
lives. This narrative is rapid, elliptical, almost expressionistic in its
extreme compressions and its violence of shape and color; and it is
perfectly contained by the monotonous frenzies of its sinister gal-

liambic meter. On one level, the story exists in its own right, as a sophisticated, a Callimachean yet Roman, reimagination of a bizarre, exotic legend; but at another, more resonant level, the story exists for the cry of anguish that it encloses. Catullus here imagines a terrifying androgyny whose meaning his character tries to understand, even as he himself tries to understand it—but it eludes such realization as it eludes the words, broken and desperate, that seek to grasp and hold it in Attis's monologue. All that can be understood, briefly, dimly, is that the encounter with the goddess has destroyed both Attis's manhood and the personality which that manhood had begun to confer. What remains, what survives this futile effort at discourse and understanding, are the shattering of perception and the music of fragmentation.

Poem 64, a long poem in which epic manner and epic matter are ironically reflected in a small, elegant space, tells something of the story of the wedding of Peleus and Thetis. But its central focus, as depicted on the ornate tapestry for the marriage bed, is on the story of Theseus and Ariadne, a story of erotic betrayal and erotic ruin; and the central focus of this central story is, as in the Attis poem, a monologue, the lament of Ariadne as she stands on the beach and watches her treacherous lover sail away. Like Attis, Ariadne wakens from her sleep to find the world upside down. The hero, who had promised her marriage, a new life in a new world, in exchange for her help against the Minotaur, has sneaked off as she lay sleeping. And she wakes to find the old world destroyed and the proffered new world a lie and a delusion. Like Attis, then, she finds that her identity has been taken from her, and she stands on the deserted beach, watching the vanishing sails, not so much a person as a frightened, angry voice:

> Where can I go?
> > What is left for me?
> Our Cretan hills?
> > There's bitter water between.
> A father?
> > Whom I abandoned in blood guilt.
> Or the love-purpose of a husband?
> Who makes the rowlocks creak
> in his hurry to get away from me.

And inland on Naxos?
              Derelict
no roof-tree
              no escape
the surcingle of sea-water
no hope
         no reason for refuge
all is dumb
              all is alone
                   all is nothing.
    (lines 177–86)

    Ariadne's lament is conventional in most of its themes and strategies, and readers of Dido's final speech in *Aeneid* IV and of the speeches of Byblis and Scylla in Ovid's *Metamorphoses*, all of which follow the same conventions that Catullus followed, will encounter nothing new here in the way of topoi. But the quality of this speech's music, at once somnolent and bitter, monotonous and hysterical, exists not to reveal this character in this situation, but rather to abet the imagination of a state of mind, of a reverberation of tangled feelings, that transcend story and conscious personality as they transcend the words that attempt to capture them. The brief clauses, the repetition of rhythmic patterns, the harsh alliterations, all combine to create a sense of compulsion, and of shock, a genuine despair that searches vainly for words, for a voice, for an identity. In the prime model in antiquity for this type-scene (the Medea and the Creusa of Euripides) as in later re-creations of it (Apollonius's Medea, various of Ovid's heroines) despair is argued with, the effort toward self-discourse is strenuously and sometimes successfully maintained. But in Ariadne's speech, as in Dido's final speech, narrative concerns give way to lyrical concerns, and a blind, obsessive emotion that uses speech only to destroy speech overwhelms both person and story:

                 . . . these moans are forced
from a feverish body,
as blind as epilepsy,
they are the truth of Ariadne's heart.
    (lines 197–98)

Ariadne's lament ends with a gasping prayer to the Furies to take vengeance on Theseus for his crime against her, for his failure of *pietas* ("piety") and *fides* ("faith"). Though the prayer is formally addressed to the Furies, it is also possible to see it as addressed to Nemesis, who makes a paradoxical and unconventional appearance at the finale of the poem. At the wedding of Peleus and Thetis the Fates sing a song about the offspring of the wedding couple, foretelling the glory of the son that will be born to them, Achilles. But as their song progresses, epic grandeur is imperceptibly transformed into horror when the vision of triumph culminates in the murder of the Trojan princess, Polyxena, an offering to the shade of the dead Achilles:

> Once Chance lets slip the Greeks inside
> the sea-born belt of stone, the young
> girl's blood will soak the barrow mound,
> who crouches to the two-edged sword
> and pitches, a headless trunk, forward.
> (lines 366–70)

The Fates conclude their song with conventional blessings on the happy pair, and the poem's conventional narrator, as opposed to its ironic, lyrical narrator, tries for a conventional coda in which the epic grandeur of the past, when gods mingled with humankind, as they do at this wedding, is seen as having given way to the faithless, godless present with all its squalors and discontent. One of the examples that is offered of the past communion of gods and men is Homeric times, when Athena and Mars helped in the creation of epic carnage on human battlefields; here they are surprisingly, but not indecorously, assisted by the *Rhamnusia virgo*, Nemesis, who understands better than Mars or Minerva what epic battlefields are for, what causes them, and what the death of Polyxena is about.[12] The present in this coda, then, is ugly, dark, and disordered, an ironic twist to the ironic gaiety of the wedding, and a suitable metaphor and closure for the anguished speech at the poem's center. But the epic past, Ariadne, Theseus, Thetis and Peleus, Achilles and Polyxena, was also discordant and horrifying, was also deficient in *pietas* and *fides*, was also food for Nemesis. In this poem, erotic encounter is imagined as catastrophic both in the inner world and in the outer world.[13] Here, in the complex fusion of lyric monologue and lyric narrative, feelings of guilt for past innocence betrayed and feelings of anger and radical inferiority find their focus in Ariadne, in whom the victim of love, the unmanned poet, finds an answering metaphor for his impotence, for his intolerable feminization: Ariadne, the quintessential victim, the woman who, having risked all for love, is betrayed and abandoned and shrieks her outrage and her suffering to the deaf winds on the deserted beach.

Poem 68 uses as its situation of discourse Catullus's response to a request from his friend Allius, who is feeling depressed, having problems with his girlfriend, fumbling awkwardly through the lonely guy blues.[14] He had tried to read the old poets in his search for solace, and he finds them useless; he therefore asks Catullus for something fresh from the latest muses, some sparkling erotic verse, to distract him from his troubles. Catullus, himself submerged in depression, answers that he cannot write, for various reasons: he feels stranded in Verona, is without the books he needs to write, misses the life in Rome; he cannot shake off the grief he feels for his brother's recent death. He would like to be a good friend to a good friend, but

> on whom do you think
>> I would sooner lavish
> love-gifts of Venus
>> and gifts of the holy muses
> than you?
>> You have turned to a friend
> and the friend's hands are empty. . . .
> How can I give what I have not got?
>> (lines 37–40)

Then, amazingly, the poem that he denies he could write appears. It begins and ends with a remembrance of the kindness that Allius had shown Catullus in providing him and his married lady friend with a safe trysting place. That seems simple enough, but the poem moves from this remembrance of things past to other things, becomes a disordered meditation on the entropy of his life, concentric circles of feeling and thought that drift toward a diminishing center: the self, again, parts of the self, dwindling to absence of self. Allius's help had been like a mountain stream that flashes into scorched fields and brings water to a thirsty traveler (lines 57–61). Remembering the house that Allius provided, he remembers, too, his woman's first entrance there:

> With supple steps
>   Catullus's bright-shining Goddess
> found her way thither,
>   her woman's sandals
> echoing
>   on the worn threshold-stone.
>   (lines 70–72)

She came desiring him as Laodamia had desired Protesilaus: but that was a doomed love, one that heaven hated because Protesilaus had neglected the proper ritual for the building of his house. Nemesis, whom the poet begs to spare him from a like fate (lines 77–78) had come for vengeance: Protesilaus had been the first to die at Troy, and Laodamia killed herself for grief. Troy, where Protesilaus died, is also the place where his brother had died (so Achilles, so Polyxena, so, in a way, Attis): it is a place of Nemesis, who sees all the sins and the stumblings. Laodamia's love was as deep as the pit (*barathrum*) that Hercules dug during one of his labors, as deep and as dangerous in its physical and psychological need for love as Catullus's own desire for Lesbia, as deep and dangerous as the memory into which the poet descends:

> And the light of Catullus's own life
> when she looked for his embrace
>   gave little
> in the matter of passion
>   to you, Laodamia.
> Cupid was clothed in saffron
>   and shone and played ˙
> in her love-movements . . . .
>   who looks (it is true)
> elsewhere
>   for other love.
> but the quests are secret and few.
> I hold my tongue remembering
> that cuckolds are a tedious lot.
>   (lines 131–37)

From this point on the poem seems to move from its unquiet mazes and lethargies back to a certain calm, a certain strength at its closure:

> Thus, Allius,
>   for the "offices of friendship"
> you have shown me,
>   this gift of a poem—
> not perhaps what you asked for
>   but what I can do . . . .
>   (lines 149–50)

The memory of Allius's kindness (his *pietas*, his *fides*) has nourished the incantation of solace. Catullus is able to forget his grief for his brother, grief for a growing sense of artistic impotence, grief for his squandered life, grief for Lesbia's treacheries; the poem ends with a gentle affirmation of her, for most important of all the good things of life is:

>   always she
> who is dearer to me than all else,
> my light and eyes
>   who, living,
> invests life for Catullus
>   with its sweet reason.
>   (lines 159–60)

lux mea, qua viva vivere dulce mihi est: "My light, and as long as she lives, my life is sweet."

Sweetness? That is a pleasant fantasy saved from the sour wreckage of the fantasies that compose the poem. The Lesbia figure may have been or may have seemed like Laodamia in her passion during the initial stages of the affair, but she is totally unlike Laodamia in her whims and fancies, her casual infidelities, in the severe and sustained cruelties which this poem glides over, circles but cannot close with. It is Catullus, not Lesbia, who resembles Laodamia in her passion and her heart-wholeness, her *fides*, in the futile, ruinous purity of her love: Catullus, once more the victim, once more the psyche in despair. He had said that he could not write the poem that could cheer up his friend. By an immense effort he does write the poem, a love poem that immortalizes Allius's kindness, that angles the story

of the poet's love delicately and that closes it with an elegantly sentimental composure, which the story will not really allow.

But art can solace and save, and poetry can imagine life in accor-
dance with our cravings. Or can it? The poetic memory is itself both
the bright stream that falls into parched fields and the dark abyss
that devours itself. Catullus could not write because too many things
were closing in on him—his brother's death, the truth of Lesbia's
real nature, the real nature of his sick desire and of his jealousy, his
loss of innocence, his loss of the glittering future for which he had
traded the stable past: hence the lethargy that closes him off from
poetry, and hence the futility of life and the futility of art. The poem
is achieved and magnificently achieved, yet we feel in it the subter-
ranean dark of the unconscious mind that no poem can placate and
no words can tame. This is *Erlebnisdichtung* ("poetry of experience")
of a kind, perhaps, but the term is almost useless here: because here
the highest art refines its perceptions not only of life but also of mis-
remembered life, of fantasies about life and of nameless fears of life,
and of the vanity of art as well. The object of mimesis here is not
emotions but rather the emotions beneath emotions, selves in their
splinterings, the pure unconscious in its unquiet searchings, its ingenious evasions and baffled, baffling self-punishments. An elaborate,
profoundly felt artistic discourse here imagines the ruin of artistic
discourse: Nemesis has come for her most devoted poet, bringing
with her something new to ancient lyric poetry, a pure, explosive
inwardness to which both the conventions and the spirit and purpose of Greek lyric are irrelevant. Horace, as we have seen, ignores
this new lyricism and reinvents for the Latin language and its heirs
the authentic Greek lyric modes. But for Virgil, the new lyricism of
Catullus was to be of supreme importance, and in his hands it finds
its supreme perfection until the Elizabethans and modern times.

The peculiar centrality of Virgil's *Eclogues* to the tradition of European pastoral was made possible by the loss of Theocritus to that
tradition in the West for almost a millennium and a half, and this
strange, accidental dominance has obscured not only the achievement of Theocritus and the nature of the pastoral genre but also the
unique quality of the *Eclogues* themselves, their essential lyricism.
Robert Coleman, in his recent commentary on the *Eclogues*, glimpses
what I take to be our essential difficulties with Virgil's pastorals when
he remarks of *Eclogue* 6 that it "recalls the tradition not of pasto-

ral but of neoteric narrative: elliptical, allusive, picturesque, and subjective."[15]

Yet, having noted the affinities of the poem with *Eclogues* 4 and 10 in its rejection of pastoral matter and manner, Coleman turns from the *strangeness* of this rejection of pastoral in a book of pastorals to address himself to "the particular synthesis of myth and reality that characterizes Virgil's conception of the pastoral"[16] and to congratulate Virgil on having explored "ways of extending the pastoral that nevertheless preserved and deepened its essential character," not least by "making the impersonal myth of Arcady the vehicle for an *intense, if oblique,* form of *personal* poetry. . . ."[17] A preliminary question, then, is: How far can a poet go in extending the limits of a genre without altering its essential character—particularly when the principal method of achieving such expansion is to renounce the genre's traditional styles, sensibility, and objects of mimesis? For it is not merely in *Eclogues* 4, 6, and 10 that Virgil emphasizes, almost to the exclusion of all else, the elliptical, the allusive, the picturesque, and the subjective, that he makes pastoral intense, oblique, and personal. In all the other *Eclogues* these same characteristics predominate and in fact end by overwhelming the genre that the poet is exploiting.

The most obvious, though by no means the easiest, way to focus on Virgilian pastoral style and structure is to compare his pastorals with their immediate models. In *Idyll* 11, the closest model for *Eclogue* 2, Theocritus provides the simplest of frames for the narrative monologue of his distraught, zany, and lovable "passionate shepherd." Nicias, a cultivated doctor to whom the poem is addressed, is reminded that there is no remedy for the sickness of passion but poetry. To prove this point, Theocritus recalls the instance of his fellow Sicilian, Polyphemus, whom he then reveals, sitting on the seashore, looking out at the sea and singing of the beautiful and ruthless Galatea, pretending to sing *to* her in order to try to mitigate his frustration. When that song is ended, Theocritus closes his poem with a brief two lines that return to the argument of his opening: "So Polyphemus shepherded his love with song / and found more comfort than money could buy"[18] (*quod erat demonstrandum*). The frame for this poem is highly artificial and highly persuasive. Theocritus is talking about poetry as well as about love, but he is characteristically modest in his claims for art, and the suave good sense of this attitude toward life, art, and himself is exactly rendered by the transparency and clean vitality of his language in his frame. Virgil, on the other hand, who is already a master of stylized concision in this early poem, does away with the Theocritean frame. His poem closes with the end of Corydon's monologue, and it opens, with only the most perfunctory notice of the poem's reader, in medias res. Corydon is on stage as the curtain rises. Though this strategy may at first seem less artificial than that of Theocritus's opening, in which the poem clearly announces that it is a poem, the more we study this opening of Virgil's, the more extreme and effective its own high artifice becomes. We are, in fact, allowed no distance from Corydon; we are plunged, as it were, immediately into his psyche. Theocritus's Polyphemus is alone in *Idyll* 11, but he is not conscious of being alone because his mind is utterly fixed on Galatea. He is un-self-conscious; he seems, indeed, unaware that he is singing, that is, he *is* naïve, and he is trying to talk things out—this is a genuinely dramatic monologue. But Corydon, singing the title role in an operatic sketch, is very much aware that, while he performs for an audience of mountains and forests, he is alone:

> Corydon, the shepherd burned for fair Alexis,
> His master's darling, and he hadn't a hope.
> The thick-set beeches, with their shady tops,
> Were his resort. There, by himself, with pointless
> Passion he rambled on to hills and woods.[19]
>
> (lines 1–5)

He, then, is very conscious of himself, of his song, of his deaf, imaginary audience, and of his art; and he is not really conscious of Alexis, who is only material for the artist and his art. Finally, the art of this lonely, shrill (*iactabat*) and polished artist is useless, empty, unreal (*studio inani*).

The essential origin of the genre to which Theocritus gave its definitive form was the mime, and Theocritus is true to that origin in his pastoral and in his urban idylls. What matters for Theocritus are his people and the stories that define them. He likes them, he wants us to like them, and he persuades us to join him in liking them. Theocritus is, to some degree, Alexandrian (to a degree he is even somewhat Callimachean), but he never, for all his delight in artistry, loses sight of what art (as he sees it) is for: the celebration of human beings, not merely despite, but also because of their weaknesses. Behind this concept of the purpose of art there is, of course, a profound and energetic reverence for the human spirit that is as old as Homer and as new as Dickens, that is typically Greek. This reverence, whether we find it in Homer or in the late Euripides or the comedies of Aristophanes and Menander, in Plato's dialogues or Xenophon's memoirs, or even in the hymns of Romanos—this reverence shaped the poetry of Theocritus to an extraordinary degree and directed it to seek styles and poetic techniques that would provide the proper transparency and zest for this ceremony of praise. Though little in the Theocritean corpus (and little outside it) quite rivals his *Adoniazousai* for vitality, there is no question but that the conventions of pastoral, as Theocritus shaped them, are greatly enhanced by this passion for human beings in their variety and in their oddities. It is not that Theocritus's pastorals are particularly dramatic (nothing much really happens in them, certainly nothing of much importance, and their conflicts are generally trivial and even amiable); but we constantly sense in them a concern for interchange and for give-and-take, for trade-offs, for the delights and the peculiarities of human character—above all, Theocritus's people are always talking to each other and always listening to each other. In a very real way, Polyphemus is talking to Galatea even in *Idyll* 11 (so the young man in *Idyll* 3 is arguing with his young woman, begging her, entreating her, despite her silence), whereas Virgil's Corydon complains and sighs and murmurs, offers as solace to himself the poignant, incredibly lovely and unreal catalogue of flowers with its cardboard nymph in a cardboard garden (lines 45–50). We come to care for Polyphemus as a person because what he says both defines his reality and his sweetness and also convinces us of the reality of Galatea and of her extraordinary value. This man, absurd as he is, is really in love, and we love him for it. We may smile at him (which means, we are at least partly smiling at ourselves), but we do not laugh at him— malice and real mockery are not allowed in these healthy Epicurean poems with their insistence on friendship and compassion. Not the least miraculous aspect of Theocritus's art is that he finds, then suggests that we learn to trust and enjoy, what is most decent and most humane in ourselves. Sublime comic art is perhaps the rarest thing in literature, as is well known, and among its greatest masters is Theocritus.

The case with Virgil and his Corydon is very different. Virgil does invite us to laugh at Corydon and finally to despise him—he is, after all, a pompous hayseed with a yen for the trendy artsy world, he is foolish in his squalid love affairs (but are any of them *not* imaginary?) and foolish also in his Theocritean jingles and his ostentatious Alexandrian *techne* ("art") (where the cumbersome erudition of the singer of Theocritus's *Idyll* 3 becomes droll because he is as droll as he is bewildered and sweet, Corydon's idea of ornament, *Amphion Dictaeus in Actaeo Aracyntho,* 34 ["Amphion of Thebes on Attic Aracynthus"], is clumsy camp). This all seems, at first, just good clean fun, this malicious gaze at the pastoral imposter as he shows and tells just how tiresome he is. But under Corydon's funny posturings and Virgil's rich and elegant wit, there is, at last, something rather ugly. In addition to being an amusingly boring clown, isn't Corydon also hopelessly neurotic? Beneath the exquisite music and images is superb, cruel wit, and beneath the wit there is frightening loneliness and frustration. We cannot understand these terrors because we cannot really understand Corydon and his story; but we feel the hideous emotions that gnaw at him because it is they that are the central object of Virgil's mimesis in this poem, it is they that the poem exists to evoke, to suggest. *Eclogue* 2 is a lyric monologue, a lyric poem, of stunning originality, and it is "pure poetry" rather in the manner of Mallarmé.[20] Where Theocritus, true to his genre, gives us life, human character and stories whose spare clarities exist to illumine those characters and our lives, Virgil gives us fragments of a human being and fragments of a story which exist to illumine a complicated and obscure nexus of emotion: Corydon is pastoral distilled to pure lyric poetry; he is, in Hölderlin's phrase, "a metaphor for an emotion."

This lyric is dramatic only in the way that Senecan monologue or Eliot's favorite Elizabethans or Eliot himself are dramatic, or in the way that Mallarmé's *Hérodias* or Paul Valéry's *La jeune parque* or Eliot's "Gerontion" are dramatic—somewhere at its center there is a ferocious, blind conflict that wants to find and free itself, a heart without language, Rilke's "speechless heart," trying vainly to understand itself. Corydon, or the phantom who wears his mask, is in love with love; which is to say he cannot love, which is to say, he cannot, he feels, be loved: which is to say, Corydon hates both love and himself. This poem is about as far from Theocritus and his pastorals as it is possible to get. For if, as I think is the case, the hallmarks of The-

ocritus's world are freedom, simplicity, and leisure;[21] if for Theocritus
and his people it is fellowship and sympathy that matter most in our
lives; if the weather and quality of his days are defined by their sun
and fun—then Virgil's grave parody of Theocritus's people and
places shows a systematic rejection of all that Theocritus's poetry
imagines and celebrates. Virgil would later learn to mitigate and har-
ness this ferocity and bitterness, would temper his profound sense of
taedium vitae ("disgust," "weariness with life") with reason and discipline; but the young, unhappy epicurean seems here quite conscious
of what he is trying to do to the work of his older, cheerful epicurean
master. And beyond the rejection of the world view he wished to
share with Theocritus (and could not share and so transformed),
there is in this and in the other *Eclogues* a clear rejection of classical
mimesis. The young lyrical mannerist here fiercely renounces artistic
modes that, as he grows older, he will partially accept and will then
be able to adapt to his own *maniera* ("mannerism"). The *studium*
("zeal") is *inane* ("useless") here, as art in the *Aeneid* is often *inane*,
because this mannerist distrusts art no less than he distrusts life; and
the lyricist, poaching on pastoral territory, is less concerned with
imagining humans as they are in their dealings with each other than
he is in the imagination of inwardness, of the fearful, speechless
heart.

Another, similar lyricization of Theocritean pastoral occurs in the
second monologue of *Eclogue* 8, from which its model, the wonderful *Idyll* 2, Simaitha and her story, has all but vanished. What remains, what Virgil chooses to retain, having jettisoned what matters, are Simaitha's gestures and her poses. This part of *Eclogue* 8 is a
superb collage of Theocritus's images and rhetoric set to unforgetta-
ble music: the husk has been exquisitely gilded, and the hollowness
resonates grandly. Theocritus's creation is, to be sure, a crazy lady
doing crazy lady things, but she is very much alive and kicking. As
Theocritus's Simaitha screams and whimpers to her maid, what is
bothering her gradually comes to light—we come to know her because we come to *see* what has happened to her, and she and her
poem come to life (higher praise cannot be offered) in the manner of
Browning's great dramatic monologists. Simaitha's character unfolds
from her story as it moves, point by point, through delicate modulations, constantly pausing at crucial details, constantly gathering momentum, to its subtle and poignant conclusion. She is as gullible

and sentimental as her Delphis is shrewd and fancy free (the delicacy with which this funny and sad encounter, this fragile complexity, is revealed in such small compass is one measure of Theocritus's art); she is hysterical and endlessly vulnerable; she is, as I think she guesses, not very skilled in magic; she knows she is going to lose Delphis; and she claims and gets our sympathy—because she does love the charming, worthless Delphis, because she is lost and foolish and has, beyond her silliness, a shy, mysterious dignity and an awkward trust in life.

By getting rid of this or any story, by stripping his character of every vestige of personality, of her name and her local habitation (as Michael Putnam remarks: "In *Eclogue* 8, there is little suggested save the inner darkness of a house, a confined and private world within a rural setting"),[22] Virgil is able to concentrate solely on the frightening, ferocious emotion into which Theocritus's poem is dissolved. What remains of Theocritus's poem is the imagery of magic, which, deprived of its psychological causes, becomes sinister and obsessive, becomes morbid ornament that somehow devours the poem's form. Only in the following stanza are these frenzied recollections of Simaitha's innocent putterings with witchcraft not compressed to mere nightmare:

> May love grip Daphnis, as a heifer, weary,
> Seeking her bull through woods and lofty groves,
> Sinks down in green sedge by a running water,
> Desperate—nor thinks to stir when darkness falls.
> Such love be his: his cure no care of mine.
>
> (lines 85–89)

> talis amor Daphnin qualis cum fessa iuvencum
> per nemora atque altos quaerendo bucula lucos
> propter aquae rivum viridi procumbit in ulva
> perdita nec serae meminit decedere nocti,
> talis amor teneat nec sit mihi cura mederi.

The enchantress projects her own despair and helpless erotic suffering on the object of her love-hate, and the measure of her hatred and her pain is the tangle of image and syntax. The anger of this poem churns to its abrupt, surprising, and deliberately unsatisfying conclusion: *ab urbe venit* ("he has returned from the city"). But has he?—*credimus? an qui amant ipsi sibi somnia fingunt?* ("Is it true? or do

lovers wrap themselves in dreams?"). Or are we perhaps left with the
enchantress imagining Delphis's return because, for the moment,
she can no longer endure the savagery within her?

This poem, this part of *Eclogue* 8, is wonderfully effective, is a
model for dark lyric monologue. Here Virgil has, in fact, perfectly
achieved an ancient symbolist poetry that, like its modern counter-
part, relies for its effects and for the intensities of its meanings on
carefully chosen and carefully scumbled images that are set, and
kept, in motion by supreme incantation, by an obsessive, beautiful,
inhuman music; and this music, having renounced the world of phenomena, incarnates its fantasies and thereby embraces yet profounder unrealities, yet profounder sorrows.

Real melancholy and real danger are carefully excluded from Theocritus's landscape and its figures, not because Theocritus is frightened of them but because, good epicurean that he is, he knows them
to be illusions. Polyphemus in *Idyll* 11 and Boukaios and Milon in
Idyll 10 intuit the possibility of melancholy love, but they reject it in
favor of common sense, of a realization of the normal rhythm of happiness and unhappiness that shapes human life. Polyphemus does
not really convince himself that there is "another Galatea," but he
really does regain some self-esteem and fights free, for the time
being, of his deepest illusions about himself. Corydon, however,
when we last hear him, is struggling to maintain them throughout
his song. The charming sentimentality of Boukaios in *Idyll* 10 is
nicely balanced by the dry but welcome prudence of Milon. The
poem is tolerant of infatuation, but in its reconciliations it points
beyond suffering to moderate hopes and moderate joys, to ordinary
lives and ordinary destinies. In *Idyll* 1, which is supreme of its kind,
the idea of untimely death, of mysterious and extraordinary fate, is
carefully weighed against the disciplined vitality of pastoral art and
its vision of the everyday world with its small conflicts and small,
irritating discomforts; and the wonderful closure of the poem insists
on our slender yet sufficient capabilities and therefore our reasons for
having some faith in life and in ourselves.

> Sweeten your sweet mouth with honey,
> Thyrsis, and with honeycomb. Eat your fill
> of Aegilus's finest figs, for your voice
> outsings the cricket's. Here's the cup:
> smell, friend, its sharp freshness—

you would think it had been dipped
and bathed in the holy well of Hours.
Here, Dusky; she is yours to milk.
You others, stop that frisking,
or you'll get the ram worked up.

(lines 146–52)

The calm, humorous coda of the goat-herd advises us to accept "our walk at noon," "the colors of Sunday," and our easy, simple, possible pleasure. In this celebration of things as they are, untimely death is nothing more than the foil, the exception, that is part of the pattern.

In Virgil's pastoral world the ordinary becomes the extraordinary, the real becomes the symbolic surreal, the dramatic becomes the lyrical, and danger and disorder become the principles of artistic order. In short, Virgil colors the clarities of Theocritus's pastoral world with indelible melancholy. This is not so surprising because each genre that he touched, his melancholy lyric genius transformed.[23] The "form, figures, and subject matter" of Theocritus's pastorals have no authentic existence in Virgil's *Eclogues*. Instead, ironic phantoms, deliberately imprecise imitations of pastoral form, figures, and subject matter, recall their origins in order to destroy them, and Virgil's unique, pervasive melancholy replaces the tactful affirmations of Theocritus. In Theocritus, art exists to mirror life; in Virgil, life (or a dim, painful memory of it) exists to serve art. It is now (briefly, one hopes) fashionable to believe that all poems are somehow about poetry; having come to believe that life is impossible, we doubt that poetry is possible and now write and read, almost exclusively, poems about that impossibility. This radical disbelief in our own reality, this despair over art, and this cultivation of style for style's sake, are of the essence for mannerism. No lyric poetry surpasses the *Eclogues* in the mimesis of this kind of despair. Theocritus's greatest poem, *Idyll* 7, includes a celebration of poetry, whose worth and truth the presence of the marvelous Lycidas utterly confirms; but in this poem, poetry is only a part of the process. We sing it and listen to it as we go on our common road to our separate destinations; it is a mutual delight and a mutual solace; we joke about it and about each other because we are fairly sure of life, and poetry, and our fellowship. Poetry helps unite us. But it is a means, not an end.

Larks and linnets made their song, the dove his moan,
bees hummed and hovered round the springs.
The harvest's richest smells were everywhere;
the air was filled with fruit-time's fragrance. . . .
I pray that I may one day plant again
the great winnowing fork in her (Demeter's) heap of corn
as the goddess smiles her blessing on us,
with wheatsheaves and poppies in either hand.
      (lines 141–43, 155–57)

The end, in this poem, is the superb garden and its quiet, gentle festival: fruition, gratitude, calm—a sense of our place in things.

Virgil's grim parody of this poem, *Eclogue* 9, utterly negates the Theocritean vision. The bitterness of Moeris and the confused naïveté of *this* vague Lycidas aptly combine to emphasize the failure of Arcady to provide a refuge from the anxieties of contemporary life. Will the vanished master-poet, Menalcas, return to them, bringing with him the solace of his poetry? The two men quote to each other choice pieces of his pastoral, Theocritean poetry to cheer each other up, to cheer themselves up. But the poem itself dissolves into disquieting ambivalences. The singing stops. Menalcas will not return.[24] What the fragments of Theocritean poetry are used to prove in Virgil's poem is the unreality of Theocritus's pastoral solace. But this is not really the judgment of a stern, modern realist on an older, frivolous romantic. Theocritus had not claimed that his poems would cure contemporary ills; they were not intended as a narcotic against pain but as an image of a tendance of soul that offered to help the reader to reform himself, to persuade him not to imagine that his freedom and his reason were illusory. Virgil's first mistake was to assume that Theocritean pastoral tendance was a narcotic, that it would take away the pain, that the pleasance was a place of shelter from reality rather than reality itself. Then, having found that the pain continued (and that the narcotic was therefore useless and deceptive), he compounded his first mistake with a second one: he converted the real pleasance into an illusory, interior Arcady, a symbolic world in which real pain (and real pleasure) could be systematically transmuted into sad but harmless and exquisite illusions. And, finally, he completed this process of creative perversion by criticizing his model as being frivolous and unreal in order to exalt the integrity and "reality" of his own creation.

Virgil chose to interpret his experience and his sensibility by means of the genre least suited to them. Pastoral form, at least as Theocritus developed and perfected it, cannot order this content. Thus, in Virgil's *Eclogues*, disintegrating pastoral form mirrors disintegrating religious content (for the idea of Rome was central to Roman religion), and thus the haunting multiple ironies of failed cosmos, failed refuge, failed identity, and failed poetry begin their intricate, endlessly beautiful, endlessly mournful configurations. As in Catullus's Poem 64 and in Eliot's *The Waste Land*, public ruin becomes a metaphor for the private sorrows of lyric monologue. Virgil had misunderstood Theocritus's pastorals from the beginning, and as his own desperations proliferated, he kept creating ironic surface beauties to mask what he took to be emptiness—the emptiness, as he thought, of Theocritus and the emptiness (*Geistlosigkeit*) of his own world. The "synthesis of myth and reality" that Coleman posits to explain the unique power and the disturbing beauty of these poems is Virgil's most effective illusion among the many illusions that combine to shape his pastoral symbolist lyric. But there is no synthesis of anything in these poems—only lyric monologue, only mirror after mirror, each reflecting its neighbors perfectly, infinitely:

> . . . a myth of captivity
> Which we might enter: an unpeopled region
> Of ever new-fallen snow, a palace blazing
> With perpetual silence as with torches.[25]

> Issues from the hand of time the simple soul
> Irresolute and selfish, misshapen, lame,
> Unable to fare forward or retreat,
> Fearing the warm reality, the offered good,
> Denying the importunity of the blood,
> Shadow of its own shadows, spectre in its own gloom,
> Leaving disordered papers in a dusty room;
> Living first in the silence after the viaticum.[26]

Like the other *Ariel Poems*, "Animula" (from which the latter lines are taken), written in 1929, the year before *Ash Wednesday*, marks a turn in Eliot's poetry, not only toward the church, but also away from the intense, private lyricism of his earlier work, which is dominated by the lyric monologue. After *Ash Wednesday* Eliot would move to public voices and public themes, in the theater and in the choral lyric of "The Rock" and *Four Quartets*. In "Animula" the vanishing soloist looks back to the world of *Prufrock*, of "Gerontion," and of *The Waste Land* almost for a last time. The world here rejected by the anonymous speaker is "a flat world of changing lights and noise, / To light, dark, dry or damp, chilly or warm" (lines 2–3), of "The pain of living and the drug of dreams" (line 21). It is, in fact, the world of lyric monologue, of vulnerability, of bad inwardness and bad solitude, in which the hidden speaker of this poem sees personality in its unfoldings only as a "shadow of its own shadows." What this poem manages to imagine is the *animula*, the "little soul," moving from its childhood safeties into the disorders and the isolations of unquiet maturity:

> The heavy burden of the growing soul
> Perplexes and offends more, day by day;
> Week by week, offends and perplexes more
> With the imperatives of "is and seems"
> And may and may not, desire and control.
>
> (lines 16–19)

But this movement, this growth, is really, against all expectation, toward prayer:

> Living first in the silence after the viaticum.
>
>   Pray for Guiterriez, avid of speed and power,
> For Boudin, blown to pieces,
> For this one who made a great fortune,
> And that one who went his own way.
> Pray for Floret, by the boarhound slain between the yew trees,
> Pray for us now and at the hour of our birth.
>
> (lines 31–37)

This passage recalls the closure of "Gerontion":

> . . . De Bailhache, Fresca, Mrs. Cammel, whirled
> Beyond the circuit of the shuddering Bear
> In fractured atoms.
>
> (lines 68–70)

But those discontinuities and fatalities, which the speaker can only ponder fitfully, anxiously ("Thoughts of a dry brain in a dry season") are here gathered by prayer into the life ("living first," "the hour of our birth") that "the silence after the viaticum" bestows.[27] Vanity, one's own and that of others, once felt as being both absurd and terrifying, succumbs to charity, to prayer for others and for oneself. The pain of the *animula*, once destructive and incomprehensible, is now seen to have significance and purpose. It is an agent of prayer: the self no longer vainly deliberating with the self, muttering to itself, but the self addressing, really addressing, something other than itself, something beyond itself and its pains and drugs, its fears and shadows and discontinuities.

The imagination of the private world of lyric monologue, which "Animula" recalls and dismisses, has been a powerful, perhaps *the* powerful, solo lyric mode from Tennyson's "Tithonus" and "Lucretius" and Mallarmé's *Hérodias* down to John Berryman's "Homage to Mistress Bradstreet" and his incomparable *Dream Songs*. Lyric monologue suits the modern temper very well because it can be made to mime, even to incarnate, the self in its isolations, its manifold disorders, and its unrealities. It can, in the most natural way (a person speaking to himself) imagine and attempt to order the most intense and the most discordant experiences without the need to communicate them; in the mode of lyric monologue the anguished private world, carefully hidden in and structured by a private, intricate, ironic art, is allowed its pure, full voice.[28] This, then, is a paradoxical lyric mode: peculiarly powerful, yet peculiarly, perhaps deliberately, unsatisfying; it is made public, in a sense, yet it remains "merely personal." And in its failure to become truly shared—as against the modes of Sappho or Horace or Shakespeare or Goethe or Pushkin, poets for whom lyric discourse is what matters—this lyric mode seems to exacerbate and to widen the very emotions it seeks to order or, failing that, to exorcise; for instead of setting them out in the situation of discourse, in the common light of day, it impersonates an inwardness so intense, so irremediable, that genuine discourse is impossible. Which is precisely what this mode and the poems that employ it are really saying—I am alone:

> I would meet you upon this honestly.
> I that was near your heart was removed therefrom
> To lose beauty in terror, terror in inquisition.
> I have lost my passion: why should I need to keep it

Since what is kept must be adulterated?
I have lost my sight, smell, hearing, taste and touch:
How should I use them for your closer contact?
("Gerontion," lines 55–61)

or:

"My nerves are bad to-night. Yes, bad. Stay with me.
Speak to me. Why do you never speak. Speak.
What are you thinking of? What thinking? What?
I never know what you are thinking. Think."
I think we are in rats' alley
Where the dead men lost their bones.
(*The Waste Land*, lines 111–16)

For an I so intricate and so vulnerable, no other solo lyric mode had been possible but lyric monologue, and for Eliot the burdens and the terrors of disordered selfhood were intolerable—it is that intolerability that his early poems, before *Ash Wednesday* and the *Ariel Poems*, deepen and unfold. There seems a good chance that *The Waste Land*, with its intricate, manifold lyric monologues and their dark harmonies, will remain the great solo lyric in English of its century.[29] The poem's greatness depends, of course, both on Eliot's extraordinary sensitivity to his own experience and on the extraordinary precision of the art that ordered that sensitivity and that experience; but the poem's impact on twentieth-century literature depends not only on its inherent greatness but also on its uncanny capacity for offering what the century demands in the way of lyric poetry. When the self had come to see itself as discontinuities, and when, accordingly, decorum required that lyric itself become discontinuous, this powerful, essential mimesis of disorder became, and, despite mild currents of disapproval and neglect, remains, the supreme example of solo lyric for a world whose sense of lyric discourse had all but disappeared. But Eliot, when the demons had at last departed, or when the initial inspiration had been exhausted, or the inwardness had become intolerable, moved, slowly, patiently, to the other great lyric mode and to a new, less anguished achievement.

VI

The Amplitude of Time:
Whitman and Modern Choral

As the name and idea of lyric in the past two hundred years have tended to take on the narrow connotations of solo poetry and *Erlebnisdichtung* ("poetry of experience"), so the name and the idea of selfhood have increasingly come to define only the private individual in his inwardness or in his isolation from, his opposition to, his victimization by, the world outside him. That concept of selfhood, in a way, suits solo lyric in all times and all places, whether the self is celebrating, praising its loves and its sense of fulfillment and ecstasy, or whether it is condemning, blaming its hates and fears, its sense of frustration and failure. Whether the solo lyricist attempts to imagine his expansions and unfoldings and praises himself and the world, or whether he attempts to imagine his contractions and his withdrawals and blames himself or blames both himself and the world for his suffering, in the essential solo lyric situation, the poet experiences, shapes his consciousness of self and world, by contrasting himself with the world. The quality of that contrast focuses either on the power and beauty or on the weakness and suffering of the individual as he discovers what it means to be becoming in space and time. But, as we have seen, in ancient formulations of lyric, both solo and choral poetry were equally valid and equally important, each of them necessary to the total shaping of the human personality. The sense of this dual, interdependent nature of lyric has all but vanished from our modern ways of thinking about poetry, about literature. For all that, if the name of choral has almost disappeared from our literary vocabulary, the choral imagination and the choral act have, so far from disappearing, made an extraordinary comeback in modern times.

Human beings have, after all, not only private emotions and selves but also public emotions and selves. For solo lyric and the private emotions that it shapes, the lyric situation is *Ich und Welt* ("I and world"); for choral poetry, as we have seen with Pindar, that situation is *Wir und Welt* ("we and world"), and, unlike that of solo lyric, this situation does not define opposition or otherness. Its function is not to clarify the limits and the nature of the private self; rather in *Wir und Welt* the choral poet imagines those emotions which lead us to want to understand both the possibility of our communion with each other and the possibility of our communion with the world. As it is possible to use solo lyric to lie about the nature of the self, to magnify both its powers and its vulnerabilities rather than to attempt to define the private self truly, so it is possible to use choral poetry to distort the nature and meaning of community and of communities in their relations to the divine. As solo lyric can be forced to promote varieties of solipsism, so choral lyric can be forced to promote varieties of evil nationality and of totalitarianism. In either case, the possibilities for good are in exact proportion to the possibilities for evil. For the most part, the modern choral that I am about to describe has been on the side of the angels, and the reasons for this are not far to seek. In our technological societies, when the individual human began more and more to feel cut off from his fellows and from the world, when inwardness became less a matter of fruition and beauty and more a matter of anger and terror, the modern choralists, in their different ways, attempted to countervail this process of alienation by reaffirming our kinship with each other and with the world that begets us and nourishes us, by denying that the exploitations of empire and the degradations worked by the machine had or would or could succeed in isolating us from each other or from the earth and the universe. Fragmented persons fashion fragmented worlds, and fragmented worlds produce fragmented persons.

What modern choral attempts to do is to put an end to this vicious circle and to reestablish the great metaphors for *communitas* as the proper and central metaphors for the human condition.

In describing this kind of modern poetry as choral, I am, of course, tampering with the ancient idea of choral. There is here no choral music and, more importantly, there is no dance; for ancient Greek choral, beyond its music, the dance was a visual metaphor for the emotions of fellowship, for the faith in renewal that its text shaped and affirmed verbally. Yet, as we have seen, when Catullus wrote his wedding songs and when Horace reinvented Simonidean and Pindaric choral for his Rome, both music and dance were absent as they were to be absent when Jonson undertook his reinventions of Pindar and of Horace. What matters, for literary choral, is that the agent and the object of choral mimesis be present: the universal representative of the community singing for and to the community about the hopes and passion for order, survival, and continuity that they all share. This shift in the outward look of choral in no way alters its essential character. The idea of a genre is defined not by its accidents of representation, its material causes[1] (meter, music, dance) but by its substance, that is, by its content, its agents, objects, and purposes of mimesis. Whatever its alterations in accidents, from Pindar to Horace, from Horace to Jonson, from Jonson to Whitman and other modern choralists, the substance of choral is what it has always been.

There is no need to undertake here a sketch of the history of choral, but one might point out that between Horace and Jonson, choral poetry is by and large confined, and gloriously confined, to the Christian hymn, to the great poems of Romanos, the great Byzantine hymnist, and to the tradition of the Latin and later of the Protestant hymnists. But this topic is essentially outside the scope of this book; it is essentially secular choral that concerns us here, even when we think of the choral poetry of an Eliot or of a Charles Péguy. As my chief emblem of what modern choral is, I take Walt Whitman, or rather, early Whitman, who seems to me at once the most original, influential, and powerful of modern choralists. But before we look at Whitman, it would be well to glance at what Ben Jonson accomplished in his imitations, or rather, his re-creations of ancient choral.

The Cary-Morison ode opens as a eulogy on Sir Henry Morison, who died in his young manhood, but, almost imperceptibly, it becomes a celebration of the friendship of Morison and his older companion and fellow soldier, Sir Lucius Cary. In its opening stanzas, the poem trembles on the brink of lamentation, but these temptations are steadfastly refused. It is not Morison's death that matters but the quality of his life, and the poem praises the virtues, the courage, and the decency that drew these two young men together and held them together until untimely death parted them. Yet the death was untimely only as the foolish world judges such things:

> Alas, but Morison fell young;
> Hee never fell, thou fall'st, my tongue.
> Hee stood, a Souldier to the last right end,
> A perfect Patriot, and a noble friend,
> But most a vertuous Sonne.
> All Offices were done
> By him, so ample, full and round,
> In weight, in measure, number, sound,
> As though his age imperfect might appeare,
> His life was of Humanitie the Spheare.
>   (lines 43–52)

This imperfection, then, against appearance, has paradoxically reached perfection. On the other hand, some nameless man who lived to be eighty and who

> . . . vexed time, and busied the whole State:
> Troubled both foes, and friends:
> But to no ends:
> What did this Stirrer, but die late?
> How well at twentie had he falne, or stood!
> For three of his foure-score, he did no good.
>   (lines 27–32)

Perfection is something the eye and mind may miss because the values that shape our perceptions may be perverted by a perverse society; the function of this choral poem is to reshape our perceptions accurately by reordering our values:

> In small proportions, we just beauties see:
> And in short measures, life may perfect be.
>   (lines 72–73)

Perfection, then, is the pivotal idea in the poem, and what perfection may be is slowly unfolded before our eyes as the poem, alternating between praise of Morison and then of Cary and blame for those who are unlike them, circles slowly, carefully to its still center. These young men, separated by death, are in fact still joined by bonds of fellowship that death cannot undo; they are like the Dioscuri, at once separate yet eternally inseparable: "But fate doth so alternate the designe, / Whilst that in heav'n, this light on earth must shine" (lines 95–96). But even the friendship is not the perfection but the means to the perfection. Ordinary friendships may be founded on "pleasures vaine," "rimes or ryots," "orgies of drink, or fain'd protests" (lines 102–04); what defines this friendship is "simple love of greatnesse, and of good; / That knits brave minds, and manners, more than blood" (lines 105–06). Love of greatness, and love of good, the *knitting* of brave minds and manners: what drew them together to become "this bright Asterisme" (line 89) and makes them a paradigm of virtue ("such a Law / Was left yet to Man-kind," lines 120–21) was their shared sense of community, their pure sense of their responsibilities toward the larger fellowship of England, of which their personal fellowship, in thought and in action (their courageous deeds on England's behalf), is the radiant, abiding symbol. Perfection, then, is the yielding of the self to the larger good and the unity of brave minds and manners which that yielding confers, the unity on which the felicity and the moral greatness of society depend. Here, as in Pindar and in Horace's *Roman Odes*, is the knowledge that the individual most nearly finds and is himself when he accepts his place in and responsibilities to the society into which he was born, that he lives most perfectly in the present when he preserves the past and works to conserve the future of that society. To some minds, all this may smack of bourgeois or chauvinist thought control; if so, that is a pity. Not the least generous, noble, and sane aspect of the choral idea is its insistence that the perfection of self grows from the disciplines and the freedoms of selflessness.

In the Cary-Morison ode Jonson seeks to re-create—and does so with astonishing success—the shapes and modulations of Pindar. "To Penshurst" is choral only in its essential content, not in its modes or form, and it therefore looks forward to what I am calling modern choral. Despite its pastoral motifs, the poem focuses, again, on a celebration of the goodness of society and on the roots of that goodness. The lush opening, with its praises of fertility and abundance, glides, almost halfway through the poem, into praise for the lord and lady of Penshurst and their unostentatious generosity, their easy acceptance of their responsibilities to their community. (Once again, Jonson is at pains to contrast genuine nobility with spurious greatness and its "envious show.") The exact quality of their rich, unassuming hospitality is defined by a surprise visit to Penshurst by King James and his son and by the regal praise for the "high huswifery" of Lady Mary Wroth. But the definition of fertility and decorum, of the virtues that create and sustain Penshurst and what it symbolizes, is not here complete, for this poem also circles to its perfection:

> These, Penshurst, are thy praise, and yet not all.
> Thy lady's noble, fruitfull, chaste withall.
> His children thy great lord may call his owne:
> A fortune, in this age, but rarely knowne.
> They are, and have been taught religion: Thence
> Their gentler spirits have suck'd innocence.
> Each morne, and even, they are taught to pray,
> With the whole household, and may, every day,
> Reade, in their vertuous parents noble parts,
> The mysteries of manners, arms, and arts.
>
> (lines 89–98)

Chastity, piety, unity, and humility (the whole household) but, above all, again, paradigms of virtue, the living representatives of the truly good past who teach goodness and pass it on to a future that they guard and shape by what they do and what they are.

> Now, Penshurst, they that will proportion thee
> With other edifices, when they see
> Those proud, ambition heaps and nothing else
> May say, their lords have built, but thy lord dwells.
>
> (lines 99–102)

Dwells: lives an authentic life by accepting his responsibilities as lord, as husband, as father, carefully, passionately. In the Cary-Morison ode, Jonson had asked:

> For what is life, if measur'd by the space,
> Not by the act?
> Or masked man, if valu'd by his face,
> Above his fact?
> (lines 21–24)

The answer there had been as it is here. Living, truly living, is defined by the acts and facts of moral imagination, by the continuities of families and societies, by the efforts made for their purification and constant renewal. In this sense, most lives are squandered on fraudulent building of one sort or another, are run through; lived they are not: *"thy lord dwells"* because his selfhood is shaped, strengthened and clarified in the power and precision of good community.[2]

It is a long leap from the civilities and the approaching hazards of Jonson's aristocratic England to the mess and tumult of Whitman's democratic, newly industrial America, but, chorally speaking, the distance is not as great as it may seem. In a very real sense, every society is in jeopardy, every society needs the lessons and the solace of choral poetry. What choral poets do is not so much to state the fact of good community as to imagine the possibility of good community, to persuade the choral audience that both their hopes of goodness and their fears of social and moral danger are genuine, and thus encourage the necessary marshaling of energies and strengthening of wills and of faith. What confronted Whitman as a choral poet we have discussed in some detail in the first chapter and need not rehearse it at length here; another crisis of selfhood, the dehumanizations not of science but of technological science, a profound *Weltwende* ("world change") in which European traditions, never strong in America, began their long deterioration. Whitman's solutions to his choral difficulties, at once simple, complex, and mysterious, turn on his audacious reinvention of an archetypal choral voice.[3]

It is through his extraordinary fusion of solo and choral voices that Whitman achieves his unique invention.[4] In *Song of Myself* especially, but throughout the whole of the 1860 edition of *Leaves of Grass*, what we keep hearing is a strangely harmonious discord between the Whitman who joys and grieves in a personal way and the Whitman who imagines, represents, and clarifies the common joys and griefs of humankind. In the great twentieth section of *Song*,[5] having addressed the individual reader in this fashion, "This hour I tell things in confidence, / I might not everybody, but I will tell you" (section 94), he gives his fullest description of himself as the speaker of this poem and of "you" (each and every hearer of the poem):[6]

> Who goes there! hankering, gross, mystical and nude?
> How is it I extract strength from the beef I eat?
>
> What is a man anyhow? What am I? What are you?
>
> All I mark as my own, you shall offset it with your own,
> Else it were time lost listening to me.
> > (sections 95–97)

In the 1855 and 1860 editions "Who goes there" is an exclamation, *ecce!* Only in the later revisions does it become a question. Look who goes there! A thing of desire, born from the good earth, its mind bent on heaven, pure and powerful in its nakedness. This vision of desire and strength is Whitman and is us. He does not ask us, he commands us, to look at it, suddenly, unprepared, without our preconceptions and without our comforting, tormenting cultural conditioning. For those preconceptions and that conditioning impede our vision and harm our hearts. Know, he says, know we are a certain kind of animal, not the maimed creature of hypocritical outworn superstitions, but this existing thing, this complex tangle of lust and aspiration, this newness. Ralph Waldo Emerson, worried that America was as barbarous as Europeans said it was, worried, too, that America was not emerging from its chaotic origins, had asked the question, Who are we? persistently and eloquently. Whitman takes up the challenge. His repetition of the question, What am I? What are you? is impatient, almost contemptuous. For the answer stares us in the face. We are this vision, something at once immanent and transcendental, something universal and unique, aspiring after our perfection yet perfect already.

> I do not snivel that snivel the world over,
> That mouths are vacuums, and the ground but wallow and
> > filth,
> That life is a suck and a sell, and nothing remains at the end
> > but threadbare crape, and tears.

> Whimpering and truckling fold with powders for invalids—
>   conformity goes to the fourth-removed,
> I cock my hat as I please, indoors or out.
> (sections 98–99)

He fully realizes the crisis of selfhood in modernity, sees that humans are coming to see themselves as impotent, ephemeral, irrelevant, that Americans, lacking even the trappings of the dying cultural heritage of Europe, will feel this crisis with special violence and danger. The dying superstitions teach men that they are doomed beasts; a growing secular materialism teaches them that the earth, their home, is a random, an insignificant, clod of dirt to be pillaged in the interests of progress and then abandoned, that our lives are defined by the banalities of our funerals. He refuses to snivel or whimper; he brushes aside this new and old and fatal denigration of humans and their earth with a flick of his wrist as he cocks his hat, gracefully, defiantly. Then, having abjured bad religion, he announces:

> Having pried through the strata, analyzed to a hair, counsell'd
>   with doctors, and calculated close,
> I find no sweeter fat than sticks to my own bones.
>
> In all people I see myself—none more, and not one a
>   barleycorn less,
> And the good or bad I say of myself I say of them.
>
> And I know I am solid and sound,
> To me the converging objects of the universe perpetually flow,
> All are written to me, and I must get what that writing
>   means.
> (sections 101–03)

The various scientists, dismembering their particular objects of investigation, seem sometimes to find nothing there when the process of dismemberment is complete: the earth nothing after such analysis, the heavens nothing, man nothing. He parodies their techniques wittily—but, as always in Whitman, it is humor more than wit, for there is always a touch of large-hearted, amiable self-mockery in such strategies; he presents himself gravely as a fellow scientist, doing to himself what they do to the rest of reality. But when he has completed *his* experiment, he finds sweetness in his fleshly truth; more important, he finds, joyously, his unity with all human creatures, their exact equality, their difficult, necessary, mysterious blend of good and bad. So, when his anatomy of life is completed, because of the sweetness and the equality and the harmony of good and bad, he knows that the pessimistic, the cynical, conclusions are utterly and dangerously mistaken. Hence, he can affirm his wholeness and his health; there is no sick fragmentation of the self here, only a joyful connection with the universe, a sense that all of reality is, like his poem, a good text that is meant for him to read and that the significance of his own being depends upon his reading that text passionately, precisely. Some of his contemporaries who were reading the same text—but it was not the same—were reading it differently. Those sniveling, whimpering, despairing, invalid readings are exuberantly rejected by the readings he now offers:

> I know I am deathless,
> I know this orbit of mine cannot be swept by a carpenter's
>   compass,
> I know I shall not pass like a child's carlacue cut with a burnt
>   stick at night.

> I know I am august,
> I do not trouble my spirit to vindicate itself to be understood,
> I see that the elementary laws never apologize,
> I reckon I behave no prouder than the level I plant my house
>   by, after all.
>   (sections 104–05)

The meaning of the world's text, then, and the essential meaning of this poem, is his kinship with the objects of the universe converging upon him in their perpetual flow, in their rhythm, of which he is a part; is his kinship with all humans and all creatures who are also part of this zigzag unfolding, this blossoming of space and of time. To have mastered this text is to have lived genuinely, absolutely; to have glimpsed, however briefly, the kinship is to possess and to be possessed by the eternal present. *Hic et nunc* ("here and now") becomes part of *illud tempus* ("that time"), and in this still center, this timeless present, there is no death; nor are there other boundaries, for the "orbit of mine" becomes the orbit of reality. This is not pantheism or solipsism or animism or any ism; this is not a philosophical poem. True, there are bits and pieces of the *Upanishads* here, fragments of Lucretius, but there are also fragments of everything and everybody. In a passion of belief he accepts everything and rejects nothing; for discovering himself to be an elemental law of reality among other elemental laws of reality, there is nothing to be spurned and everything to be embraced. This is, poetically speaking, a super-sensual ontology, in which identity and existence, sundered in modern cultures, find again the possibility of their real and ideal, their unsunderable, marriage.

> I exist as I am—that is enough,
> If no other in the world be aware, I sit content,
> And if each and all be aware, I sit content.

> One world is aware, and by far the largest to me, and that is
>   myself,
> And whether I come to my own today or in ten thousand or
>   ten million years,
> I can cheerfully take it now, or with equal cheerfulness I can
>   wait.

> My foothold is tenoned and mortized in granite,
> I laugh at what you call dissolution,
> And I know the amplitude of time.
>   (sections 106–08)

Paradoxically perhaps, he accepts possible isolation from the kinship just after he has grandly affirmed the kinship. Yet at the closure of Chant 20 he is also concerned to affirm his independence, his contentment and his cheerfulness, all of which define and prove his faith in the kinship. In the eyes of the world, man's time and space may have been reduced to a meaningless infinitesimal irrelevance by the news from geology and astronomy and biology, but in the center of this bad news, which turns out to be more good news, Whitman is still "solid and sound," his foothold on reality still perfectly secure, his natural existence sufficient (I exist as I am—that is enough). "Time is the evil," say other poets who feel their identities and cultures threatened with destruction. This poet who has read the text of reality, even as he has allowed himself to be read by it, will have none of that. Again, good-hearted, casually but firmly, he laughs at the misconceptions of dissolution and glories in the amplitude of time, that incalculable immensity of scientific measurement that had tried to challenge and unnerve him. In the amplitude there is nothing but the kinship, the identity, and the flowering. Very early in the poem,

> A child said, *What is the grass?* fetching it to me with full
>   hands;
> How could I answer the child? I do not know what it is any
>   more than he.
>   (section 26)

He cannot answer the question, though he proposes various possible answers, among them, "the handkerchief of the Lord," "a uniform hieroglyphic." The entire poem will be the answer. Toward the final closure the impassioned ignorance reechoes:

> I hear and behold God in every object, yet understand God
>   not in the least,
> Nor do I understand who there can be more wonderful than
>   myself.
>
> Why should I wish to see God better than this day?
> I see something of God each hour of the twenty-four, and
>   each moment then,
> In the faces of men and women I see God, in my own face in
>   the glass,
> I find letters from God dropped in the street—and every one
>   is signed by God's name,
> And I leave them where they are, for I know that others will
>   punctually come forever and ever.
>
> And as to you Death and you bitter hug of mortality, it is idle
>   to try to alarm me.
>   (sections 345–47)

In the amplitude of time the messages of God are constant, infinite; the absolute perfection of the message may be beyond us, but, humanly speaking, the message is clear enough:

> Urge, and urge, and urge,
> Always the procreant urge of the world.
>
> Out of the dimness opposite equals advance—always
>   substance and increase, always sex,

Always a knit of identity—always distinction—always a breed
of life.

To elaborate is no avail—learned and unlearned feel that it is
so.
(sections 10–12)

Far-swooping elbowed Earth! Rich, apple-blossomed Earth!

Smile, for YOUR LOVER comes!
(section 116)

The knit of identity that weds us to ourselves and weds us to each
other, despite of, because of, our distinctions, also weds us to an
earth that surpasses the Lucretian earth in her variety and fertility:

Prodigal, you have given me love! Therefore I to you give
love!
O unspeakable passionate love!
(section 117)

And blessed by this dialectical knit and distinction, we can forget
the bitter hug of mortality to pursue our proper business—the procreant urge of the world. And when we have finished the poem and
put it aside—but we never do quite finish it, always return to it—
why is it that this strange, vulgar, incomparable voice can turn us
back away from nightmare to the procreant urge?

I think he teaches us to trust him because, in fact, instead of arrogance and instead of vulgarity, he shows constant tact. Early in the
poem he tells us firmly:

You shall not look through my eyes either, nor take things
from me,
You shall listen to all sides, and filter them from yourself.
(section 7)

So, toward the end of the poem, he reminds us, gently, of our freedom and our responsibility:

But each man and each woman of you I lead upon a knoll,
My left hand hooking you round the waist,
My right hand pointing to landscapes and a plain public road.

Not I—not any one else, can travel that road for you,
You must travel it for yourself.
(sections 324–25)

Furthermore, the plain public road that he points out to us is not, as
is sometimes maintained, an idiot's delight of mindless progress and
vapid hedonism and smug appetite. For his own purposes he may, in
a wildly funny burst of self-approval, say,

I dote on myself—there is a lot of me and all so luscious,

Each moment, and whatever happens, thrills me with joy,

O I am so wonderful!
(sections 152–53)

But when he tells us, "I am large—I contain multitudes" (section
362), it is not in the same mood; here he reminds us that he has
shown us not only the joy of life but the grief of it:

Through me many long dumb voices,
Voices of the interminable generations of slaves,
Voices of prostitutes, and of deformed persons,
Voices of the diseased and the despairing, and of thieves and
    dwarfs. . . .

Through me forbidden voices,
Voices of sexes and lusts—voices veiled, and I remove the
    veil,
Voices indecent, by me clarified and transfigured.
(sections 141–42)

He has become, throughout the poem, not only the decent and
the lucky but also the insulted and the injured, the luckless and the
hopeless. In the moments of these "impersonations," we hear echoes
of the personal voice of *Children of Adam*, *Calamus*, and "Out of
the Cradle." The poet who wrote "Of the Terrible Doubt of Appearances" and who could say, in "As I Ebb'd with the Ocean of
Life":

Oppress'd with myself that I have dared to open my mouth,
Aware now that amid all that blab whose echoes recoil upon
    me I have not once had the least idea who or what I am,

> But that before all my arrogant poems the real Me stands yet
>   untouch'd, untold, altogether unreach'd,
> Withdrawn far, mocking me with mock-congratulatory signs
>   and bows,
>
> With peals of distant ironical laughter at every word I have
>   written,
> Pointing in silence to these songs, and then to the sand
>   beneath
>   (section 5)

—this poet, complex yet simple, universal yet unique, can be trusted
to point out the signs to us and let us do our own work to find out
what they signify. He has imagined for us the possibility of the kinship, the identity, and the flowerings; he leaves us to struggle for ourselves, but not without the most gentle and selfless of benedictions:

> I bequeath myself to the dirt, to grow from the grass I love,
> If you want me again, look for me under your bootsoles.
>
> You will hardly know who I am, or what I mean,
> But I shall be good health to you nevertheless,
> And filter and fibre your blood.
>
> Failing to fetch me at first, keep encouraged,
> Missing me one place, search another,
> I stop somewhere waiting for you.
>   (sections 370–72)

"Few poets," said Randall Jarrell, "have shown more of the tears of
things, and the joys of things, and of the reality beneath either tears
or joy."[7] This perfection of praise and blame Whitman managed to
fashion because he confronted squarely the problems of community
and identity in modern times, even as he kept clearly and passionately in his mind and heart their perennial meaning and value.
Song of Myself is the greatest, the fundamental poem in American
literature; it heartens us, yet also haunts us, eludes us, because we
keep trying to take its imagination of community and identity as a
promise that neither its poet nor we have kept. But Whitman promised us nothing; rather, with immense patience, cunning, understanding, and love he coaxed and scolded, pleaded and warned,
blamed and praised: that we might accept the fact of our being and

then meet the challenge of cultural transition which he defined for us so well.

How delicate and difficult that definition is and how much it cost him can best be seen in the tragic failure of nerve that fastened on him after the Civil War, when the vision of community and identity and its unique voice of praise and blame could no longer be sustained:

> With the bright crispy Autumn weather, WALT WHITMAN again makes his appearance on the sidewalks of Broadway. His large, massive personality,—his grave and prophetic, yet free and manly appearance,—his *insouciance* of manner and movement,—his easy and negligent, yet clean and wholesome dress,—go to make up a figure and an individuality that attracts the attention and interest of every passer-by.

This is an advertisement for himself that Whitman sent to the *New York Times* for its October 1, 1868 issue.[8] The poet of "Crossing the Brooklyn Ferry," "Out of the Cradle," "The Sleepers," *Drum Taps*, and "When Lilacs Last in the Dooryard Bloom'd," was getting ready to write *American Vistas*; then, as if remembering this caricature that he had written for the daily press, he began to convert himself into it. The jingoistic *vates* ("seer"), whom the tensions of good choral had kept in check, now emerges from the ruin of good choral to celebrate various kinds of mediocrity. But before this catastrophe, he had reinvented choral poetry, a bookish choral, unsung, undanced, for the modern world that needed it. Although the accidents of ancient choral were absent, its substance lived again vital and fresh: the singer imagined choral identities for his audience as he imagined a choregic identity for himself; and the great themes, the center of choral, renewal of society, praise for the flowerings of space and time, faith in the rhythm of the universe and for man's place in that rhythm—these were all, from 1855 to 1868, alive and well in Brooklyn.

To my mind, modern choral is the most powerful and most attractive of modern poetic forms, and when the current fashion for anonymous monologue, masquerading as philosophical meditation, has passed, perhaps the preeminence of choral will be recognized. I take Whitman as my example of choral in modern poetry because he seems to me to have focused all the force of his gifts and sensitivities on investigating the kind of consciousness that is proper to choral and thereby to have given choral its most perfect modern shape. But that choice may well reflect merely a certain kind of taste. The idea and the act of choral poetry are clearly at the heart of Hölderlin's poetry and account for his greatest achievements; some of the best of Wordsworth and most of the best of Shelley are informed by the choral instinct. The idea of choral struggles to win mastery in the poetry of Victor Hugo and fails to do so, but the failure is spectacular. In Baudelaire, a more than reluctant choralist in an age of high capitalism, the ceremony of praise may resound in peculiar ways, and the praise may seem overwhelmed by the blame, but a unique choral compassion for the now agonized kinship of humankind and a deathless love of Paris belie the prevalence of anger and despair and reveal the necessary shaman.[9] The choral spirit and the choral gesture are of the essence for Paul Claudel and for Charles Péguy. It was, in part, by his slow, patient and powerful development of choral consciousness that William Butler Yeats transformed supreme artistry to supreme genius. Without his choral instincts Pablo Neruda is unthinkable, as is the later, great Anna Akhmatova. In astonishing ways, Rilke, the least likely of choralists on the surface, comes to his full fruition in the *Sonnets to Orpheus* by virtue of a complex, subtle, yet genuine choral inspiration. In her "Epitaph for the Race of Man," Edna St. Vincent Millay escapes an exquisite near-triviality and finds high permanence. In many of his poems from the late thirties, the forties, and the early fifties, W. H. Auden manages to find an authentic passion which collects that amazing, scattered intelligence when he is moved "to find or form a genuine community."[10] Finally, in *Four Quartets*, Eliot defines modern man, himself and us, with a clear, unpersuadable humility that has no parallel in modern poetry. This poem is rather unpopular now, perhaps because we are estranged from the particular forms of community that Eliot fought to imagine. Moreover, the fresh clarity of the poem—not just its formal perfections, which are also now suspect—distresses us, but that tells us more about us than it does about him. As long as the fierce passions of Allen Ginsberg's *Howl* and *Kaddish* sound in our ears, Eliot's controlled passion is bound to seem feeble if not false; but for the force and precision of its desire to gather us together, no less than for its astonishing technical control, *Four Quartets* is the perfect modern choral.[11] It is our *Georgics*, that masterly choral of another age that needed choral desperately and found it abundantly.[12]

And, at last, there is Pound, who is always the special case. In no poet after Whitman, as I think he sometimes realized, was the choral gift purer or stronger than it was in Pound. I am not concerned here to defend his cranky Yankee economics and politics, which are not worthy of attack; nor will I waste time pondering the causes of his having nearly ruined his art by systematically confusing art with life. As the early Pound had attempted to escape selfhood, so the middle and late Pound attempted to escape his choral vocation; or rather, he tried to legitimate his choral poems with bogus history and fertile cant, believing perhaps that the world, which he knew loathed poets, might listen to an erudite man of action. For all that, Pound's passion for *communitas* was extraordinary both for its intensity and for its delicacy, and his reverence for fertility and renewal, beautifully rendered page after page, is among the most precious things in modern poetry. More than anyone, he saw *communitas* being wantonly, cynically, sacrificed to the velleities of secular materialism, and he saw fertility and renewal being annihilated by the greed of uncontrolled technologies. So, great choral poet that he was, he tried to imagine paradise, which is what every choral poetry tries to imagine.[13] He seems to have died thinking that he had failed:

> M'amour, m'amour
> > what do I love and
> > > where are you?
> That I lost my center
> > fighting the world.
> The dreams clash
> > and are shattered—
> and that I tried to make a paradiso
> > > > > terrestre—[14]

But he had not. The poem is there, in *The Cantos*, and we have only to ferret it out. If this seems an arrogant suggestion, I remind you that what all Pound's critics in fact do is to construct the fragments of the fragments that, each for his own reason, they prefer. Even people who read the whole poem do not really read the whole poem because it is unreadable, and it is unreadable because, as they cheerfully admit, it exists only *in potentia*.[15] Since Pound himself had no illusions about this, no more should we. This is not to say that the improvisations, which are sometimes brilliant and sometimes not, the patching and doodlings, are without their own interest, but it will no more do to muddle it all together and call all of it poetry than it will do to muddle it all together and call none of it poetry.

As I say, each reader not only reads his own *Cantos* (which is how reading any poem is done), but each reader of *The Cantos* is required by its poet to construct his own *Cantos*. My choral *Cantos* is composed of 2, 13, 45, 47, 49, 81, and 106; when I have worked at it long enough, other bits and pieces will have been added, but, for the present, that is its essential form, though I would be tempted to add *The Pisan Cantos* entire, which is clearly a poem about the world's renewals:

> It comes over me that Mr Walls must be a ten-strike
> with the signorinas
> and in the warmth after chill sunrise
> an infant, green as new grass,
> has struck its head or tip
> out of Madame La Vespa's bottle
> mint springs up again
> > in spite of Jones' rodents
> as had the clover by the gorilla cage
> > with a four-leaf
>
> When the mind swings by a grass-blade
> > an ant's forefoot shall save you
> the clover leaf smells and tastes as its flower.
> > (Canto 83, pp. 532–33)

And it is, paradoxically, also about the survival of *communitas*, in its utter ruin, beyond all hope. Bereft of the kinship, muttering only to himself, suddenly and amazingly he begins at last to talk to all of us, *for* all of us; he becomes the *choregos* he had tried to be before and could not become—not until he found himself alone and humiliated, forced to meditate not only on his suffering and on the errors that had led him to that suffering, but also on what was valuable, what was enduring, what could be saved from the wreckage of the dream. He found that he loved and praised only what Pindar and

Horace and Jonson and Whitman had loved and praised: perfection of good order, the kinships of earth, the earth herself in her epiphanies of fertility, nature and culture, the paradises of earth and the unearthly paradises that engender them, the dignity of humankind and of the universe. Like his predecessors in choral, he had also blamed what offered to harm or destroy what he loved and praised— but he had spent too much time in blaming. And the joy and the celebration survived even that.

Notes

I. *Swans in Crystal: The Problem of Modern Lyric and Its Pronouns*

1. See Lewis Freed, *T. S. Eliot: The Critic as Philosopher* (Lafayette, Ind.: Purdue University Press, 1979), pp. 174–80.

2. Tertullian, *De pallio* 3.1–2.

3. All English translations are mine unless otherwise noted.

4. For Catullan monologue, see Gordon Williams, *Tradition and Originality in Roman Poetry* (Oxford: Oxford University Press, 1968), pp. 461–63.

5. By lyrical discourse I mean the process by means of which the lyric poet describes (and so evokes) an emotion or complex cluster of emotions while simultaneously submitting that evocative description to dialectical scrutiny, to deliberation, to argumentation (e.g., Sappho, Pindar, Horace, Shakespeare, Herbert, Baudelaire, Cavafy—masters of lyrical deliberation). For a discussion of description and deliberation as the higher forms of language, see Sir Karl Popper, *Of Clouds and Clocks: An Approach to the Problem of Rationality and the Freedom of Man*, The Arthur Holly Compton Lecture (St. Louis: Washington University Press, 1965), pp. 18–20. For a critique of "unshaped" pure expression, see Benedetto Croce, *Philosophy, Poetry, and History: An Anthology of Essays*, trans. Cecil Sprigge (Oxford: Oxford University Press, 1966), pp. 274–78.

6. Sir Thomas Browne, *Religio Medici* 2.9.

7. See M. H. Abrams, "Structure and Style in the Greater Romantic Lyric," in *From Sensibility to Romanticism*, ed. Frederick Hilles and Harold Bloom (Oxford: Oxford University Press, 1965), pp. 527–60; Ross Garner,

Henry Vaughan: Experience and the Tradition (Chicago: University of Chicago Press, 1959), pp. 110–12.

8. But see the reasonable remarks of Christopher Caudwell, *Romance and Realism: A Study of English Bourgeois Poetry*, ed. Samuel Hynes (Princeton: Princeton University Press, 1970), pp. 124–30. See also David Craig, "Towards Laws of Literary Development," in *Marxists on Literature*, ed. David Craig (Baltimore: Penguin Books, 1975), pp. 135–60.

9. William Wordsworth, *The Prelude: 1798–1799*, ed. Stephen Parrish (Ithaca: Cornell University Press, 1977).

10. A lucid summary of the orthodox notion of fragmentation is Karl Malkoff's *Escape from the Self: A Study of Contemporary American Poetry and Poetics* (New York: Columbia University Press, 1977). For a useful discussion of historical alterations in the concept of the self (but not necessarily in the substance of the self), see Lionel Trilling, *Sincerity and Authenticity* (Cambridge, Mass.: Harvard University Press, 1972).

11. Cavafy is also, in a sense, a solitary poet, but his solitude, informed not only by artistic discipline but also by patient observation and loving memory, is a good solitude. Nor, though he seldom speaks of it, is he forgetful of his audience, from which he distances himself, yet to which he is, paradoxically, very close. See, e.g., the closing stanza of "Very Seldom," in *The Poems of C. P. Cavafy*, trans. John Mavrogordato (New York: Grove Press, 1952), p. 56.

12. Aristotle, *Politics* 1253a.

13. For various views of the failure of the lyric I or the triumph of impersonalism, see M. L. Rosenthal, *The New Poets: American and British Poetry Since World War II* (Oxford: Oxford University Press, 1967), pp. 5–17; Arnold Hauser, *Mannerism* (London: Routledge & Kegan Paul, 1965), 1:48–50, 357; Walter Sokel, *The Writer in Extremis: Expressionism in Twentieth-Century German Literature* (Stanford: Stanford University Press, 1959), pp. 110–16; Robert Pinsky, *The Situation of Poetry* (Princeton: Princeton University Press, 1976), pp. 72–88, 145–55; Hugo Friedrich, *The Structure of Modern Poetry*, trans. Joachim Neugroschel (Evanston: Northwestern University Press, 1974), passim; Karl Pestalozzi, *Die Entstehung des lyrischen Ich* (Berlin: De Gruyter, 1970), pp. 342–56. For a striking discussion of poetic personality, see Krishna Chaitanya, *Sanskrit Poetics: A Critical and Comparative Study* (Bombay: Asia Publishing House, 1965), pp. 335–41.

14. Stephen Spender, *The Struggle for the Modern* (Berkeley: University of California Press, 1963), pp. 133–43.

15. For an excellent and sympathetic discussion, see Andrew Welsh, *Roots of Lyric* (Princeton: Princeton University Press, 1979), pp. 79–99.

16. For the reader of English poetry, chief among these perhaps are A. E. Housman, Edward Thomas, and Thomas Hardy, all of them favorites of the young Auden who himself continued the tradition.

17. See William Butler Yeats, *Explorations*, ed. Mrs. W. B. Yeats (New York: Macmillan, 1962), pp. 163, 220–21.

18. See Richard Ellman, *The Identity of Yeats* (Oxford: Oxford University Press, 1954), pp. 129–38; see also Alexander N. Jeffares, *W. B. Yeats: Man and Poet* (London: Routledge & Kegan Paul, 1966), p. 215.

19. Delmore Schwartz, *Summer Knowledge: Selected Poems 1938–1958* (New York: Doubleday, 1959; rep. New York: New Directions, 1967).

20. See Schwartz's "O Love, Sweet Animal," "The Heavy Bear Who Goes with Me," "Prothalamium," and "Coriolanus and His Mother: Act One."

21. Sylvia Plath, *Ariel* (New York: Harper & Row, 1966).

22. William Carlos Williams, *Selected Poems* (New York: New Directions, 1963).

23. Josephine Miles, *Poetry and Change* (Berkeley: University of California Press, 1974), pp. 161–94.

II. *Praise and Blame: Greek Lyric*

1. Yvor Winters, *Forms of Discovery* (Denver: Alan Swallow, 1967), pp. 356–57.

2. A. M. Dale, *Collected Papers*, ed. T. B. L. Webster (Cambridge: Cambridge University Press, 1969), p. 161.

3. For ancient restrictions, see E. A. Barber and J. U. Powell, *New Chapters in the History of Greek Literature* (Oxford: Oxford University Press, 1921), p. 33; and Warren D. Anderson, *Ethos and Education in Greek Music* (Cambridge, Mass.: Harvard University Press, 1966), p. 3.

4. See Dale, *Collected Papers*, p. 162.

5. On the distinctions between monody (solo) and choral, see Rudolph Pfeiffer, *The History of Classical Scholarship* (Oxford: Oxford University Press, 1968), pp. 282–83.

6. See Thomas G. Rosenmeyer, James Halporn, and Martin Ostwald, *The Meters of Greek and Latin Poetry* (Indianapolis: Bobbs-Merrill, 1963), pp. 39–40; Dale, *Collected Papers*, p. 164.

7. Dale, *Collected Papers*, p. 168; A. Pickard-Cambridge, *Dithyramb, Tragedy, and Comedy* (Oxford: Oxford University Press, 1927), pp. 17ff.

8. See Hermann Koller, *Musik und Dichtung im Alten Griechenland* (Bern: Francke, 1963), pp. 177ff.

9. The translations of Archilochus, hitherto unpublished, are by T. G. Rosenmeyer; the numbering of the fragments follows that of the Greek texts in David A. Campbell's *Greek Lyric Poetry: A Selection of Early Greek Lyric: Elegiac and Iambic Poetry* (London: Macmillan, 1967).

10. I exclude Mimnermus and other elegists, together with the iambists, from my discussion since the speakers in this poetry, unlike Archilochus,

seem rather impersonal for the most part, do not dramatize the situation of their discourse, and are less interested in imagining emotion than in constructing lapidary gnomes; they are closer to the essayist and the modern epigrammatists than to the lyric poet. But see Hugh Parry, *The Lyric Poem of Greek Tragedy* (Toronto: S. Stephens, 1978), p. 9.

11. C. Day Lewis, *The Lyric Impulse* (Cambridge, Mass.: Harvard University Press, 1965), pp. 3, 144–45.

12. Aristotle, *Rhetoric* I.3.1358a.·

13. See Joseph Russo, "The Inner Man in Archilochus and the *Odyssey*," *Greek, Roman, and Byzantine Studies* 15(2) (1974): 139–52; Kenneth J. Dover, "The Poetry of Archilochus," *Archiloque, Entretiens Fondation Hardt* 10 (1963): 195.

14. T. S. Eliot, "Shakespeare and the Stoicism of Seneca," *Selected Essays* (London: Faber & Faber, 1951), p. 137. See also Anthony D. Moody, *Thomas Stearns Eliot: Poet* (Cambridge: Cambridge University Press, 1979), pp. 12–14.

15. See Dover, "Poetry of Archilochus," p. 212; and Gordon M. Kirkwood, *Early Greek Monody* (Ithaca: Cornell University Press, 1974), p. 224. The new Cologne Papyrus of Archilochus does nothing to resolve the problem of a personal versus a merely literary voice; see H. D. Rankin, *Archilochus of Paros* (Park Ridge, N.J.: Noyes Press, 1977), pp. 68–72.

16. See K. K. Ruthven, *A Guide to Ezra Pound's Personae, 1926* (Berkeley: University of California Press, 1969), pp. 20–21.

17. See Campbell, *Greek Lyric Poetry*, p. 157.

18. On these grounds, Bacchylides seems to me only marginally lyrical: his central concern is with story. See Gordon M. Kirkwood, "The Narrative Art of Bacchylides," in *The Classical Tradition: Literary and Historical Studies Presented to Harry Caplan*, ed. Luitpold Wallach (Ithaca: Cornell University Press, 1966), pp. 98–114; and D. S. Carne-Ross, "The Gaiety of Language," *Arion* 1(3) (1962): 65–88.

19. Walt Whitman, *Song of Myself* in *Leaves of Grass: Facsimile Edition of the 1860 Text*, ed. Roy Harvey Pearce (Ithaca: Cornell University Press, 1961), sec. 211.

20. The classical formulation of the personal lyric I is Emil Staiger's *Grundbegriffe der Poetik* (Zurich: Atlantis Verlag, 1946, 1968); see Paul Hernadi, *Beyond Genre: New Directions in Literary Classification* (Ithaca: Cornell University Press, 1972), pp. 23–34. For a discussion of modernist rejections of *Erlebnisdichtung*, see K. O. Conrady, "Moderne Lyrik und die Tradition," in *Zur Lyrik Diskussion*, *Wege der Forschung*, 111, ed. Richard Grimm (Darmstadt: Wissenschaftliche Buchgesellschaft, 1966), pp. 425–26; see also René Wellek, "Genre Theory, the Lyric, and *Erlebnis*," in *Discriminations: Further Concepts in Criticism* (New Haven: Yale University Press, 1970), pp. 236–52.

21. Ezra Pound, "Vorticism," in *Ezra Pound*, ed. John Sullivan (London: Penguin Books, 1970), p. 50.

22. Herbert N. Schneidau, *Ezra Pound: The Image and the Real* (Baton Rouge: Louisiana State University Press, 1969), p. 168.

23. The translations of Sappho, hitherto unpublished, are by T. G. Rosenmeyer. The numbering of these fragments, as for those of Anacreon and Simonides, follows that of Denys L. Page, *Lyrica Graeca Selecta* (Oxford: Oxford University Press, 1968).

24. See D. A. Russell, *Longinus* (Oxford: Oxford University Press, 1970), 10.1–2, for a good discussion of the ancient critic's appreciation of the poem. Perhaps the funniest contribution to the personalist view that has been made in recent years is George Devereux's "The Nature of Sappho's Seizure," *Classical Quarterly* n.s. 20 (1970): 12–31.

25. See Denys L. Page, *Sappho and Alcaeus* (Oxford: Oxford University Press, 1955), p. 26.

26. See Dionysius of Halicarnassus, *De compositione verborum*, 23, ed. William R. Roberts (London: Macmillan, 1910), p. 241.

27. Page, *Sappho and Alcaeus*, p. 30.

28. For Sappho's gift for "perfected meditation," see Anne Burnett, "Desire and Memory," *Classical Philology* 74 (1979): 16–27.

29. Page, *Sappho and Alcaeus*, p. 18.

30. Aristotle, *Poetics* 1451b.

31. Ruth Finnegan, *Oral Poetry* (Bloomington: Indiana University Press, 1978).

32. See Harry Caplan, *Ad Herennium* (London: Loeb, 1954), p. 398.

33. See Hermann Fränkel, *Early Greek Poetry and Philosophy*, trans. Moses Hadas and James Willis (Oxford: Blackwell, 1975), p. 162.

34. Ibid., pp. 303, 325.

35. Ibid., p. 323.

36. See A. Harvey, "The Classification of Greek Lyric Poetry," *Classical Quarterly* 49 (1955): 170–73.

37. Bruno Gentili, "Lirica greca arcaica e tardo arcaica," *Introduzione allo studio della cultura classica* (Milan: Marzorati, 1972), pp. 76–78.

38. See Edward E. Sikes, *The Greek View of Poetry* (London: Methuen, 1921), pp. 11–13; and J. A. Davison, "Literature and Literacy in Ancient Greece," *Phoenix* 16 (1962): 222–23.

39. St. Augustine, *De magistro* 11.

40. Arthur Rimbaud, Letter to Georges Izambard, May 13, 1871, in *Oeuvres complètes*, ed. Antoine Adam (Paris: Gallimard, Bibliothèque de la Pléiade, 1972), p. 249.

41. Pindar does not address his audience as You since he is speaking both to them and for them in addition to addressing gods and athletes; nor does he need to say We since he and the other choral performers and the au-

dience form a single entity. His I wavers firmly between personal and choral, as, e.g., does Whitman's. This precision of ambivalence gives the choral much of its richness—the consciousness of consciousness in its unities and its shimmerings.

42. See Paolo Vivante, "On Time in Pindar," *Arethusa* 5 (1972): 107–13; and Bruno Snell, *The Discovery of the Mind*, trans. T. G. Rosenmeyer (Cambridge, Mass.: Harvard University Press, 1953), pp. 44–45.

43. Homer, *Iliad* 2.484ff.

44. E. L. Bundy, *Studia Pindarica* (Berkeley: University of California Press, 1962).

45. David C. Young, "Pindaric Criticism," *Pindaros und Bakchylides, Wege der Forschung*, 134, ed. William Calder and Jacob Stern (Darmstadt: Wissenschaftliche Buchgesellschaft, 1970), pp. 87–88.

46. Barbara Hardy, *The Advantage of Lyric* (Bloomington: Indiana University Press, 1977), pp. 1–17.

47. For a criticism of the theory of parts, see Claude Calame, "Réflexions sur les genres littéraires en Grèce archaïque," *Quaderni urbinati di cultura classica* 17 (1974): 123.

48. Archibald MacLeish, "Ars Poetica," in *Collected Poems* (Boston: Houghton Mifflin, 1952), pp. 40–41.

49. For a dismissal of the importance of pronouns in any and all lyric, combined with an interesting discussion of lyric modes and their objects of mimesis, see Gemino H. Abad, *A Formal Approach to Lyric Poetry* (Quezan City, Philippines: University of Philippines Press, 1978), pp. 15–16, 27, 28, 65–72, 376–77. For "deictic" pronouns in lyric, see Jonathan Culler, *Structuralist Poetics* (Ithaca: Cornell University Press, 1975), pp. 168–69.

50. See Aristotle, *Rhetoric* 1371a–b.

51. See Parry, *Lyric Poems*, pp. 13–14.

III. *On the Absence of Ancient Lyric Theory*

1. For a reasoned statement of the attitudes behind this sad mistake, see Quintilian, *Institutes* 1.8.6.

2. See C. O. Brink, *Horace on Poetry* (Cambridge: Cambridge University Press, 1963), 1:182.

3. See Joel E. Spingarn, *The History of Literary Criticism in the Renaissance* (New York: Columbia University Press, 1924), pp. 27–99.

4. Brink, *Horace on Poetry*, 1:169–70.

5. See Hans Färber, *Die Lyrik in der Kunsttheorie der Antike* (Munich: Neue Filser, 1936), pp. 3ff. The translations of Plato are by M. E. Hubbard, those of Aristotle by D. A. Russell, in *Ancient Literary Criticism: The Principal Texts in New Translations*, ed. D. A. Russell and Michael Winterbottom (Oxford: Oxford University Press, 1972).

6. Färber, *Die Lyrik*, pp. 23–4.

7. See Paul Vicaire, *Platon, Critique Littéraire* (Paris: Klincksieck, 1960), p. 146; see also Plato, *The Laws* 799b.

8. What Aristotle does, in fact, is to reduce the means of literary mimesis to narrative (mixed and unmixed being fused) and dramatic. See Färber, *Die Lyrik*, pp. 4ff.; and P. Steinmetz, "Gattungen und Epochen der griechischen Literatur in der Sicht Quintilians." *Hermes* 92 (1964): 461. For his apparent neglect of lyric, see Gerald Else, *Aristotle's Poetics: The Argument* (Cambridge, Mass.: Harvard University Press, 1957), pp. 567–68; Luigi E. Rossi, "I generi letterari e le loro leggi scritte e non scritte nelle letterature classiche," *Institute of Classical Studies, University of London Bulletin* 18 (1971): 78. For the difficulties with the triad of modes, see Claudio Guillen, *Literature as System* (Princeton: Princeton University Press, 1971), pp. 383–405.

9. Emily Dickinson, *Selected Letters*, ed. Thomas H. Johnson (Cambridge, Mass.: Harvard University Press, 1971), letter 268, p. 176. For lyric mimesis of an action, see Charles Batteux, *Principes de la littérature* (Paris: Nyons, 1775; reprt., Geneva: Slatkin Reprints, 1967), 1:316–28. For an elegant criticism of antimimetic theories, see Gerald Graff, *Literature Against Itself* (Chicago: University of Chicago Press, 1979), pp. 179–205.

10. See Francis Cairns, *Generic Composition in Greek and Roman Poetry* (Edinburgh: Edinburgh University Press, 1972), p. 6.

11. See Plato, *The Laws* 700a–b. For useful descriptions of the species of Greek lyric, see Herbert W. Smyth, *Greek Melic Poets* (London: Macmillan, 1900), pp. xxiii–cxxxiv; Calame, "Réflexions sur les genres," pp. 116–120; Steinmetz, "Gattungen und Epochen," pp. 458ff.

12. See Cairns, *Generic Composition*, p. 14. For the possible influence of Callimachus, see Pfeiffer, *History of Classical Scholarship*, p. 130. See also P. M. Fraser, *Ptolemaic Alexandria* (Oxford: Oxford University Press, 1972), 1:459–63.

13. See Cairns, *Generic Composition*, pp. 71–72, 75.

14. See Stanley Edgar Hyman, *Poetry and Criticism* (New York: Atheneum, 1961), passim.

15. See C. O. Brink, *Horace on Poetry (Ars Poetica)* (Cambridge: Cambridge University Press, 1971), 2:172–73.

16. See Cairns, *Generic Composition*, p. 138.

17. Calame, "Réflexions sur les genres," pp. 114–15, shows clearly why we should not; see also Douglas E. Gerber, "Studies in Greek Lyric Poetry," *Classical World* 70 (October 1976):69. If, as seems likely, this Proclus is the neoplatonist (fifth century A.D.), we are here assuming, and it is a large assumption, that Proclus recapitulates the entire late tradition from Didymus to his own time. See Pfeiffer, *History of Classical Scholarship*, pp. 182–84, 277; and Rossi, "I generi litterari," pp. 74–75.

18. See Albert Severyns, *Recherches sur la Chrestomatie de Proclus, Bibli-*

otheque de la Faculté de Philosophie et Lettres de l'Université de Liège 79 (1938): 33–40, 115. See also Färber, *Die Lyrik*, pp. 31ff.; and Pfeiffer, *History of Classical Scholarship*, p. 184.

19. Much of Statius's *Silvae* and some of Martial may be thought to represent this category adequately.

20. See Cairns, *Generic Composition*, p. 6.

21. Ibid., pp. 10, 75.

IV. *In the Birdcage of the Muses: Ancient Literary Lyric*

1. The Cynic philosopher Bion of Borysthenes coined the phrase "the birdcage of the muses" in order to twit the more orthodox philosophers who had shut themselves up in the Ptolemaic academe, but it has some use as well for the paradox of literary lyric; see Athenaeus, *Deipnosophistae* 22d.

2. See Jacquiline de Romilly, *Magic and Rhetoric in Ancient Greece* (Cambridge, Mass.: Harvard University Press, 1975), pp. 8–9. The translation of Isocrates is by La Rue Van Hook in Isocrates, *Orations* (London: Heinemann, Loeb Library, 1945), p. 3.

3. See Auguste Couat, *Alexandrian Poetry*, trans. James Loeb (London: Heinemann, 1931), pp. 199–206.

4. See Davison, "Literature and Literacy," pp. 219–33.

5. For good sketches of Alexandrian poetry, see Constantine Trypanis, "The Character of Alexandrian Poetry," *Greece and Rome* 16 (1947) 1–12; and E. Howald, *Die Kultur der Antike* (Zurich: Rentsch, 1948), pp. 108ff.

6. A. E. Housman, "The laws of God, the laws of man," in *Last Poems* (New York: Holt, Rinehart and Winston, 1922; reprt. in *Collected Poems*, Holt, Rinehart and Winston, 1965).

7. See Couat, *Alexandrian Poetry*, pp. 178–98.

8. See Kirkwood, *Early Greek Monody*, pp. 200ff.

9. Translations of Meleager are by Peter Whigham, *The Poems of Meleager* (Berkeley: University of California Press, 1975).

10. Translations of Catullus, both in this and in the following chapter, are by Peter Whigham, except for the prose paraphrase of the final stanza of Poem 51, which is mine. See *The Poems of Catullus* (Baltimore: Penguin Books, 1966; reprt. in bilingual ed., Berkeley: University of California Press, 1969).

11. For this collection, possibly made by Catullus himself, see Wendell Clausen, "Catulli Veronensis Liber," *Classical Philology* 71(1) (1976): 37–43; and Marilyn B. Skinner, "Catullus's *Passer*: The Arrangement of the Polymetric Poems," Ph.D. dissertation, Stanford University, 1977. I realize that this question is uncertain, but I am personally persuaded by these formulations. The question of the chronology of the Catullan corpus is vexed and

will doubtless remain so, for neither objective nor subjective criteria are quite adequate to the difficulties that proliferate here. Frankly, I must beg the question. Some of the elegiacs seem to me contemporary with the polymetric poems; some of them seem contemporary with the long Alexandrian poems.

12. See Pietro Pucci, "Il carmine 50 de Catullo," *Maia* 13 (1961): 249–56.

13. See Wendell Clausen, "Callimachus and Latin Poetry," *Greek, Roman, and Byzantine Studies* 5(3) (1964): 181–96.

14. The poem is neither a translation of Sappho nor a careless paraphrase. It is a re-creation—the poem recast for his own purposes, fresh ironies reverberating from the transformation.

15. For this group, not school, of poets, see T. P. Wiseman, "Cinna the Poet," in his *Cinna the Poet* (Leicester: Leicester University Press, 1974), pp. 44–58.

16. See David O. Ross, *Style and Tradition in Catullus* (Cambridge, Mass.: Harvard University Press, 1969), pp. 76–95.

17. Nemesis appears in Poems 50.20, 66.71, 68.77, and, as I believe, in 64.395. Her central function in Catullus's consciousness of erotic and moral ruin, to punish those who abuse the power of love, is echoed in the prayer to Cybele in Poem 63 and in the prayer to the Furies in Poem 64. See also the Ovidian imitations in *Metamorphoses* 3.406; 14.694.

18. See Wiseman, *Cinna the Poet*, p. 118: "Catullus's tragedy was that he had not fully rejected the moral standards of the Valerii of Verona when he tried to live in the world of the patrician Claudii."

19. See Eduard Fraenkel, *Horace* (Oxford: Oxford University Press, 1957), pp. 339ff., 365.

20. I pass over the *Epodes*, which seem to me experimental and generally unsatisfying. See, however, the lucid appreciations of Gordon Williams, *Horace: New Surveys in the Classics* (Oxford: Oxford University Press, 1972), 6:6–14.

21. Cicero: *De officiis* 1.114.

22. See H. Bardon, *La littérature latine inconnue* (Paris: Klincksieck, 1952), 2:113.

23. For the Romans' difficulty with even relatively simple lyric meters, see Cicero, *Orator* 55.183. The *Carmen Saeculare* was performed by a chorus, but we know very little about this performance, and it is hardly clear that the poem was sung rather than, say, chanted. See Fraenkel, *Horace*, pp. 378–82.

24. See Statius's *Silvae* 4.5, which is written in timid Alcaics, and see also his mechanical Sapphics in 4.7; in 5.3 brevity proffers form. See Pierre Grimal, *Le lyrisme à Rome* (Paris: Presses Universitaires de France, 1978), pp. 200–06.

25. See L. P. Wilkinson, *Golden Latin Artistry* (Cambridge: Cambridge University Press, 1970), p. 219.

26. These arguments are lucidly and fairly stated by K. E. Bohnenkamp, *Die horazische Strophe: Studien zur "Lex Meinekiana,"* Spudasmata, 30 (Hildesheim: Olms, 1972), pp. 321–36, but the weight of the evidence is still against his thesis. "Musical Horace" is elaborately argued for by Günther Wille, *Musica Romana* (Amsterdam: P. Schippers, 1967), pp. 234–53.

27. It is possible that these ladies sang in life even as they sing in the poems, but what they would probably have been singing was golden oldies and new hits—in Greek. Cf. Wille, *Musica Romana*, pp. 139–40, 245–46, 249–50.

28. On this aspect of his poetics, see Archibald Y. Campbell, *Horace* (London: Methuen, 1924), pp. 5–18, 224–28; and C. O. Brink, *Horace on Poetry*, 2:275–76, 502–03.

29. Ben Jonson, *Epigrammes* CXXIV; *The Underwood* XXII.

30. For Horace's sense of his future eminence, typically ironic and typically shrewd, see *Epistles* 1.20.17–18; *Odes* 2.20, 3.30.

31. See Grimal, *Le lyrisme à Rome*, pp. 31–50.

32. See *Odes* 4.3.13–16; and Williams, *Tradition and Originality*, pp. 2ff., 25–28, 568–69.

33. See Bardon, *La littérature latine inconnue*, 2:20ff.; and *Odes* 4.2.45–60.

34. Tacitus, *Dialogue on the Orators* 41.

35. Horace, *Epistles* 1.10.22.

36. See Monroe K. Spears, *The Poetry of W. H. Auden: The Disenchanted Island* (Oxford: Oxford University Press, 1963), pp. 230, 335–37.

37. See Steele Commager, *The Odes of Horace* (New Haven: Yale University Press, 1962), pp. 307–52.

38. Horace, *Epistles* 2.2.144.

39. Ibid., 1.1.41–42.

40. Although his speculations remain incapable of proof and will perhaps remain so, a great contribution to the problem of the place of Maecenas in Horace's lyrics is A. W. Verrall, *Studies Literary and Historical in the Odes of Horace* (London: Macmillan, 1884), pp. 65–67.

41. See Cairns, *Generic Composition*, pp. 74–75.

42. Horace, *Epistles* 1.11.27.

43. For Lucretius, see *De rerum natura* 3.1060–69; on Epicurus, see Hans P. Syndikus, *Die Lyrik des Horaz* (Darmstadt: Wissenschaftliche Buchhandlung, 1973), 2:254–70.

44. Horace, *Epistles*: 1.4.40–45; 1.11.8–10; 1.14.10–21; 1.16.5–16; 1.18.104–12.

45. See also Horace, *Epistles* 2.2.141–42; 214–16.

V. *The Figure of Ariadne: Some Lyric Mongrels and Lyric Monologue*

1. See Parry, *Lyric Poems*, passim.
2. Charles Baudelaire, "Le cygne" ("The Swan"), lines 37–52.
3. See Wolfgang Schadewaldt, *Monolog und Selbstgespräch*, Neue Philologische Untersuchungen 2 (Berlin: Weidemann, 1926), pp. 250–54.
4. Homer, as always the exception to and the perfection of the rule, complicates such formulations. The poet of the *Iliad* mingles narrative, drama, and lyric with intricate modulations; the more novelistic poet of the *Odyssey*, though he puts much of his narration in the mouth of Odysseus, invariably provides admirable distance for himself and his speakers and is sparing with lyrical interlude.
5. Robert Penn Warren, "Hemingway," *Kenyon Review* 9 (Winter 1947): 28, describes Hemingway in these terms: "a lyric writer rather than a dramatic writer: for the lyric writer's virtue depends upon the intensity with which personal vision is rendered rather than upon the creation of a variety of characters whose visions are in conflict with themselves." Recall Hemingway's own formula: "The real thing, the sequence of motion, and the fact which made the emotion. . . ."
6. See Charles Chadwick, *Symbolism*, The Critical Idiom 16, ed. John D. Jump (London: Methuen, 1971), pp. 3–7.
7. George Chapman, *Bussy d'Ambois*, ed. Nicholas Brooke (London: Methuen, 1964), Act 5. Sc. 1, lines 80–94.
8. Ibid., introduction by Brooke, p. xlviii.
9. Robert Browning's monologues, like those of Propertius, Tibullus, and Ovid, are, if anything, antilyrical; they are truly dramatic, yet they are also novelistic: they try to imagine the personality in terms of its relations to and conflicts with society: in very important ways, the personality of the speaker in these poems is used to describe and to criticize his society.
10. For the myth, see Maarten J. Vermaseren, *Cybele and Attis: The Myth and the Cult* (London: Thames & Hudson, 1977), pp. 90–92; for the tradition of this kind of monologue, see Williams, *Tradition and Originality*, pp. 205–06.
11. The translations are Whigham's; see Chapter 4, n. 10.
12. For Nemesis, see Chapter 14, n. 17. In this section Catullus is again concerned to emphasize and empathize with the innocent female victim; for his own sense of victimization and feminization, see Eve E. Adler, "Catullan Self-Revelation," Ph.D. dissertation, Cornell University, 1971.
13. See Wiseman, *Cinna the Poet*, p. 54; J. K. Newman, *Augustus and the New Poetry*, Collection Latomus 88 (Brussells: Revue des études latines, 1967), p. 50; Michael Putnam, "The Art of Catullus 64," *Harvard Studies in Classical Philology* 65 (1961): 165–205; and Leo Curran, "Catullus 64 and the Golden Age," *Yale Classical Studies* 21 (1969): 171–92.

14. For a good discussion of the probable unity of Poem 68, see Kenneth Quinn, *Catullus: An Interpretation* (New York: Barnes & Noble, 1973), pp. 179–88.

15. Robert Coleman, *The Eclogues*, Cambridge Greek and Latin Classics (Cambridge: Cambridge University Press, 1977), pp. 34–35.

16. Ibid., p. 35; see also pp. 26, 91, 178, 196.

17. Ibid., p. 35; emphasis is mine.

18. The translations of Theocritus are by Anthony Holden, *Greek Pastoral Poetry* (Baltimore: Penguin Books, 1974).

19. The translations of Virgil are by Paul Alpers, *The Singer of the Eclogues: A Study of Virgil's Pastorals* (Berkeley: University of California Press, 1979).

20. See Ernst Howald, *Das Wesen der Lateinischen Dichtung* (Zurich: Rentsch, 1948), pp. 70–73; Newman, *Augustus*, pp. 437–54; Hauser, *Mannerism* 1:365–71; and Ernst Curtius, *European Literature and the Latin Middle Ages*, trans. William Trask (New York: Pantheon, 1953), pp. 301, 392.

21. Thomas G. Rosenmeyer, *The Green Cabinet* (Berkeley: University of California Press, 1969), p. 129.

22. Michael Putnam, *Virgil's Pastoral Art: Studies in the Eclogues* (Princeton: Princeton University Press, 1970), p. 211.

23. See Sebastian Posch, *Beobachtungen zur Theokritnachwirkung bei Vergil*, Commentationes Aeniponteae 19 (Innsbruck: Wagner, 1969), pp. 13–14.

24. Coleman, *Eclogues*, pp. 273–75.

25. Geoffrey Hill, "Funeral Music," in *Somewhere Is Such a Kingdom: Poems 1952–1971* (Boston: Houghton Mifflin, 1975).

26. T. S. Eliot, *Collected Poems* (New York: Harcourt, Brace, 1970).

27. See the excellent discussion by Moody, *Thomas Stearns Eliot*, pp. 135–37; see also Elizabeth A. Drew, *T. S. Eliot: The Design of His Poetry* (New York: Scribners, 1949), pp. 124–26.

28. See Marion Montgomery, *T. S. Eliot: An Essay on the American Magus* (Athens: Georgia University Press, 1970), pp. 68–90, for a good discussion of Eliot's use of monologue.

29. See James E. Miller, Jr., for the significance of the Poundian revisions in his *T. S. Eliot's Personal Waste Land: Exorcism of the Demons* (University Park: Pennsylvania State University Press, 1977), pp. 60–61.

VI. *The Amplitude of Time: Whitman and Modern Choral*

1. See Aristotle, *Poetics* 1447a.

2. For Jonson's borrowings from Martial, see Harold A. Mason, *Humanism and Poetry in the Early Tudor Period* (London: Routledge & Kegan Paul,

1958), pp. 273–86; Mason's vigorous reading of the poem shows how the originals were ennobled.

3. See Pearce's discussion in his introduction to *Leaves of Grass, 1860 Text*, p. xxvi.

4. James E. Miller, Jr., calls the public voice "epic"; see his *American Quest for a Supreme Fiction: Whitman's Legacy of the Personal Epic* (Chicago: Chicago University Press, 1979), p. 43. A number of the poems that Miller treats as epic in this stimulating book I would describe as choral.

5. For a fine description of the structure, i.e., the movement of *Song of Myself*, see Malcom Cowley, *Walt Whitman's Leaves of Grass: The First (1855) Edition* (New York: Viking, 1959), pp. xvii–xx.

6. Section numbers for the poem are given here as they are found in Pearce, *Leaves of Grass*, which is the text I use, and always will.

7. Randall Jarrell, *Poetry and the Age* (New York: Knopf, 1955), p. 112.

8. Gay W. Allen, *Walt Whitman: Man, Poet, and Legend* (Carbondale: Southern Illinois University Press, 1961), p. 16.

9. Georges Poulet, *La conscience critique* (Paris: Corti, 1971), pp. 30–31, gives a good description of the compassion and the sense of community that are central to Baudelaire's public lyrics.

10. See Auden's introduction to the *Oxford Book of Light Verse* (Oxford: Oxford University Press, 1938), p. xix.

11. Ginsberg is, of course, the most powerful choralist of his generation. If in the past decade and more, his voice became shrill beyond hearing and his craftsmanship random, uncertain, who would dare to offer him blame? For that world, he composed and performed the only kind of choral that was possible in it.

12. For the choral origins of the *Four Quartets*, rejected verses from a choral passage in *Murder in the Cathedral*, see Helen Gardner, *The Composition of the Four Quartets* (Oxford: Oxford University Press, 1978), pp. 14–16, 39.

13. For the prevalence of this central idea, see Ezra Pound, *The Cantos* (New York: New Directions, 1970), pp. 229, 250, 436, 460, 643, 747, 797, and, the final page and the final beautiful canto, 803.

14. Ibid., "Notes for Canto 117 et seq.," p. 802.

15. See Michael J. Alexander, *The Poetic Achievement of Ezra Pound* (Berkeley: University of California Press, 1979), p. 138 and passim, for a balanced, deeply reasoned, and imaginative defense of the discontinuity.

Index of Names

Abad, Gemino H., 202n49
Abrams, M. H., 6
Adler, Eve E., 207n12
Aeschylus, 60, 68, 146, 147
Akhmatova, Anna, 192
Alcaeus, 92, 94, 114, 136
Alcman, 53–54, 102–103
Alexander, Michael J., 209n15
Allen, Gay W., 209n8
Alpers, Paul, 208n19
Anacreon, 2, 26, 49–53, 80, 82, 94, 114, 115, 134, 135
Anderson, Warren D., 199n3
Archilochus, 2, 29–38, 40, 92, 94, 114, 115, 134, 135, 199n9
Archpoet, The, 51
Aristophanes, 146, 164
Aristophanes of Byzantium, 84–88, 91
Aristotle, 30, 78, 80–83, 198n12, 201n30, 202n50, 203n8, 208n1
Athenaeus, 204n1
Auden, W. H., 74, 140, 192, 198n16
Augustine, St., 74, 201n39

Bacchylides, 28, 53, 54, 59
Barber, E. A., 199n3
Bardon, H., 205n22, 206n33
Barthes, Roland, 10

Bassus, 124
Batteux, Charles, 203n9
Baudelaire, Charles, 8, 10, 11, 12, 18, 36, 147–48, 154, 192
Beddoes, Thomas, 153
Benn, Gottfried, 12, 21
Berryman, John, 174
Blake, William, 7
Boethius, 124
Bohnenkamp, K. E., 206n26
Bowra, C. M., 25–26
Brink, C. O., 202n2, 202n4, 203n15, 206n28
Browne, Sir Thomas, 5
Browning, Robert, 140, 207n9
Buffet, Jimmy, 37
Bundy, E. L., 68
Burnett, Anne, 201n28
Burns, Robert, 7, 52

Caesar, Julius, 125
Cairns, Francis, 90, 91, 203n10, 203n12, 203n13, 204n20, 206n41
Calame, Claude, 202n47, 203n11, 203n17
Callimachus, 82, 98, 100–104, 110, 112, 127, 130, 131, 139, 154, 156, 164
Campbell, Archibald Y., 206n28

211

Campbell, David A., 199n9, 200n17
Caplan, Harry, 201n32
Carne-Ross, D. S., 200n18
Catullus, 2, 3–4, 36, 37, 108–23, 127, 130, 134, 154–62, 178, 204n10, 204n11
Caudwell, Christopher, 198n8
Cavafy, C. P., 11, 12, 198n11
Cézanne, Paul, 14, 37
Chadwick, Charles, 207n6
Chaitanya, Krishna, 198n13
Chapman, George, 152–53
Chaucer, 84
Cicero, 76, 77, 117, 123, 125, 131, 205n21, 205n23
Claudel, Paul, 192
Clausen, Wendell, 204n11, 205n13
Coleman, Robert, 162–63, 171
Coleridge, Samuel Taylor, 3, 7, 153
Commager, Steele, 206n37
Conrady, K. O., 200n20
Couat, Auguste, 204n3, 204n7
Cowley, Malcolm, 209n5
Craig, David, 198n8
Croce, Benedetto, 197n5
Culler, Jonathan, 202n49
Curran, Leo, 207n13
Curtius, Ernst, 208n20

Dale, A. M., 199n2, 199n4, 199n6
Dante, 33
Davison, J. A., 201n38, 204n4
De Romilly, Jacqueline, 204n2
Devereux, George, 201n24
Dickens, Charles, 164
Dickinson, Emily, 11, 48, 83
Dionysius of Halicarnassus, 41
Donne, John, 6
Doolittle, Hilda (H. D.), 24
Dover, Kenneth, 200n13, 200n15
Drew, Elizabeth A., 208n27
Du Bellay, Joachim, 90

Eliot, T. S., 1–3, 5, 8, 22, 43, 71, 73, 102, 153, 172, 172–75, 178, 192–93
Ellman, Richard, 16
Else, Gerald, 203n8
Emerson, Ralph Waldo, 183
Euripides, 107, 146, 157

Färber, Hans, 202n5, 203n6, 203n18
Fergusson, Francis, 24
Finnegan, Ruth, 49

Fitts, Dudley, 24
Fitzgerald, Robert, 24
Fraenkel, Eduard, 205n19, 205n23
Fränkel, Hermann, 55, 201n33, 201n34, 201n35
Fraser, P. M., 203n12
Freed, Lewis, 197n1
Friedrich, Hugo, 198n13

Gardiner, Helen, 209n12
Garner, Ross, 197n7
Gentili, Bruno, 201n37
Gerber, Douglas E., 203n17
Ginsberg, Allen, 22, 192, 209n11
Goethe, Johann Wolfgang von, 7, 91, 174
Graff, Gerald, 208n8
Grimal, Pierre, 205n24, 206n31
Guillen, Claudio, 203n8

Halporn, James, 199n6
Hardy, Barbara, 202n46
Hardy, Thomas, 198n16
Harvey, A., 201n36
Hauser, Arnold, 198n13, 208n20
Hawthorne, Nathaniel, 11
Heine, Heinrich, 36
Hemingway, Ernest, 149
Herbert, George, 6, 91, 140
Hernadi, Paul, 200n20
Herrick, Robert, 51
Hill, Geoffrey, 208n25
Holden, Anthony, 208n18
Hölderlin, Friedrich, 18, 63, 166, 192
Homer, 55, 66, 81, 82, 146, 207n4
Hopkins, Gerard Manley, 11
Horace, 2, 4, 13, 56, 62, 77, 88, 90, 92–95, 123–45, 174, 178, 180
Housman, A. E., 198n16, 204n6
Howald, Ernst, 204n5, 208n20
Hugo, Victor, 192

Ibycus, 54, 114
Isocrates, 96–97

Jarrell, Randall, 190
Jeffares, Alexander N., 199n18
Johnson, Samuel, 125
Jonson, Ben, 5, 13, 90, 128, 178–82

Keats, John, 8, 149
Kirkwood, Gordon, 200n15, 200n18, 204n8

Knight, Etheridge, 22
Koller, Hermann, 199n8
Kyd, Thomas, 152

Lamartine, Alphonse, 7
Lattimore, Richmond, 24
Leopardi, Giacomo, 7
Lewis, C. Day, 30, 48, 51
Li Po, 51
Lucretius, 143, 186

MacLeish, Archibald, 202n48
Malkoff, Karl, 198n10
Mallarmé, Stéphane, 8, 10, 153, 166, 174
Marlowe, Christopher, 151
Martial, 108, 204n19, 208n2
Marvell, Andrew, 7
Mason, Harold A., 208n2
Meleager, 104–107, 116
Menander, 164
Miles, Josephine, 22
Millay, Edna St. Vincent, 192
Miller, James E., Jr., 208n29, 209n4
Mimnermus, 199n10
Montgomery, Marion, 208n28
Moody, Andrew D., 200n14, 208n27

Neruda, Pablo, 192
Newman, J. K., 207n13, 208n20
Nietzsche, Friedrich, 54, 150

Ostwald, Martin, 199n6
Ovid, 157, 205n17, 207n9

Page, Denys L., 201n23, 201n25, 201n27, 201n29
Parrish, Stephen, 198n9
Parry, Hugh, 199n10, 202n51, 207n1
Parton, Dolly, 37
Pearce, Roy Harvey, 200n19, 209n3, 209n6
Péguy, Charles, 178, 192
Pestalozzi, Karl, 198n13
Petrarch, 91, 122
Pfeiffer, Rudolph, 199n5, 203n12, 203n17
Philodemus, 130
Photius, 88
Pickard-Cambridge, A., 199n7
Pindar, 25, 26, 28, 54, 59–71, 94, 124, 131, 133, 137, 138, 139, 147, 177, 178, 180, 201n41

Pinsky, Robert, 198n13
Plath, Sylvia, 19–21
Plato, 78, 79–80, 81, 165, 203n7, 203n11
Poe, Edgar Allan, 82
Popper, Sir Karl, 197n5
Posch, Sebastian, 208n23
Poulet, Georges, 209n9
Pound, Ezra, 22, 28, 34–37, 48, 139, 193–95
Proclus, 88–90
Propertius, 36, 37, 207n9
Pucci, Pietro, 205n12
Pushkin, Alexander, 174
Putnam, Michael C. J., 168, 207n13

Quinn, Kenneth, 208n14
Quintilian, 202n1

Racine, Jean Baptiste, 125
Rankin, H. D., 200n15
Rich, Adrienne, 22
Rilke, Ranier Maria, 166, 192
Rimbaud, Arthur, 62
Romanos, 165, 178
Ronsard, Pierre, 5
Rosenmeyer, Thomas G., 199n6, 199n9, 201n23, 208n21
Rosenthal, M. L., 198n13
Ross, David O., 205n16
Rossi, Luigi E., 203n8, 203n17
Rousseau, Jean-Jacques, 7
Russell, D. A., 201n24, 202n5
Russo, Joseph, 200n13
Ruthven, K. K., 200n16

Sappho, 4, 25, 26, 38–49, 51, 80, 82, 92, 114, 116, 136, 174
Schadewaldt, Wolfgang, 207n3
Schneidau, Herbert N., 36
Schwartz, Delmore, 17–19
Seneca, 76, 107, 124, 150–51, 166
Severyns, Albert, 203n18
Shakespeare, 33, 122, 150, 151, 174
Shelley, Percy Bysshe, 192
Sikes, Edward E., 201n38
Simonides, 4, 50, 53–59, 80, 95, 131, 133, 137, 138, 139, 178
Skinner, Marilyn B., 204n11
Smyth, Herbert W., 203n11
Snell, Bruno, 202n42
Socrates, 57, 131
Sokel, Walter, 198n13

Sophocles, 68, 82, 146, 147, 150
Spender, Stephen, 13
Spingarn, Joel E., 202n3
Staiger, Emil, 200n20
Statius, 124, 204n19, 205n24
Steinmetz, P., 203n8
Stesichorus, 53, 54
Sullivan, John, 201n21
Syndikus, Hans P., 206n43

Tacitus, 138
Tennyson, Alfred Lord, 84, 153, 174
Tertullian, 2
Theocritus, 163–72
Thomas, Edward, 198n16
Tibullus, 207n9
Tourneur, Cyril, 152
Trilling, Lionel, 198n10
Trypanis, Constantine, 204n5

Upanishads, 185

Valéry, Paul, 14, 91, 166
Van Hook, La Rue, 204n2
Vaughan, Henry, 6
Vermaseren, Maarten J., 207n10
Verrall, A. W., 206n40
Vicaire, Paul, 203n7

Villon, François, 36
Virgil, 107, 126, 132, 137, 148, 149, 157, 162–72
Vivante, Paolo, 202n42

Warren, Robert Penn, 207n5
Webster, John, 152
Wellek, René, 200n20
Welsh, Andrew, 198n15
Whigham, Peter, 204n9, 204n10, 207n11
Whitman, Walt, 178, 182–91, 200n19
Wilde, Oscar, 31, 52
Wilkinson, L. P., 206n25
Williams, Gordon, 197n4, 205n20, 206n32, 207n10
Williams, William Carlos, 22
Winterbottom, Michael, 202n5
Winters, Yvor, 24–26
Wiseman, T. P., 205n15, 205n18, 207n13
Wordsworth, William, 3, 7, 192

Xenophanes, 55
Xenophon, 165

Yeats, William Butler, 15–17, 192
Young, David C., 202n45

Designer:	Al Burkhardt
Compositor:	G & S Typesetters, Inc.
Printer:	Vail-Ballou Press
Binder:	Vail-Ballou Press
Text:	10/12 Goudy Old Style
Display:	Goudy Old Style